*To the many friends, neighbors, co-workers,
and family members (you know who you are!)
whose questions about Windows XP inspired this book.*

Table of
Contents

Acknowledgments

During the course of working on this book, I had the privilege of working with a truly gifted team of professionals at Microsoft Press. Without their hard work and dedication, this book would never have come into being. I would like to thank Alex Blanton at Microsoft Press for his inestimable assistance on getting this project started, and to the tireless and talented project editor Sandra Haynes for seeing it through to completion. Project manager Susan McClung kept track of all the details, and desktop publishing specialist Patty Fagan is responsible for turning this collection of words and pictures into great-looking typeset pages. Copyeditor Marcia Allen and proofreaders Jan Cocker, Jackie Fearer, and Robert Saley swept away all the typos that my spelling checker missed and helped keep the whole book stylistically consistent. Technical editor Bob Hogan read every word of every chapter to make sure the text was accurate and that every set of instructions worked properly. Kathy Murray contributed her expertise to Chapters 9 and 10 and made my job considerably easier. Finally, I owe special thanks to my longtime friend and collaborator Carl Siechert, who pitched in to help with Chapters 13 and 14. Many thanks to one and all!

Introduction

For more than a decade, I've been helping ordinary people wrestle with Microsoft Windows. Friends, neighbors, and family members pepper me with questions about their computers every day. I get phone calls and e-mails, and occasionally someone stops me in the gym and says, "I'm having this problem with Windows and I wonder whether you can help me figure it out..." In the past few years those questions have become much tougher: How do I keep my computer safe from viruses? How can I get these photos out of my new digital camera and burn them onto a CD? Why is all this offensive e-mail landing in my Inbox, and what can I do to get rid of it? What do I need to do to share my high-speed Internet connection with all the PCs in my house?

Those are all great questions, and I'll bet you've got a few of your own that are just as tough. You know that today's Windows-powered computers are amazingly powerful and complicated. Windows XP has more gizmos, gadgets, bells, whistles, and cool features than any single piece of software Microsoft has ever produced. So where do you begin? If you don't have a hotline to your favorite Windows expert, how do you find the fastest, smartest way to tame this amazing operating system?

If you're like other people I've talked with, you're probably frustrated with computer books that overpromise and underdeliver—you know, the ones that assume you're an imbecile or an idiot or some kind of dummy. After you get past the cornball jokes and the step-by-step instructions on how to click the mouse, those books don't leave much room for answers to the really tough questions, do they?

That's why I wrote this book.

This Book Could Be for You

Throughout this book, I assume that you have some experience with earlier versions of Windows, especially Windows 95, Windows 98, and Windows Millennium Edition (Windows Me). I won't waste your time showing you how to click mouse buttons or move a window around on the screen. You're smart enough to figure out how the Start button works, and I'll bet you've used the Web, so you don't need me to tell you how to click a hyperlink or what *www* stands for. You want answers, and you don't want me to waste your time.

I've started by identifying the essential tasks you need to do every time you sit in front of a computer running Windows XP. I explained each of those tasks in plain English, with step-by-step instructions, strategies to help you work smarter, and pointers to places where you can find more information.

Of course, if you want to read this book from cover to cover, I've organized it so you can quickly get up to speed on Windows XP. For a fast, no-nonsense introduction to the features of Windows XP, especially those that are different from the Windows version you already know, I recommend reading Chapter 1, "You've Got Windows XP...Now What?" and Chapter 2, "How Windows Works (and How to Work with Windows)," before you go any further.

Want to dig deeper? Just keep reading. If you're concerned about viruses, hackers, spam, and other unpleasantries, don't miss Chapter 8, "Protecting Your Privacy and Your Computer's Security," where I explain how to use a firewall to block Internet intruders and how to protect yourself from viruses, worms, and Trojan horses. Wondering what to do with your new digital camera? See Chapter 12, "Picture-Perfect Digital Photography." And if you're thinking about setting up a network, you'll find step-by-step instructions in Chapter 14, "Setting Up and Running a Small Network."

You don't have to read this book from front to back, though. If you're stumped by a Windows feature that isn't working the way you expect, feel free to dive into the chapter that covers that feature for quick answers; if there's relevant advice or essential instructions about that task in a different chapter, you'll find a "See Also" note that leads you to that information.

Throughout this book, you'll find a variety of helpful elements designed to turn you into an instant Windows expert. Whenever possible, I've tried to steer clear of jargon and technobabble. On those occasions when it's unavoidable, look for a Lingo box that translates the term into plain English. You'll also find tips, notes, and "Try This!" elements scattered throughout the text, all with the goal of helping you work (and play) faster and smarter.

What Hardware and Software Do You Need?

This book is all about Windows XP. If you're thinking about upgrading to Windows XP, you'll find helpful advice in the first two chapters. Throughout the rest of the book, I assume you already have a computer with Windows XP installed and running. I expect that most people who read this book are running Windows XP Home Edition, but I also cover some of the features you'll find in Windows XP Professional. If you're running Windows XP at home or in a small business, everything you read in this book should match what you see on your screen. If you use Windows XP on a large corporate network, however, you may notice some differences—I've tried to point these differences out whenever possible.

Support

Every effort has been made to ensure the accuracy of this book. Microsoft Press provides corrections for books at the following address:

> http://mspress.microsoft.com/support/

If you have comments, questions, or ideas regarding this book, please send them to Microsoft Press via e-mail to:

> *mspinput@microsoft.com*

or via postal mail to:

> Microsoft Press
> Attn: Faster Smarter Series Editor
> One Microsoft Way
> Redmond, WA 98052-6399

Please note that product support is not offered through the above addresses.

Chapter 1

You've Got Microsoft Windows XP... Now What?

Every day, several hundred million people use Microsoft Windows. You're probably one of them. After all, a personal computer isn't a techie toy anymore—it's an essential tool for gathering information about the world we live in, doing business, and staying in touch with friends and family. If you've already learned how to work with your current version of Windows, upgrading to Windows XP should be easy, right? How different can it be?

If you're just getting started with Windows XP, be prepared to be pleasantly surprised—and perhaps just a little bit overwhelmed. At first glance, Windows XP may look a lot like your old familiar Windows, but the more you work with it, the more differences you'll discover. Mysterious lockups and crashes, for instance, are dramatically reduced, and many of your everyday tasks are simpler and less complicated. Best of all, some chores that used to stump even certified rocket scientists—like setting up a home network or connecting a digital camera—are completely automated.

What's New in Windows XP

In this chapter, I'll give you an overview of the most important features of Windows XP, and I'll show you how to make sure that your system files are absolutely, positively up to date. If you've just purchased a new computer with Windows XP already installed, I'll show you how to safely move your files and settings from the old computer to the new one.

User Accounts, Passwords, and Security

In Windows XP, you have to log on—that is, identify yourself with a unique user name—before you can begin using the computer. By logging on, you gain access to your own personalized work space, with a folder for your personal documents, a desktop that's yours to customize, and a Start menu containing your own shortcuts. If you add a password to your account, you can prevent other users of your computer from looking at your private files or tinkering with your desktop and Start menu. On a home computer, you can create separate accounts for every member of the family, with no worries that the kids will accidentally erase Mom and Dad's financial records to make room for a hot new music download.

If you're used to Windows 95, Windows 98, or Windows Millennium Edition (Windows Me), you might be wondering: What's the big deal? After all, earlier versions of Windows allowed you to create separate accounts and add a logon dialog box at startup. The difference is crucial, however. With those older versions of Windows, anyone could bypass the logon box by tapping the Escape key, and the password offered no protection for your personal files. By contrast, with Windows XP, every user is required to log on, and if you configure the system correctly, your files are safely locked away from anyone who lacks the correct password.

Tip   For maximum security, be sure you format your hard disk using the NTFS file system and add a password to your account.

See Also   To learn more about the NTFS file system, see the section "Working with Hard Disks," on page 31.

Differences in the Way Windows Works

Anyone who's used earlier versions of Windows knows how to double-click an icon, how to make a window bigger or smaller, and how to use the taskbar to switch between running programs. Windows XP keeps those familiar elements but adds a host of new features that make your computer easier to use. For instance, you'll find that the reorganized Start menu (shown in Figure 1-1) gives you easier access to commonly used locations like My Computer and Control Panel, as well as making it easier to perform tasks like searching for a file or looking for answers in Help And Support. The taskbar automatically groups similar buttons together to reduce clutter. Icons located in the notification area (at the bottom right corner of the screen) automatically hide when they're not needed, giving you more room to work with programs. And at regular intervals, Windows offers to file away desktop icons you haven't used recently—again, all in the name of clearing away clutter.

Figure 1-1 The Windows XP Start menu uses two columns instead of one, giving you easier access to the programs and folders you use most.

Digital Photos, Music, and Video

Windows XP includes an assortment of programs and widgets that make it easier for you to work with a digital camera. In fact, if you bring home a new digital camera and plug it into your computer running Windows XP, you might be pleasantly surprised to discover that the Scanner And Camera Wizard pops up automatically, as shown below, and offers to download your pictures for you. After your pictures are safely transferred to your My Pictures folder, you can view each one individually, display the entire collection as a slide show, or send copies to friends and family members via e-mail.

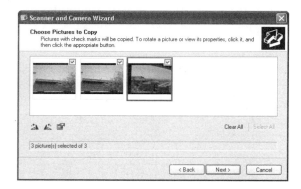

See Also   *To learn more about digital cameras, see Chapter 12, "Picture-Perfect Digital Photography."*

Windows XP also includes the most recent version of Windows Media Player, an amazingly versatile program that lets you play CDs and (with the help of a software decoding program) DVDs, copy music tracks to your PC, transfer songs to a portable music player, and keep your music collection perfectly organized. With a CD-RW drive and Windows XP, you can even select a group of songs and burn your own custom CD to play in your living room or car stereo.

See Also   *To learn how to organize music files on your computer, see Chapter 11, "Managing Music (and More) with Windows Media Player."*

Home Networking

How many computers do you have in your home? If the answer is more than one, you're a candidate for a home network. The benefits are practically irresistible: You can share files without having to deal with the hassle of floppies or Zip disks, and you can use a single Internet connection for every computer on the network. The cost of networking hardware has plummeted in recent years to prices that just about anyone can afford. Thanks to the Network Setup Wizard, anyone running Windows XP can set up a network with just a few mouse clicks.

See Also   *For step-by-step instructions to help you get your home network up and running, see Chapter 14, "Setting Up and Running a Small Network."*

Help and Support

Windows XP is an enormously powerful program, packed with literally thousands of features. If you can't figure out how to do something (and you don't find the answers in this book), try looking in the new Windows XP Help And Support Center, shown below. You can browse the index, search for topics, or look up specific words and phrases. The answers that appear are generally easy to read, and in many cases you can find tutorials, troubleshooters (like the one shown here), and walkthroughs that can help you complete a task or solve a problem quickly.

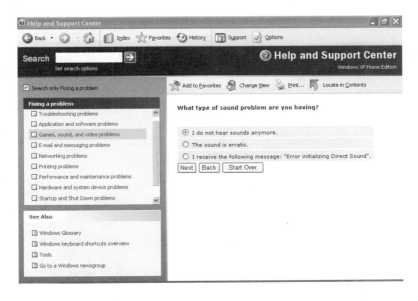

See Also To learn how to work with the Help And Support Center, see the section "How Do I...?" on page 52.

Browsing the Internet

Windows XP includes Microsoft Internet Explorer 6, a full-featured and thoroughly up-to-date Web browser. It makes short work of finding information anywhere on the Internet, thanks to easy-to-use search tools and an intelligent way of organizing shortcuts to your favorite Web sites. This version of Internet Explorer also includes significant enhancements in security and privacy protection, most notably a system that lets you take complete control of cookies, the small text files that can give away your personal information if you're not careful.

See Also   *For complete instructions on how to work with the Web, see Chapter 6, "Connecting to the Internet and Browsing the Web."*

Organizing Your Files and Folders

You'll be amazed at the sheer variety of files you can download, create, and tinker with in Windows XP—digital pictures, business reports, greeting cards, custom CD playlists, and much more. Keeping track of all those individual files can be a challenge until you learn the ins and outs of Windows Explorer, the basic file-management tool in Windows XP. If you've worked with files and folders in a previous version of Windows, you probably already understand the basics of files and folders. Windows XP adds some handy new tools like the *task panes* along the left side of the Windows Explorer window shown below, which make it easier to find the folders you use most often and to perform everyday tasks like renaming, moving, and copying files.

Tip   If you see a list of folders instead of the task pane when you open Windows Explorer, click the Folders button on the toolbar at the top of the window. This button acts as a toggle, switching between the list of available folders and the task pane.

See Also   *You'll find everything you need to know about Windows Explorer in Chapter 10, "Organizing Your Files."*

Personalizing Windows

As I noted earlier, you can set up Windows XP so that each person who logs on has his or her own desktop, a private place to store files, and shortcuts to favorite programs. You can go much further, though, and really make your PC your own. Change the fonts, use your favorite digital photo as your desktop background, add custom sounds, install a collection of fonts, and do much more.

See Also *For step-by-step customization instructions, see Chapter 9, "Making Windows Work Your Way."*

Home Edition or Professional: What's the Difference?

If you stroll through the software section of your local computer superstore, you'll notice that Windows XP is available in two different versions. What's the difference between Windows XP Home Edition and Windows XP Professional? One distinction is obvious: the Home Edition costs considerably less than its Professional counterpart. Does that mean that Home Edition is somehow inferior? Not at all.

At their core, both editions of Windows XP are exactly the same. Most of the basic features of the operating system—including all the new features I described earlier in this chapter—are absolutely identical, regardless of which Windows XP edition you use. As you might guess from the name, Windows XP Professional includes a few extra features that are primarily intended for use in businesses. For instance:

- Windows XP Professional is designed to work on large corporate networks; Windows XP Home Edition can connect to a corporate network to access shared files, but it can't permanently join the network.

- With Windows XP Professional, you get access to some expert-level security features not available in Windows XP Home Edition, such as the capability to encrypt files so that no one can read them without a password and dialog boxes that let you assign user-by-user permissions to files and folders.

- A feature called Remote Desktop, which is available only in the Professional edition of Windows XP, lets you set up your computer so that you can operate it remotely. This capability comes in handy if you want to leave the office at the end of the day, have dinner, and then use your home computer to continue working on your office files.

> **Note** To set up a Remote Desktop connection, you may need some expert help, especially if the remote computer is behind a firewall or on a corporate network.

■ If you have a computer with two *central processing units (CPUs)*, you need the Professional edition of Windows XP to take advantage of the additional CPU. Most of us are perfectly happy with a single CPU in our computer and have no need for such exotic hardware!

> **Lingo** The *central processing unit*, or CPU, is the silicon chip that runs programs and performs calculations—in other words, your computer's "brain." Most PCs that run Windows use an Intel or AMD chip. The CPU is sometimes referred to as a *processor* or *microprocessor*.

As you can tell, the advantages of Windows XP Professional are most obvious for advanced users who are part of large Windows networks. If you're using your computer primarily at home or in a small office, you'll probably find that Windows XP Home Edition is more than adequate for your everyday tasks.

How can you tell which edition of Windows XP is on your computer? You'll find this information in Control Panel, under System. Here's one easy way to reach this display:

1 Click Start, and then click Control Panel.

2 If your Control Panel window is organized by categories (the default view in Windows XP), select Performance And Maintenance, and then click the System icon. If you're using the Classic view of Control Panel, double-click the System icon.

3 Look on the General tab, where you'll see a display like Figure 1-2.

Figure 1-2 Use the System dialog box to see detailed information about your computer, including which version of Windows you're using.

Before You Upgrade...

So, you're thinking of upgrading to Windows XP but haven't done so yet? Congratulations. The smartest thing you can do before upgrading is to figure out whether any of your currently installed software or hardware will cause problems or fail to work under Windows XP. You'll be much better off if you find out about any potential problems in advance rather than discovering after the upgrade is complete that your favorite program crashes when you start it or that your expensive scanner no longer works!

Will Your Software and Hardware Work with Windows XP?

If you have the Windows XP CD, you can use the Upgrade Advisor to check your computer for potential problems. This handy compatibility-checking program normally runs as the first step in the process of upgrading to Windows XP, but you can use it all by itself, too. It works with almost any version of Windows, including Windows 95, Windows 98, Windows Me, and Windows 2000. Here's how to use it:

1 Insert the Windows XP CD in your computer's CD-ROM drive.

2 From the Welcome To Microsoft Windows XP page, click Check System Compatibility.

Tip If the Welcome To Windows XP page doesn't appear, open the My Computer window and double-click the icon for your CD-ROM drive. In the CD window, double-click the Setup icon.

---

3 On the next page, click Check My System Automatically.

4 Follow the prompts to check your system. If the wizard asks your permission to download updated setup files, click Yes.

When the Upgrade Advisor finishes its inspection, it produces a report detailing every software and hardware issue it finds. Figure 1-3 shows the initial summary from a computer running Windows Me. Click Full Details to see a full discussion of the issues and possible solutions for each item in the report shown here. If the list is lengthy, click Print so you can read the report and make notes on it as you go about fixing problems.

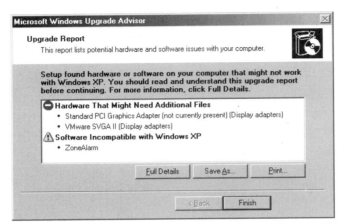

Figure 1-3 The Upgrade Advisor inspects your system and lists compatibility problems you're likely to encounter when you upgrade to Windows XP.

Tip   If you're thinking of upgrading to Windows XP but don't yet have the CD, you can still run the Upgrade Advisor. Go to *http://www.microsoft.com/windowsxp/pro/howtobuy/upgrading/advisor.asp*, download the software, and follow the instructions given above. This is the same software found on the Windows XP Professional CD, so don't be confused when you run the program and see references to the CD.

Fixing Problems Before You Upgrade

After you run the Upgrade Advisor, read its report carefully! You can read the entire report by scrolling through the Upgrade Report dialog box. In general, possible problems will fall into one of the following three categories:

■   **Software that is incompatible with Windows XP**   If you're running Windows 98 or Windows Me, your antivirus software probably falls into this category. Check with the company that makes the software to see if a patch or a new version is available. You might need only a small download to update it, or you might need to pay for a full upgrade. Whichever route you take, make sure you get a guarantee that the updated software is compatible with Windows XP.

■   **Hardware that needs additional files to work**   Your old scanner might work just fine with Windows XP, but only if you update the driver files first. Using the Upgrade Advisor report, check with the manufacturer of each device to see if they have a new driver that is certified as compatible with Windows XP. If so, download the new driver so you can install it after upgrading.

■ **Hardware that will not work with Windows XP** Some older devices won't work with Windows XP at all, and no updated driver is available. If you have one of these "orphans"—say, your trusty old scanner—you have to decide what to do next: Do you replace the device with a new one that works with Windows XP? Or is it so valuable to you that you want to hold off on your Windows upgrade?

In some cases, the Upgrade Advisor may recommend that you uninstall a particular program before upgrading to Windows XP. After the upgrade, you can reinstall it. When you've worked through every item on the list, you can safely replace your old Windows version with Windows XP.

Moving Your Files and Settings to a New Computer

You've just brought home a shiny new computer, loaded with Windows XP. The trouble is, all your programs and files are on your old computer. How do you move everything to the new computer? Windows XP can help with some, but not all, of this task.

Unfortunately, there's no easy way to move all your programs to the new computer. To get those programs working properly, you'll need to dig up the program CDs or downloaded program files and reinstall each one on the new computer. I recommend you do that task first. After you've successfully set up your collection of programs, you can use a nifty utility called the Files And Settings Transfer Wizard to move your data files—including letters, pictures, e-mail messages, and e-mail address book—to the new computer. During the process, the wizard also restores custom settings for Windows, such as your desktop colors, fonts, and wallpaper, as well as those for a long list of programs, including Microsoft Office, Microsoft Works, Microsoft Outlook Express, Adobe Acrobat, and RealPlayer, among many others.

See Also *If you're not sure about how to reinstall a program, see the section "Installing a New Program," on page 59.*

The Files And Settings Transfer Wizard is powerful, but it can be a bit confusing to use. You run the wizard on both the old and new computers. It goes through your old system, gathering all the files in your My Documents folder and on your desktop (and in a few other locations). It also searches your entire hard disk for any files that appear to be data files, regardless of where they're stored. Finally, it goes through your customized settings for Windows and for certain other programs. After the wizard gets all your files and settings together, you're ready to move them to the new computer. You can choose one of two ways to make the transfer:

■ If you set up a network connection between the old computer and the new one, you can transfer all the files and settings directly. After you reinstall all your old programs on the new computer, you should be ready to go.

■ No network? No problem, as long as you have a Zip disk, a CD burner, or some other way to save the files and settings from the old computer so you can physically carry them to the new one. You can even use floppy disks, but only if your collection of data files is very, very small! If you have a huge collection of digital pictures or music files, you'll need to use a disk format with more storage capacity.

> **Tip**　If you're planning to give your old computer to the kids and make it part of a home network, do yourself a big favor and set up the network first. (You can read all about this task in Chapter 14, "Setting Up and Running a Small Network.") Using a network is the fastest, smartest way to transfer files between computers.

The following sections describe how to use the Files And Settings Transfer Wizard (these instructions assume that your old computer is using Windows 95, Windows 98, or Windows Me).

> **Tip**　I strongly recommend that you run Windows Update on your new computer before using the Files And Settings Transfer Wizard. (See the section, "Get the Latest Windows Updates," on page 18, for an explanation of how you can use Windows Update to make sure that your copy of Windows contains the latest bug fixes and security patches.) Install all the Critical Updates and go through the list of Windows XP updates as well. If you're using the original release of Windows XP, one of the available updates is designed specifically to fix problems with this wizard!

Prepare Your New Computer

Start by getting your new computer ready to receive the transferred files. Install all your programs, get your network set up, and download any required updates. Then perform the following steps:

1 On the new computer, click Start, and choose All Programs. Choose Accessories, then System Tools, and finally click Files And Settings Transfer Wizard.

2 Click Next to skip past the wizard's opening page.

3 In the Which Computer Is This? page, shown below, choose New Computer and click Next.

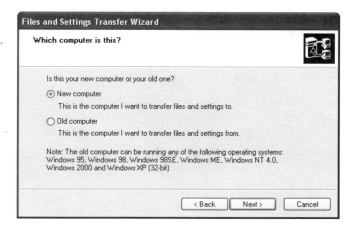

4 On the Do You Have A Windows XP CD? page, shown below, specify how you plan to run the wizard on your old computer. Choose the option to use the Windows XP CD if you have the CD handy. If you don't have the CD at hand, choose the option to make a Wizard Disk. (You'll need a blank, formatted disk for this task.)

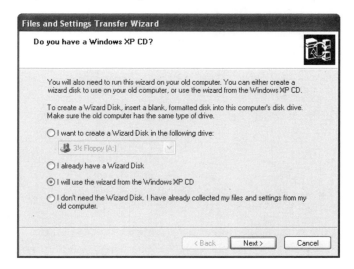

5 Click Next.

For now, you're through with the new computer. Figure 1-4 shows the dialog box you'll see if you chose the option to use the Windows XP CD. (If you chose to create a Wizard Disk, you'll be prompted to insert a blank floppy disk.

After the wizard finishes creating the disk, you'll see a screen that's similar to Figure 1-4, with instructions that refer to the floppy disk instead of your CD.) Leave this dialog box open and go to the old computer.

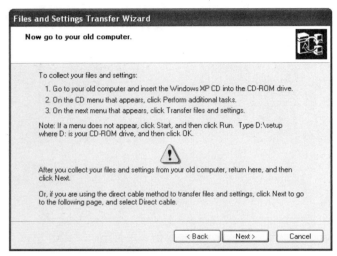

Figure 1-4 These instructions will be slightly different if you chose to use a floppy disk instead of a CD to start the Files And Settings Transfer Wizard.

Gather Your Old Files and Settings

After you finish setting up your new computer, you're ready to go to the old computer and gather the files and settings you want to transfer. Here's what to do:

1   Go to the old computer and start the Files And Settings Transfer Wizard. You have the following options:

- If you're using the Wizard Disk, insert the floppy disk into the drive, click Start, choose Run, type **a:\fastwiz**, and press Enter.

- If you're using the Windows XP CD, insert the CD into the drive. The Welcome To Microsoft Windows XP page should appear automatically; if this doesn't happen, open My Computer, double-click the icon for your CD drive, and double-click the Setup icon. On the Welcome page, click Perform Additional Tasks. On the What Do You Want To Do? page, click Transfer Files And Settings.

2   Click Next to skip the wizard's opening page.

3   On the Select A Transfer Method page, shown on the next page, choose one of the following options and click Next:

- **Direct Cable**   This refers to a special type of cable that connects the two computers' serial ports. Most people don't have one of these cables, and they're painfully slow anyway. I don't recommend this option.

● **Home Or Small Office Network**   If you followed my advice and set up your network before using the wizard, this option is available to you. If this choice is unavailable, you'll need to fix your network connection or choose a different option.

● **Floppy Drive Or Other Removable Media**   The drop-down list below this option shows all available removable drives installed in your computer, including floppy and Zip drives. Select a floppy drive *only* if you know you have very few files to copy. If you choose this option, make sure the same type of drive is available on the new computer.

● **Other**   Select this option if you want to save the files to a location on your computer, on your network, or to a removable hard drive, such as a USB drive. You'll need to enter the location where you want to save the files in the box below this choice.

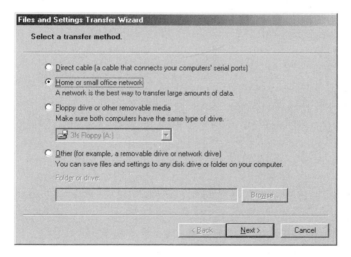

4   On the What Do You Want To Transfer? page, shown on the next page, select whether you want to transfer Settings Only, Files Only, or Both Files And Settings.

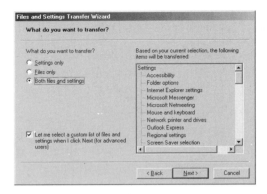

If you want to pick and choose from items on the list of available settings and files, click the Let Me Select A Custom List Of Files And Settings check box. Don't be intimidated by the warning that this is for advanced users; anyone can use this option, and if you've made it this far you should be able to figure it out.

Tip   The Settings Only option includes all your e-mail accounts, messages, and address book, but only if you've chosen to use a network or removable drive. If you have lots of messages in your Outlook Express folders, this option can take up a lot of space, so the wizard doesn't transfer e-mail with the Settings Only option if you choose a floppy drive as the destination where you want to save your files and settings. If you select a Zip drive, on the other hand, the wizard knows you have hundreds of megabytes of available storage and thus includes your e-mail.

---

5   Click Next to continue. If you chose the option to customize the list of settings, you'll see the dialog box shown in Figure 1-5. Add or remove any items if you want, and then click Next.

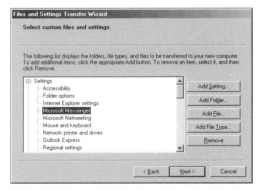

Figure 1-5 You can add or remove items from the list of files and settings.

Tip   The Files And Settings Transfer Wizard automatically picks up all the files on your desktop and in your My Documents and My Pictures folders. Use the Custom List option if you regularly store data files in a folder that is not in one of these locations. Click Add Folder, then browse to the folder where your files are stored, and click OK. Repeat this process if you have multiple folders where data files are stored.

After you finish these steps, the wizard begins collecting your files and settings. On a computer that includes lots of files to transfer, this process can take a long time, so be patient.

If you're transferring files over a network, the wizard displays a randomly selected password on the new computer and asks you to enter that password on the old computer. This is a security precaution that prevents someone from using this wizard to try to steal files from your old computer without your permission.

If you're transferring files to a disk or to a location on your computer or your network, you can see a dialog box that estimates how much disk space the collection will take (and, if necessary, how many floppy or Zip disks you'll need). If you don't have enough disk space or disks, you can cancel and start over. You may need to use different settings—or get another box of disks!

6   When the process of gathering files and settings is complete, click Finish. You're done with the old computer.

Transfer the Files

If you chose to make the transfer over your network, Windows handled everything for you automatically. If you saved your files and settings to disk, go back to the new computer and click Next. Tell Windows where the files are located and click Next, at which point the wizard handles the rest of the details.

After the transfer is complete, click Finish, log off, and log back on. All the files and settings from your old computer should be ready for you to work with on your new computer.

Tip   Don't be in too much of a hurry to delete the files from your old computer. It's possible that the wizard missed one or two files. Use your new computer as much as you can for a week or so, until you're certain that you've got all the files you need. At that point, you can safely delete your files from the old computer.

Get the Latest Windows Updates

After you finish upgrading your computer to Windows XP, are you done? Not on your life. Microsoft regularly releases updates to Windows. These updates fix bugs and repair security problems. If you want to avoid sudden crashes and other problems, it's essential that you keep your copy of Windows up to date.

After upgrading to Windows XP, you might be surprised to see that a long list of updates is available. If you stop and think about it, though, it makes perfect sense. The CD you used probably includes the original version of Windows XP, which was released in October 2001; you'll need to install all the updates that have been released since that time.

To check for updates manually, follow these steps. (Note that you must be logged on as a member of the Administrators group, and you must be connected to the Internet in order to perform this procedure. If you installed Windows XP on your home computer, you're automatically a member of the Administrators group.)

1   Click Start and then click Help And Support.

2   In the Help And Support Center window, choose Keep Your Computer Up-to-date With Windows Update. Click Yes if you see any security dialog boxes that ask you to install software from Microsoft.

3   When you reach the Windows Update screen, click Scan For Updates.

4   Windows Update connects to Microsoft's server and compares the list of available updates to those already installed on your computer. You see a personalized list of updates in the column at the left of the window, as shown in Figure 1-6.

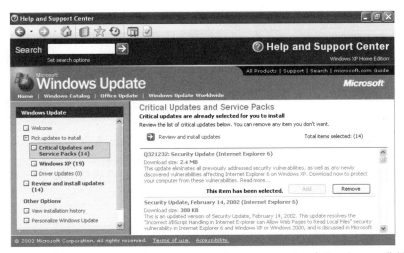

Figure 1-6   When you run Windows Update manually, you see a list of all updates available for your computer.

5 Click a category to see details for each group of updates. All Critical Updates are already selected for you. Updates in the other categories are optional; you can go through each one, read the description for each one, and decide whether you need to install it or whether you can safely skip it. Use Add and Remove to customize the list of updates you plan to install.

6 After you've gone through the entire list and added those you want to download, click Review and Install Updates. This step shows you a list of all the updates you selected, with descriptions. If you're satisfied, click Install Now. (Depending on the number of updates you selected and the speed of your Internet connection, this process could take awhile.)

Lingo   *Critical Updates* are those that fix a serious problem with Windows, one that can potentially cause you to lose data or fall victim to a virus or hacker. *Recommended Updates* fix problems that are less serious and often apply only to Windows users with specific hardware or software. *Service Packs* are comprehensive updates that consolidate many individual fixes into a single package.

Checking for Updates Automatically

If you're like me and you sometimes have trouble remembering the date of your anniversary or where you put the car keys, don't rely on manual updates to Windows XP. It's all too easy to let a few weeks or a month go by, and that sort of delay can be disastrous if a virus comes out that attacks computers that don't have the latest security updates installed. Instead, let Windows check for updates automatically. Here's how to set it up:

1 Go to Windows Update and install all available Critical Updates for your computer. If you do not have Service Pack 1 installed, be sure you also choose the Windows Automatic Updating option in the list of Recommended Updates. After completing the update process, restart your computer.

2 Click Start and open Control Panel. From the Performance And Maintenance category, click the System icon.

3 In the System Properties dialog box, select the Automatic Updates tab, as shown on the next page.

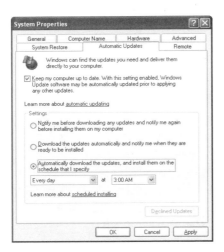

Inspect this dialog box carefully. If the one shown on your computer doesn't look like the one shown here, click Cancel and repeat Step 1. Make sure you install the Windows Automatic Updating option.

4 Make sure the Keep My Computer Up To Date check box is selected. In addition, choose one the three options below it:

- **Notify Me Before Downloading Any Updates...** This option checks the Windows Update servers and pops up an alert message in the notification area of the Taskbar when a new update is available. It does not download or install any software.

- **Download The Updates Automatically...** This option is similar to the previous one, except that it downloads all available updates for you. When you see the alert message, you can decide when it's convenient to install the updates. This is the best option for most people.

- **Automatically Download The Updates, And Install Them On The Schedule That I Specify...** By default, this option checks for new updates every morning at 3:00 a.m., automatically downloading and installing them for you. You can change the automatic update to once a week, on a specific day of the week, and you can change the time as well. Although this option is the safest way to keep your computer up to date, it also has one serious problem: If an update requires restarting your computer, Windows does so, potentially losing changes to any files you have open. Choose this option *only* if you leave your computer on but close all files at the end of the day before the update is to take place!

5 Click OK to save your changes.

From now on, Windows handles the updates for you.

Everything You Need to Know About Windows Product Activation

When you upgrade your computer to Windows XP, one of the final steps in the installation process is to activate your copy of Windows. Although you can postpone activation for up to 30 days, you can't delay it any longer or else Windows stops working and displays the dialog box shown in Figure 1-7.

Figure 1-7 If you see this message, you must activate your copy of Windows before you can continue to use it.

Why does Windows make you jump through this hoop? Activation is an antipiracy measure, intended to ensure that each copy of Windows XP is installed only on a single computer. If you purchase a copy of Windows XP at your local computer superstore, you can install it on your computer and activate it without any problems. If you then try to install that software on another computer in your own house, or if you loan the software to a friend or relative so they can install it, Microsoft's servers refuse to activate the second copy over the Internet. You'll encounter the same problem if you uninstall Windows XP from your old computer and then try to install it on a new PC, because the Product Activation servers see this as an unauthorized second copy. You can, however, call Microsoft's Product Activation hotline (a toll-free call), explain the circumstances, and have your copy activated over the phone.

For most people, product activation will never be an issue. If you purchase a new computer with Windows XP already installed, you might find that the computer manufacturer already took care of the Product Activation step. If you purchase a retail copy of Windows XP and install it on your computer, you'll need to connect to the Internet and enter the 25-digit code (found on the back of the CD case). If you enter the code correctly, the Product Activation process should be automatic and fast.

If Product Activation doesn't work or if you don't have access to a working Internet connection, choose the option to activate over the telephone. After you select your country from the list, you'll see the dialog box shown here. Call the toll-free phone number, read off the combination of letters and numbers that you see to the operator, and enter the code that the operator supplies in return. At that point, you're ready to begin working with Windows XP again.

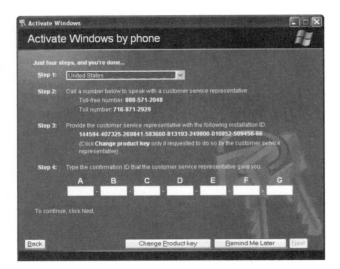

Key Points

- Windows XP is significantly different from older versions, especially Windows 95, Windows 98, and Windows Me. Make sure you understand what's new.

- Before you upgrade to Windows XP, use the Upgrade Advisor to check your computer for compatibility problems.

- If you get a new computer with Windows XP, you'll need to reinstall all your old programs, but you can use a wizard to transfer your files and settings from the old computer to the new one.

- Before you can use Windows XP, you have to activate it, either over the Internet or over the phone.

- Protect yourself by setting up Windows to download updates automatically on a regular schedule.

Chapter 2

How Windows Works (and How to Work with Windows)

You know about the basics of Windows, like the Start menu and the taskbar, but what's really new in Microsoft Windows XP? If you previously used Windows 98 or Windows Millennium Edition (Windows Me), you're used to doing things a certain way, and you'll need to make a few adjustments in Windows XP. You'll need to log on with a user name and (optionally) a password. The Control Panel looks different than you remember. Formatting a disk requires a different set of steps. Even the simple job of shutting down your computer is different.

In this chapter, I'll walk you through what's new, with a special emphasis on the basic building blocks of Windows—the Welcome screen, Control Panel, the Disk Management console, and other tools that you can use to keep your computer running at top speed with no stalls.

Getting Started

When you power on your PC, you set off a fairly complex chain of events. First, your computer runs through a series of checks called the power on self test (POST), in which the computer verifies that it has all the hardware it needs: *random access memory (RAM)*, disk storage, a video card, a mouse and keyboard, and other essential hardware components. Some computers display a series of black and white text screens during this phase, while others hide these informative messages behind a logo screen of some sort.

Lingo   *Random access memory (RAM)* is often referred to as just *memory*. This is the area where Windows stores data, programs, and parts of the operating system you're using right now. RAM is temporary storage; the data is available in the chips that make up your computer's memory banks, and when you turn off your computer, the contents of your computer's memory go away. In contrast, you use disks for long-term storage. The disks record the data on magnetic surfaces that continue to store data even when power is unavailable.

Assuming that all your hardware checks out all right, the computer then hands off control to Windows, which begins loading the operating system, hardware drivers, and some services. While the initial phase is going on, you see the Windows logo and a progress bar (whose purpose is to assure you that the computer really is doing something).

In its final phase, Windows shifts into graphical mode, replacing the logo screen with the standard blue background and displaying the Welcome screen shown in Figure 2-1.

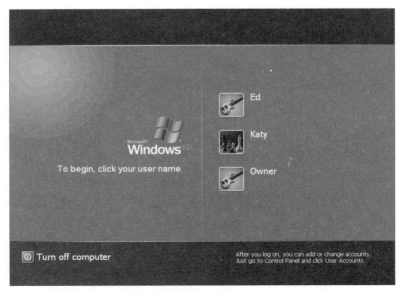

Figure 2-1 Before you can begin working with Windows, you have to log on by clicking your user name and, if necessary, entering a password.

As I'll explain shortly, you can choose to bypass this screen and log on automatically, and you can replace the Welcome screen with a different sort of logon dialog box. For most people, though, logging on at the Welcome screen is an essential security precaution.

Logging On

Why do you have to log on at all? Why doesn't Windows XP just start up, the way it did with older versions such as Windows 98 and Windows Me? The answer is simple: Unlike those older versions of Windows, Windows XP was designed from the ground up to be a secure operating system. With your unique user name and password, you can store your private files and e-mail in a place where they're completely safe from prying eyes. You can also set up the Windows desktop and other preferences exactly the way you like them. When you log on to the computer, you can be assured that no one else has come along and accessed your data or changed your settings without your permission.

See Also   Want to add a new user account to your computer? You'll find instructions in the section "Creating a New Account," on page 283.

Your account actually consists of three distinct elements.

■ Your *user name* is the name that Windows associates with your account. This name can contain punctuation and spaces. Windows ignores any differences in capitalization, however. You cannot change the user name after you create an account except by using advanced computer management tools that are beyond the scope of this book.

■ Your *full name* is what appears on the Welcome screen and at the top of the Start menu. Normally, this name is identical to your user name. However, you can change this name at any time by opening the User Accounts option in Control Panel. If the user names for accounts on your computer are in a "techie" format, like *ebott* and *jbott*, you can change their appearance on the Welcome screen to a friendlier format like *Ed* and *Judy*.

Note   Why would you want to have a user name and full name that don't match? This scenario is most common on a network, where the administrator wants all users to have names that follow a certain format, such as *ebott* or *ed.bott*. Changing the name to *Ed* on the Welcome screen makes it easier to see who that user really is.

■   A *password* is optional for user accounts, and in fact Windows leaves the password blank when you create a new account. I highly recommend that you create a password that's easy to remember and hard to guess if you share your computer with other people or if you have a network.

Try This! If you don't have a password, it's easy to create one. If you do have a password, you can change it anytime you want. If you're concerned that someone else has discovered your password, by all means change it right away! Here's how to create a password if your account doesn't have one already:

1   Click Start and then click Control Panel.

2   Choose the User Accounts option.

3   At the bottom of the User Accounts window, click the icon for your account.

4   On the What Do You Want To Change About Your Account? page, click Create A Password.

5   Enter your password in the top two boxes (entering it a second time ensures that you don't accidentally mistype it and create the wrong password by mistake), as shown below. You can enter a password hint in this dialog box as well; just make sure that your hint doesn't make it too easy for someone else to guess your password!

6   Click Create Password.

7   Close all running programs, click Start, and choose Log Off. When you return to the Welcome screen, click your name and enter the password you just created.

If you already have a password, the steps are almost identical. In place of Create A Password, you'll find Change My Password. Click that button and follow the prompts. As a security precaution, you'll need to enter your current password before entering the new one.

> **Tip** Forget your password? If you don't have a password reset disk, you can change your password by logging in using another account that is a member of the Administrators group. (For more information, see the instructions below to learn how to create this handy rescue tool.) If you don't have such an account, restart your computer and press F8 repeatedly during the text-based start-up screens. This displays the Windows Advanced Options menu. Select Safe Mode. At the Welcome screen, click the entry for Administrator (no password is required). After logging on, click Start, open Control Panel, and double-click the User Accounts option. From the bottom of the User Accounts window, click the entry for your account and then choose Change My Password. Enter a new password, and then restart your computer in normal mode and use the new password to log on to your account.

After you create or change your password, be sure to create a password reset disk. If you forget the password, you can use this floppy disk to reset it. Here's how.

1 Insert a blank disk in your computer's floppy disk drive.

2 Click Start, click Control Panel, and double-click the User Accounts option.

3 Click the icon for your account.

4 In the task pane at the left side of the window, under Related Tasks, click Prevent A Forgotten Password. The Forgotten Password Wizard appears, as shown below.

5 Click Next twice.

6 Enter your current user account password and click Next.

7 When the progress bar shows that it's reached 100% complete, click Next, and then click Finish.

8 Label the disk "Password Reset Disk" and store it in a safe place.

If you ever forget your password, you can use the password reset disk to regain access to your files. Click your account name on the Welcome screen, enter an incorrect password, and then click the Use Your Password Reset Disk prompt. Follow the wizard's prompts to change your password.

Caution   The password reset disk is designed to work only with your account. Anyone who finds it can use it to reset your password, access your account, and view sensitive information or steal your files. Don't leave this disk where an intruder can find it. Keep it under lock and key.

Switch Users Without Shutting Down

If you share a computer with other family members, you know how annoying it is when you want to check your e-mail but someone else is using the computer. With older versions of Windows, the other person had to shut down all his or her programs so that you could log in. Then, after you were finished, you had to log off and let the other person log back on, and then that person had to open all his or her programs again. With Windows XP, you can skip all this rigmarole, thanks to a cool feature called Fast User Switching.

As you might guess from the name, this feature allows two or more people to log on to the same computer and then switch between accounts quickly, leaving programs running in the background. This feature makes it easy for you to log on to your account, check your e-mail or look at a Web page, and then allow the other user to get right back to work in a matter of seconds. In fact, you can even continue downloading a file or check your e-mail in the background, while other users are using their account on the computer.

To switch to your account without shutting down another user's session, click Start and choose Log Off. The Log Off Windows dialog box appears, as shown below.

Click Switch User. This action returns you to the Welcome screen, as shown in Figure 2-2.

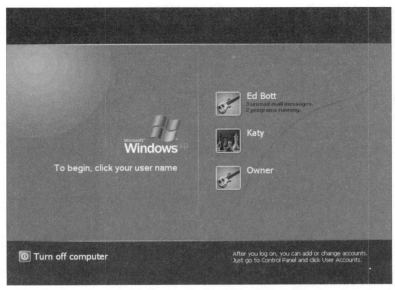

To begin, click your user name

Ed Bott
3 unread mail messages.
2 programs running.

Katy

Owner

Turn off computer

After you log on, you can add or change accounts.
Just go to Control Panel and click User Accounts.

Figure 2-2 When you switch between running user accounts, the Welcome screen changes to remind you that you have programs running and messages in your e-mail Inbox.

Note   When should you use the Log Off choice? Only when you want to shut down all your running programs and return to the Welcome screen. Use this option if your computer is short on memory and you want to allow other users to have full access to all of your system's resources.

What's different? When you use Fast User Switching, the Welcome screen adds details under each user account name, showing the number of programs running and the number of e-mail messages waiting in your Inbox (if you use Microsoft Outlook Express or Microsoft Outlook).

Tip   Get in the habit of locking your computer whenever you step away from your desk. It's easy, if you know the keyboard shortcut. Hold down the Windows logo key and press L (for *lock*). Whatever you're working on is covered instantly by the Welcome screen (don't worry—your programs are still running in the background and are there when you log on again). No Windows logo key? No problem. Press Ctrl+Alt+Del to open the Windows Task Manager dialog box, click the Shut Down menu, and choose Switch User.

Disks, Drives, Files, and Folders

With Windows XP, you have a dizzying array of options when it comes to storing data for later retrieval. You can save the files on a hard disk for fast retrieval or put them on a floppy disk or a Zip disk (if a Zip drive is installed on your machine) to move them from computer to computer. If you have a CD-R or CD-RW drive, you can copy up to 700 megabytes (MB) of data onto a CD that can be read on any computer with a CD drive. You also have a large assortment of removable storage devices, including portable hard disks and readers that work with Compact Flash and SmartMedia cards typically found in digital cameras and music players.

Disks? Drives? What's the Difference?   The terminology used to describe storage devices can be confusing. Here's a quick course that can help you sort out the vocabulary of storage devices.

A *hard disk* is the physical device in your computer that contains a motor, magnetic heads, and metal platters on which data is stored.

Drives are subdivisions of a hard disk used to help organize data. In Windows, each drive typically has its own *drive letter*. Thus, a 40-gigabyte (GB) hard disk might be divided into drive C and drive D, each with a maximum capacity of 20 GB.

Partitions and *volumes* are the technical terms used to describe the divisions on a hard disk. When preparing a hard disk for the first time, you have to create at least one partition, format it, and assign it a drive letter before you can store data on it. Windows recognizes two types of partitions: *primary* and *extended*. You are limited to a maximum of four partitions on a single disk; however, within an *extended partition*, you can create as many *logical drives* as you want, each with its own drive letter.

Removable drives are the physical devices into which you insert *removable media*, such as floppy disks, CDs, and Zip disks.

What's in My Computer?

When you're looking for data, the most logical place to begin your search is from the My Computer window. You'll find a link to this essential system folder on the Start menu. Using the My Computer window isn't always the fastest way to get to a specific file, but it's the easiest place to start when you're not sure where data is located.

In Windows XP, the My Computer window is organized by default into groups, each representing a different type of data storage. The My Computer window in Figure 2-3, for example, shows a full range of storage options.

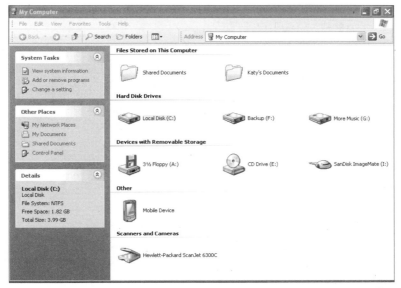

Figure 2-3 The My Computer window is an excellent starting point when searching for data.

When the task pane is visible at the left side of the My Computer window, it provides links to common tasks as well as information about the currently selected object. To toggle between the task pane and the Folders view, simply click the Folders icon on the My Computer toolbar.

Tip   When working with objects in the My Computer window, remember to right-click. The shortcut menus available when you right-click the icon for a drive or other object in the My Computer window provide direct access to functions like searching for data, exploring a drive in a new window, formatting a floppy disk, and writing files to a CD.

Working with Hard Disks

Most computers sold through retail outlets include hard disks that have already been partitioned and formatted. If you add a second (or third or fourth) hard disk to your system, you'll need to learn how to prepare it to hold data. For new and old disks alike, it's also important that you know how to check a disk for errors and repair any errors you find.

To work with hard disks and partitions in Windows XP, you use a system utility called Disk Management. With the help of this tool, you can prepare a new hard disk for use with Windows, create partitions, and format those partitions using the FAT32 or NTFS file systems. To open Disk Management, click Start, click Control Panel, select Performance And Maintenance, and open the

Administrative Tools folder. Double-click Computer Management to access the Computer Management console. In the left pane, the Storage node is open by default; select the Disk Management node.

Lingo   *FAT* stands for *File Allocation Table*. *FAT32* is the 32-bit version of this file system, used with modern hard disks. *NTFS* is the file system originally introduced with Windows NT and now standard with Windows XP.

Figure 2-4 shows the Disk Management window on a computer that contains a 100 MB Zip drive, two hard disks, a CD drive, and a CD-RW drive.

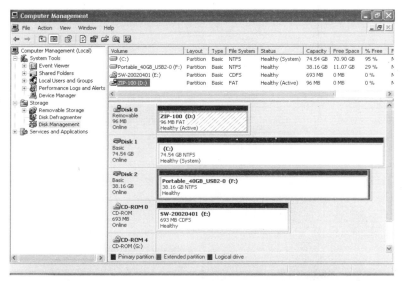

Figure 2-4 Use the Disk Management window to work with hard disks and some other types of storage devices.

The Disk Management window is divided into two parts. In the top portion, you find individual volumes, each of which typically has its own drive letter. The bottom portion contains an entry for each hard disk and removable drive installed on your computer. In either window, you can right-click the entry for a drive or disk to get information and to access the shortcut menu of available actions.

Gathering Information

From the Disk Management window, you can obtain information about any disk or drive by examining its entry. The Volume list at the top of the window contains a wealth of useful information, for instance. You can also right-click any entry from either list and choose Properties. In the case of a drive (or volume), this information is identical to what you see if you right-click the drive icon in the My Computer window and choose Properties. The General tab, shown here, tells you which disk format is in use, how much total space is available on the disk, and how much is currently in use.

Checking for Errors

Like any mechanical device, hard disks sometimes have problems. Serious problems can cause a disk to crash, but minor problems, such as a corrupted file or a slightly scrambled index, can occur as well. Your best bet is to nip these problems in the bud by occasionally checking the disk for errors. To do so, right-click the drive icon, either in the My Computer window or in Disk Management, and choose Properties. The Local Disk Properties dialog box appears, as shown below. On the Tools tab, click Check Now in the Error Checking frame.

Note   Yes, the Check Disk utility is misnamed! It doesn't actually check an entire disk for errors; instead, it checks the contents of a single drive or volume.

The Check Disk dialog box, shown in Figure 2-5, is fairly simple, with only two options to choose from:

- **Automatically Fix File System Errors**   This option looks for errors in the list of files stored on the drive you selected. If you don't select this option, the Check Disk utility reports any errors it finds but does not change them. For routine maintenance, you should always select this option.

- **Scan For And Attempt Recovery Of Bad Sectors**   This option performs an exhaustive check of the entire disk and repairs any data stored in sectors of the disk that are defective. It's a good idea to run this sort of test occasionally, but doing so adds significantly to the amount of time the job takes.

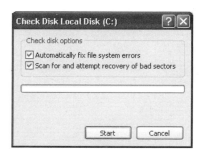

Figure 2-5 The Check Disk dialog box allows you to evaluate your disk drive for errors.

Tip   How often should you check a drive for errors? Once a month is probably sufficient, but you can and should perform this routine maintenance any time you're experiencing problems with your computer and want to rule out disk problems. Also, you should check a drive for errors before you copy a large number of files to or from the drive.

For some disks, Windows can check for errors immediately. If you see the dialog box shown here, however, you need to restart your computer so that the disk check can occur when Windows isn't running. This step is necessary, for instance, when you try to check for errors on the drive that contains your Windows system files (usually drive C).

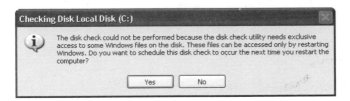

Creating and Formatting a New Partition

After you install a new hard disk in your computer, you need to create at least one partition on the disk to provide a space where Windows can store data. To create a new partition, open the Disk Management window. If this is the first time you've run Disk Management since installing the new disk, a wizard appears, offering to initialize the disk for you. Follow its instructions, being sure that you *do not* choose the option to create a dynamic disk, which is intended for use with advanced configurations and can cause problems with backups and disk-checking tools. Then follow these steps. (Note that you must be a member of the Administrators group to create a partition or format a drive.)

1   In the bottom half of the window, right-click the portion of the disk that is listed as Unallocated and choose New Partition from the short-cut menu.

Tip   Windows doesn't allow you to combine two existing small partitions into a single large one, nor does it let you shrink a big partition so you can create a new one. If you want to do tasks like these, you need a utility such as PartitionMagic, from PowerQuest Software (*http://www.powerquest.com/partitionmagic*). Don't even think about doing this sort of disk surgery, however, unless you have a current backup of your data!

---

2   Click Next after reading the Welcome page of the New Partition Wizard.

3   On the Select Partition Type page, choose Primary Partition and click Next. (If you choose the Extended Partition option, the wizard ends and you must create a logical drive before you can continue. For most home and small business users, a primary partition is the correct choice, because it's so much easier to work with.)

4   On the Specify Partition Size page, specify how much of the unallocated space on your disk you want to use for the new partition. By default, Windows selects the entire unallocated space. Keep this option if you want to create a single large partition using the entire disk.

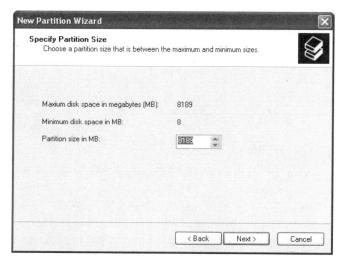

If you want to create more than one partition, enter a value here and click Next to continue.

> **Note**   The value you enter here is expressed in megabytes, but your new hard disk almost certainly contains many gigabytes of space. To convert gigabytes to megabytes, just multiply by 1024. If you want to create two 40-GB drives from an 80-GB disk, enter **40960** in the Partition Size box. (For quick approximations, feel free to multiply by 1000 instead.)

5   On the Assign Drive Letter Or Path page, choose Assign The Following Drive Letter. (The remaining two options on this page are strictly for experts.) Normally, you should accept the drive letter assignment that Windows suggests.

6 From the Format Partition page, shown in Figure 2-6, choose Format This Partition With The Following Settings (the default setting). Adjust the three options shown here as follows:

● File System—Choose NTFS or FAT32. To make the most efficient use of disk space and to maximize security, NTFS is your best choice.

● Allocation Unit Size—Keep the Default selection.

● Volume Label—This text identifies the drive in the My Computer window. The default value is New Volume, but you can change this text to be more descriptive of what you plan to store on the new drive. Volume labels can also be changed at a later time.

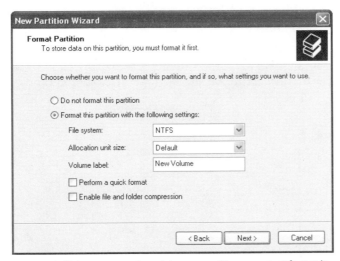

Figure 2-6 Before you can store data on a partition, you must format it.

7 Click Next to move to the final page of the wizard. Review your settings here. If you need to change anything, use Back to return to the relevant portion of the wizard. Otherwise, click Finish.

Changing Drive Letters

How does Windows assign drive letters? Drive A and drive B are always reserved for floppy drives, and drive C is almost always used for your first hard disk, the one that contains your Windows system files. After that, Windows assigns new drive letters on a first-come, first-served basis. You can change the drive letter for any drive except drives A, B, or C by using the Disk Management utility. This capability might come in handy if you install a removable hard drive to use for backups and you always want it to have X as its drive letter.

To change the letter assigned to a drive, open Disk Management, right-click the entry for the drive, and choose Change Drive Letter And Paths. Click Change and select a letter from the drop-down list of available drive letters. Click OK to save your change.

Caution Think carefully before changing the letter assigned to a drive, especially if you have programs installed on that drive. Changing the drive letter could result in your programs no longer working properly.

Formatting Floppies and Zip Disks

Setting up a hard disk should be a relatively rare event. By contrast, the option to format removable disks is one you'll use regularly. Although new floppy disks normally come pre-formatted, you can use the format option to erase a floppy disk quickly so you can copy files to it.

To format a floppy disk, insert the disk in your floppy drive and open the My Computer window. Right-click the floppy drive icon (usually A) and choose Format from the shortcut menu. Figure 2-7 shows the Format dialog box for the standard 3.5-inch floppy drive.

Figure 2-7 Click Start to format a floppy disk and prepare it to store data.

A few of the options in this dialog box are worth noting.

■ You can enter a Volume Label consisting of no more than 11 characters. (The limit for a label on a hard disk drive, by contrast, is 32 characters.) This label appears when you view the My Computer window.

- Select the Quick Format option if the disk has previously been formatted and you simply want to erase it.

- Select the Create An MS-DOS Startup Disk option if you want to create a bootable floppy disk that you can use to access your system in the event of a hard disk crash.

Tip   It's a good idea to create an MS-DOS startup disk and keep it handy. However, when you start your system using an MS-DOS boot diskette, you won't be able to read any information on a hard disk formatted with NTFS.

After choosing any applicable options, click Start to begin formatting the disk. When Windows finishes, you'll have the opportunity to format another disk or close the dialog box.

What about Zip disks? Although these high-capacity disks look like slightly oversized floppy disks, they behave quite differently. For starters, they hold the equivalent of 70 or more conventional floppy disks—100 MB or 250 MB, depending on the Zip hardware you own and the disk itself. More importantly, Zip disks typically don't need formatting.

Unlike previous versions of Windows, Windows XP can read from and write to Zip disks without requiring any special software. Moving and copying files with a Zip drive in Windows Explorer works just as it does on any other drive. One crucial difference is that Zip drives are formatted at the factory and don't normally need to be formatted. In fact, formatting a Zip disk can cause problems and should only be done as a last resort when Windows doesn't recognize a disk any longer.

Tip   If you have a Zip drive, you can gain access to many cool features—including tools for formatting and protecting Zip disks—by installing the latest version of Iomega's IomegaWare utilities. If you have an older Zip drive, don't use the software that came with the drive—it may not work properly with Windows XP. Instead, visit the Iomega Web site (*http://www.iomega.com/software*) and get the latest version, which is certified to be compatible with your new operating system.

Setting Up Your CD Drive

These days, nearly every computer comes with a CD drive. It's the standard way to install new software, including Windows itself. In addition, virtually all CD drives function as excellent audio CD players, and many types of data now arrive on CDs. Your local one-hour photo lab can probably transfer your pictures from film to a Photo CD. An increasing number of CD drives go well beyond the standard Compact Disc format and can also handle DVDs and even allow you to create your own music and data CDs.

Lingo   *CD*, of course, means *compact disc*. But what do the letters tacked onto the end of the names of CD drives tell you about their capabilities? A *CD-ROM* drive provides *read-only memory*; it cannot write data to a CD. *CD-R* drives use *recordable* media, which can be written one time only. *CD-RW* drives are *rewritable*, which means that you can erase data and record new data on the discs used in these drives. However, CD-RW disks are finicky and cannot be read by all CD drives. A CD-RW drive can also act as a CD-R drive to create data and music discs.

For most types of CD drives, no special software is required. Windows XP recognizes the different types of drives and makes their features available, although sometimes in a limited fashion. For instance, with a blank CD and a CD-R or CD-RW drive, you can copy data files from your hard disk to a CD or create a music CD from MP3 or Windows Media Audio files. However, you'll need a third-party CD-burning program to copy a music CD directly or to do anything more complicated than just copying data files.

When you insert a CD or DVD into a compatible drive, Windows XP scans the files on the disc and then uses a feature called AutoPlay to decide what to do with it. By default, AutoPlay asks you what you want to do with that type of disc. Figure 2-8, for instance, shows the dialog box that pops up when you insert a CD filled with pictures. (You would see different choices if you inserted a music CD, or a blank writable CD, or one that's filled with a variety of different file types.)

Figure 2-8 Use the AutoPlay feature to decide how to handle different types of removable media.

In this case, you can view the pictures on the CD as a slide show, copy them to the My Pictures folder, or just open Windows Explorer and work with the files there. The choice is all yours, and Windows asks you what you want to do each time it detects this type of media. If you're certain you always want to handle a certain type of disk the same way, select the Always Do The Selected Action option before clicking OK.

Tip   Does AutoPlay bug you? You can turn it off selectively or completely. Open the My Computer window, right-click your removable drive, and choose Properties. From the list at the top of the AutoPlay tab, select a content type. Then, in the list of actions below, choose Select An Action To Perform. From the list of available actions, click Take No Action and then click Apply. Repeat this process for each type of content in the list. Click OK when you're finished.

If you have a CD-R or CD-RW drive that's compatible with Windows XP, you can use the software built into Windows to burn your own CDs. You can copy files and folders from Windows Explorer, read from rewritable CDs created using third-party software, and erase rewritable CDs.

Lingo   CD *burners* and *burning* software get their name from the fact that the CD drive actually uses a laser to etch data onto a blank CD. Nothing is actually singed when you create your own custom CD, of course. In fact, if you ever see smoke coming from inside your computer, you should pull the power plug and call for help!

Before you can get started, make sure that CD recording is enabled on your drive. The easiest way to do this is to look in the My Computer window. If you've inserted a blank CD into the drive, you should see a CD-R or CD-RW label over the drive icon, as shown here.

Right-click this drive icon and choose Properties. On the Recording tab, check to see that Enable CD Recording On This Drive is selected, as shown in Figure 2-9.

Figure 2-9 Select the option at the top of the CD Drive Properties dialog box to enable CD recording in Windows.

> **Tip**   What if you prefer to use a third-party CD burning program, such as Roxio's Easy CD Creator or Ahead Software's Nero? In that case, clear the Enable CD Recording On This Drive box. This step eliminates the possibility that the Windows CD recording software will conflict with your preferred program.

Setting the other three options in this dialog box can save you a few headaches down the line. The options are as follows:

- The first option lets you select the drive where Windows stores an "image" of the CD. If you're planning to fill a blank CD completely with data (a total of 650-700 MB), ensure that you have well over 1 GB of free space available. By default, Windows suggests using drive C. If you have a different drive with lots of free space, use it instead.

- The next option lets you select a write speed. By default, Windows uses the Fastest setting, which tries to push your CD drive to the limit. If you encounter problems when writing CDs, try setting this number lower to 16X or less.

- Automatically Eject The CD After Writing is on by default. This option is intended to alert you when you've finished writing a CD. If your computer is on the floor next to your chair, however, you may not want to risk snapping off the CD drive when you swivel around! In that case, clear this check box.

Once you've enabled CD recording, the actual mechanics of copying files to a CD are straightforward. First, you select the files you want to copy. From Windows Explorer, you can drag files or folders directly onto the CD drive icon in the My Computer window or the Folders pane. Continue doing this as you work with files in different folders. You can add files at different times, over a period of hours, days, or even weeks. Windows keeps track of your selections in the CD Writing folder.

> **Tip**   Here's a time-saving trick to help you copy files to a CD without dragging them around. Select one or more files or folders, right-click, and choose the Send To menu. Select the menu choice for your CD-R or CD-RW drive.

Eventually, you'll find that you've collected enough files and it's time to burn them to a CD. To do so, go to the My Computer window and double-click the icon for your CD-R or CD-RW drive. This opens a window showing you all the files waiting to be written to your CD, as shown in Figure 2-10. Notice that the icons are fainter than normal and have a down arrow at the bottom.

Figure 2-10 All the files shown here are waiting to be written to a CD.

To begin writing the CD, click Write These Files To CD at the top of the task pane on the left. This fires up yet another wizard. In the CD Writing Wizard, shown below, type in a name for the new CD (you can use up to 16 characters), and then click Next. The remainder of the process is completely automatic.

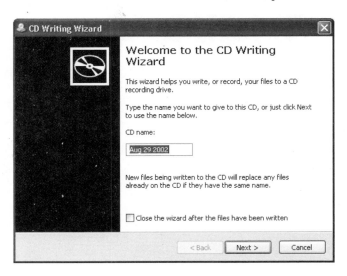

Change Settings with Control Panel

When you want to change the seemingly endless array of settings in Windows, your first stop should be Control Panel. This all-in-one window contains icons that lead to a host of options. Don't be intimidated by the Control Panel. Although some of its options might seem technical, most are easy to use and perfectly safe.

To see what options are available on your PC, click Start and then click the Control Panel icon. If you've used Control Panel in a previous version of Windows, you might be a bit confused when you see the organization of icons in the Windows XP Control Panel. As Figure 2-11 shows, icons are arranged by category, rather than being lumped together in a single window, all in alphabetical order. The result is less clutter, but it also requires that you know exactly which category contains the icon you're looking for. If you guess wrong, you must click Back and try another category.

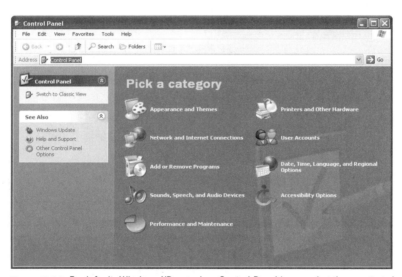

Figure 2-11 By default, Windows XP organizes Control Panel icons using these categories.

If you prefer the all-in-one-window arrangement of icons instead, click Switch To Classic View in the task pane at the left side of the window. Figure 2-12 shows the results. Note that the link at the top of the task pane changes. Click Switch To Category View to go back to the previous window.

Figure 2-12 In Classic view, all the Control Panel icons appear in a single window.

Although using Category view usually requires a few extra clicks to find the exact Control Panel option you're looking for, this view can help you avoid stumbling through dialog boxes when you can't remember exactly where a specific option is located. For instance, the Appearance And Themes category, shown below, contains a mix of links and icons, some of which take you directly to a specific tab on a dialog box, where you can accomplish a task (such as choosing a screen saver) with a minimum of fuss.

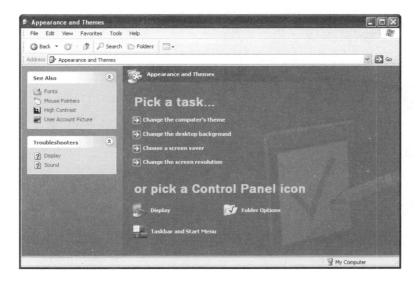

Windows includes a heaping helping of Control Panel icons—about two dozen—and other programs can add to Control Panel as well. In Classic view, these added icons appear in the same folder as the Control Panel icons. If you use the Category view, however, you'll find that most of these latecomer icons are lumped together under the catch-all label Other Control Panel Options. To find this folder, look in the task pane under the See Also group.

One potentially confusing thing about Control Panel options is that you typically have many ways to reach each one, some of which don't require you to stop at the main Control Panel window first. Some of these shortcuts require that you memorize odd keyboard combinations, but some are incredibly obvious and useful, once you learn the secrets. For an option you use every few days, learning these shortcuts can help you work faster and smarter with Windows XP. The table below lists my favorite shortcuts.

Table 2-1   Cool Control Panel Shortcuts

Option Name	Shortcut
Date And Time	Double-click the date or time in the notification area on the far right end of the taskbar.
Display	Right-click any empty space on the desktop and choose Properties.
Folder Options	From any Windows Explorer window, choose Folder Options from the Tools menu.
Fonts	Hold down the Windows logo key and press R. In the Run box, type **fonts** and press Enter.
Internet Options	From any Internet Explorer window, choose Internet Options from the Tools menu.
Network Connections	Right-click the My Network Places icon on the Start menu and choose Properties. (If this icon isn't on your Start Menu, add it by following the instructions in the section "Streamline Your Start Menu," on page 210.)
Power Options	Right-click any empty space on the desktop and choose Properties; on the Screen Saver tab, click Power.
Printers And Faxes	Add the Printers And Faxes icon to the Start menu using the instructions in the section "Streamline Your Start Menu," on page 210.
Scanners And Cameras	Double-click the device icon in the My Computer window.
System	Right-click the My Computer icon on the Start menu or in a Windows Explorer window and choose Properties or hold down the Windows key and press Break. (This rarely used key is usually in the top right corner of the keyboard.)
Taskbar And Start Menu	Right-click Start and choose Properties.
User Accounts	Click Start and click the picture to the left of your name. In the User Accounts window, click Home.

Make Windows Run Faster

It's a basic fact of life: Your computer never runs as fast as you want. If you feel the need for speed, try some of the techniques I describe in this section, which can rev up your computer to a higher gear. (As an extra bonus, some of these tips also help your computer run more reliably by reducing the risk of crashes.)

Defragment Your Hard Disk

Every time you save a file to your hard disk, Windows chops it into small pieces and stores it wherever it finds space. When you retrieve the file so you can work with it later, Windows retrieves all those pieces and reassembles them on the fly. On a freshly formatted new disk, each file gets its own block of storage space, with all the individual *clusters* lined up neatly alongside one another. The mechanical components that make up the hard disk can read these contiguous clusters easily, making the task of retrieving your file quick and efficient.

> **Lingo** A *cluster* is the minimum storage space used by Windows. When you format a disk, you divide it into clusters, each of which can hold all or part of a saved file. Even if the file contains only a few words, it occupies the entire cluster. Large files use up many clusters.

However, that neat ordering breaks down as you work with many files over time. Let's say you save 100 small files on your new hard disk, with each occupying its own cluster. Over time, you delete 20 or 30 of those files, leaving blank clusters scattered throughout the previously contiguous storage space. The next time you save a large file—one that occupies 40 or 50 clusters—Windows begins reusing the space formerly occupied by the deleted files. As a result, those first 20 or 30 clusters are scattered over a wide space, resulting in a fragmented file. When Windows instructs the hard disk to retrieve that file it has to grab each of those clusters individually, which takes more time than if the file were stored in a contiguous space. If your disk is severely fragmented, with lots of files scattered about, you'll notice that it takes longer than normal to retrieve files.

To eliminate the problems caused by fragmented files, you must physically rearrange them on the disk. Like previous Windows versions, Windows XP includes a tool designed to do exactly that. To get started, click Start and then click All Programs. From the Accessories menu, choose System Tools, and finally, click Disk Defragmenter. Disk Defragmenter is also accessible through the Computer Management console under the Storage node.

Tip   Here's a shortcut to the Disk Defragmenter. Open My Computer, right-click the icon for the drive you want to defragment, and then select Properties. On the Tools tab, click Defragment Now. Note that this only works for hard disk drives. You can't defragment a floppy disk or a CD.

As Figure 2-13 shows, the top of the Disk Defragmenter window lists all hard disk drives currently available on your computer.

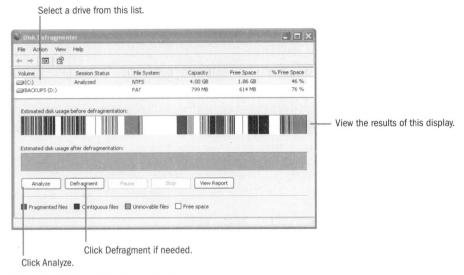

Figure 2-13   This disk is thoroughly fragmented.

Defragmenting a disk is a two-step process. First, select a drive letter from the list at the top of the Disk Defragmenter window and click Analyze. The program scans all the files on the selected disk, determines which ones are fragmented, and then shows the results in the color-coded analysis display that appears just below the drive list. A highly fragmented list is tinged with red instead of blue markers, which indicate contiguous files. After the analysis is complete (the process typically takes only a few seconds), Windows displays a dialog box advising you whether you need to proceed to the next step and actually defragment the disk, as shown below.

To proceed with the second step, click Defragment. The actual process of defragmenting can take some time, but it's completely automatic and doesn't require any extra steps on your part. As the program does its magic, you can see the changes reflected in the lower half of the analysis display (Estimated Disk Usage After Defragmentation). At any point, you can suspend the process by clicking Pause. To cancel the defragmentation operation completely, click Stop.

Tip Would you like to defragment your disks automatically? You can't do this with the Disk Defragmenter program included with Windows XP. Instead, you need a third-party program such as Diskeeper (*http://www.diskeeper.com/consumer/diskeeper/diskeeper.asp*) or Norton Utilities (*http://www.symantec.com/nu/nu_9x*).

Master Your Memory

As a general rule, having more RAM lets you do more with your computer. Adding memory lets you open more programs, work with larger files, and avoid slowdowns, error messages, and crashes, which can occur when you run out of RAM. To see how much memory is installed in your computer, open Control Panel's System option (you'll find it in the Performance And Maintenance category), and click the General tab.

When you add RAM to your system, Windows should detect it automatically and configure itself to take advantage of the extra memory. You don't need to make any changes manually.

How Much Memory Do You Need?   When your PC seems to be poking along in the slow lane, adding extra RAM is the single most important thing you can do to give it some extra zip. So how much is not enough, and how much is too much?

There's no right or wrong answer. Windows XP can run, albeit slowly, with as little as 64 MB of RAM—as long as you don't ask it to do too much. On the other hand, if you design rocket ships for a living, you'll need a lot more memory. For demanding applications, at least 512 MB is in order. Some motherboards can accommodate as much as 2 GB of RAM chips, and Windows XP can use it all.

So, how much memory do you need? My personal recommendations are based on the amount of work you do. See if you can identify yourself in this list.

■   You browse the Web, send and receive e-mail, and write letters using Microsoft Works. Aside from the occasional digital picture of your nephew in Nantucket, you rarely do anything with graphics. You're the only full-time user of your computer. You'll do fine with 128 MB of RAM, although having 256 MB wouldn't hurt.

■   You use Microsoft Office and regularly use both Outlook and Word. You have a digital camera and occasionally touch up photos to put them on your family Web site. Other family members use the computer to check e-mail and play games. You need at least 256 MB of RAM, and upgrading to 512 MB would be smart.

■   You use every Microsoft Office program, including FrontPage. You always have at least six browser windows open. You're experimenting with video editing and desktop publishing, and you use Adobe PhotoShop to clean up old family pictures. Your kids are constantly downloading music files in the background while you work. With anything less than 512 MB of RAM, you're going to find yourself drumming your fingers on the desktop waiting for your computer to catch up with you. Add as much RAM as you can afford.

Clean Up Unnecessary Files

One thing that can slow your system to a crawl is a shortage of disk space. Over time, your hard disk becomes cluttered with junk files, including temporary files that you no longer need and deleted files that are still sitting in the Recycle Bin. Use the Disk Cleanup Wizard to clear away some of the clutter. To start this wizard, click Start and choose All Programs; click Accessories, then System Tools, and finally Disk Cleanup. Figure 2-14 shows this wizard in action.

This column tells you how much disk space you'll recover.

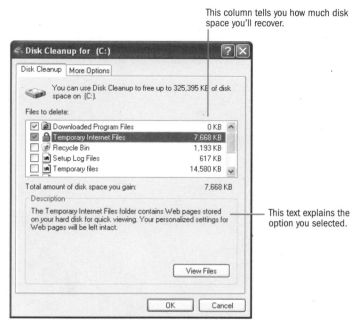

This text explains the option you selected.

Figure 2-14   Use the Disk Cleanup Wizard to reclaim some disk space.

The Disk Cleanup Wizard analyzes your hard disk and then presents options you can use to gain increased disk space. Select check boxes on the Disk Cleanup tab to carry out the indicated actions (emptying the Recycle Bin, for instance). Most of these changes are helpful, or at least harmless. Steer clear of the choice to compress old files, however, which has the potential to slow down your system. Click OK to apply the changes.

Caution   Using the Disk Cleanup Wizard is infinitely preferable to trying to prune old files by hand. One thing I suggest you never do is try to clean out files in the Windows or System folders. Some of these files are required by Windows or programs, and if you delete them you run the risk that Windows or an important program begins to experience problems or stops working altogether.

Change Advanced Visual Effects

On older, slower PCs with minimal amounts of memory and no reasonable prospects for a hardware upgrade, you might need to take some extra steps to get acceptable performance. To solve this problem, click Start, point to Control Panel, select Performance And Maintenance, and finally select the System option. On the Advanced tab, in the Performance frame, click Settings. The Performance Options dialog box, shown below, contains 16 advanced options with unbelievably technical names. (Can you tell me what Show Translucent Selection Rectangle means?)

Although you can click Custom and set each of these options individually, that's a hit-or-miss solution. Assuming you came to this dialog box because your system was sluggish, click Adjust For Best Performance and then click OK. After a bit of reconfiguring, you'll return to a simpler desktop that looks more like the old Windows interface, and hopefully everything moves with just a bit more zip!

How Do I...?

Windows XP does an amazing number of things. So many, in fact, that you probably couldn't cover every feature even in a shelf full of books the size of this one. That doesn't mean you're on your own when you need answers, though. Instead, turn to the Windows XP Help And Support Center, where you'll find instructions, overviews, tutorials, troubleshooters, and reference material on just about every aspect of Windows XP.

The information in the Help And Support Center runs the gamut, in technical terms, from step-by-step instructions suitable for a beginner to in-depth technical details that can help an expert work through a sticky problem. Next time you get stuck, the Help And Support Center should be your first stop.

Using the Help And Support Center

The Help And Support Center works like an online book. It's divided into sections and chapters, with a table of contents and an index, all hyperlinked together so you can smoothly jump between related ideas and concepts in different sections. To get started, click Start and choose Help And Support. This takes you to the Help And Support Center home page. Figure 2-15 shows the key parts of the Help And Support Center. You can retrieve information in any of the following ways, depending on the task you've tackled.

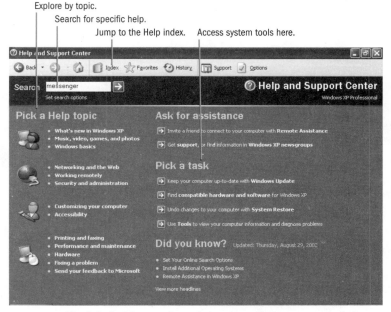

Figure 2-15 The Help And Support Center home page offers many ways to find answers.

- **By Topic**   The Pick A Help Topic column on the left side of the home page includes links to a wide variety of general topics. In essence, it functions as a hyperlinked table of contents for the entire Help "book." Pick a topic and start clicking. As you dig deeper, you'll find more and more details about the topics you're exploring.

- **By Keyword**   Click Index to view the full list of keywords in the Help Index. Start typing in the text box above the keyword list to jump to a specific keyword, and then click Display (or double-click the keyword entry) to see the matching topic, which appears in the right-hand pane, as shown below. In some cases this action returns another dialog box with a list of topics for you to select from. This strategy works well when you've seen a keyword in Windows and you want to learn more about what it means.

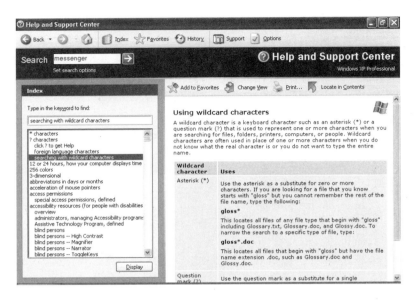

■ **By Searching** Click in the Search text box at the top of the Help And Support Center window and enter a word or phrase to search for. Then click the green arrow to the right of the text box. The Search Results list appears just below. Click any link to see that topic. This technique works well when you want to see a lot of details about a specific term. Because the results are gathered from all Help topics, the results can be too broad.

Tip When you're learning how to use a new feature, use the Favorites menu to keep track of topics that you find particularly helpful. From the topic pane, click Add To Favorites. To review your list of favorite Help topics, click Favorites at the top of the Help And Support Center.

Get Answers from the Internet

The Help And Support Center is big and fairly comprehensive, but it doesn't have every answer to every Windows question. Far from it. In addition, new problems and solutions are uncovered every day, and you won't find that sort of up-to-date information in a Help file. That doesn't mean you're out of luck. When you use the Search text box to look for information in the Help And Support Center, Windows also sends your request to Microsoft's Web site (assuming you have an active Internet connection) and checks the enormous and ever-growing Microsoft Knowledge Base. You'll find these search results at the bottom of the list, under the Microsoft Knowledge Base heading.

Tip   The Knowledge Base consists of numbered articles, ranging in length from a paragraph or two to several pages and covering the complete spectrum of technical depth. All Knowledge Base article numbers begin with the letter Q, followed by a six-digit number. If you ever see instructions to read a specific Knowledge Base article, you can hop over to the Help And Support Center, enter the article's Q-number in the Search text box, and have the exact article delivered straight to your computer over the Internet. How cool is that?

Shutting Down

Two minutes to start up. Two minutes to shut down. A minute to start up your programs and find your files again at the beginning of the day and another minute or two after lunch. If you go through this routine every day, you're wasting time. At 10 minutes a day, that's almost an hour a week, and nearly 50 hours per year down the tubes. Want to get some of that time back? Next time, instead of turning off your computer, why not use one of your other shutdown options instead?

Windows XP gives you a total of three options for shutting down. Choosing the right one can help you get back to work more quickly. All the power-saving options described here work only if your computer includes the proper power management circuitry. (Virtually every computer sold since 1998 should work with these instructions. If you have an older computer, however, you might not be able to use all these features.)

Note   Your power management options depend to a large extent on the design of the computer. In some cases, you can configure the computer so it "wakes up" when you click the mouse or press any key. You might have Standby on your keyboard, with a corresponding utility program to configure how that key works. Some computers automatically go into standby when you press the Power switch and only shut down completely if you hold this switch down for 4 seconds. To see which options are available on your computer, look in the documentation that came with the computer or visit the support section of the manufacturer's Web site.

To shut down your computer, click Start and choose Turn Off Computer. You'll see the dialog box shown here.

Stand By: Take a Short Break

The Stand By option puts your computer in a low-power mode that saves energy. Any programs that were running remain in your computer's memory. When you resume from standby (in seconds, typically, instead of the several minutes required by a normal startup), everything is just as you left it. Use this option when you plan to be away from your computer for no more than an hour or two and you want to save a few watts.

> **Caution**   Don't forget to save your work before shifting into standby! If the power fails while you're away, all the data in memory literally vanishes into thin air, and nothing can bring it back. Saving your files regularly is always a good idea, but it's essential in this case.

Hibernate: Save Your Work

If you plan to be away from your computer for more than a few hours, consider the Hibernate option. This feature saves everything in your computer's memory to a file on your disk and then shuts down the computer. When you turn your computer back on, Windows reloads the contents of the hibernation file into memory, putting you right back where you were. Resuming from hibernation takes longer than resuming from standby, but typically requires much less time than a full restart. Your data is safe from a power failure, too, because it's actually saved on the disk.

Before you can use the Hibernate option, you need to enable it. To do so, follow these steps:

1   Click Start and choose Control Panel.

2   Open the Performance And Maintenance category and click Power Options. (If you use the Classic view of Control Panel, just double-click the Power Options icon.)

3   On the Hibernate tab, select the Enable Hibernation option, as shown below.

4   Click OK to save your changes and close the Power Options dialog box.

Note   Using the Hibernate option requires a chunk of disk space equal to the amount of memory installed on your computer. This free space must be available on your drive C. If your drive C is full, you might find that the Hibernate option doesn't work. In that case, you'll have to move or delete enough files to free up the needed space.

So how do you tell Windows that you want it to hibernate? The option is hidden under Stand By in the Turn Off Computer dialog box. You can make it visible by holding down Shift when you see this dialog box. While continuing to hold down Shift, click Hibernate to put your PC to sleep. To wake up again, press the power button on your computer.

Caution   While your computer is hibernating, don't change any hardware. When it wakes up from its slumber, it expects to see exactly the same devices that were attached before you put it to sleep. If you want to add or remove a device, do so before hibernating or after resuming normal operation. For devices that are not hot-pluggable and require you to access the main board, be sure to shut down and power off your computer first.

Shut Down: Close Everything

Sometimes, of course, you just want to turn off your computer. If you're planning to do an upgrade or if you just installed a new piece of software that requires a restart, you'll need to do this. To do a full shutdown, click Start and choose Turn Off Computer. Use Turn Off to power down your PC completely. Use Restart to shut down and then automatically restart.

Key Points

- Before you can begin using Windows XP, you must log on with a unique user name.

- You can add a password to your account to protect it from snoops. You can also change your password at any time.

- With a feature called Fast User Switching, you can leave all your programs running while other users log on to their account on the same computer. After they're through working, you can return to your desktop, where all your programs are still running exactly as you left them.

- The My Computer window is the surest route to finding files and folders, regardless of where they're stored.

■ Use the Disk Cleanup Wizard regularly to clean up unneeded files from your hard disk and keep your system running smoothly.

■ Before you can use a hard disk, you have to create a partition and format it.

■ Defragmenting your hard disk and checking for disk errors are essential maintenance tasks.

■ The Help And Support Center contains an enormous amount of information, and it can even search Microsoft's Knowledge Base over the Internet.

■ Instead of shutting down your system, use the Stand By or Hibernate options, which let you resume working with your computer more quickly.

Chapter 3

Installing, Uninstalling, and Running Programs

Without software, Microsoft Windows would be pretty boring. Oh, sure, you'd still have Solitaire and Windows Media Player, so you could listen to your favorite CDs while avoiding work. But sooner or later you'll run out of CDs, and how long can you play cards, really? Fortunately, you can choose from thousands of programs, from Microsoft and other companies, to give yourself something else to do with Windows. Conveniently, when you learn how to install one Windows program, you've pretty much mastered the process. In this chapter, I'll show you how to add and remove programs, how to make it easier to start your favorite programs, and how to deal with programs that won't run right.

Installing a New Program

Most Windows programs sold in retail packages come on CD-ROM. When you pop the CD in the drive, the Setup Wizard runs automatically. Answer a few simple questions, and before you know it, you're ready to use your new program.

If you download a new program from the Internet—either a commercial program that you purchased for *electronic delivery*, or a *shareware* or *freeware program* downloaded from a site like *http://www.download.com*—you may need to go through an extra step or two before you can install it. Downloaded programs are usually stored in compressed (Zip) files, which means you first have to extract the files and then double-click the Setup or Install icon to get started.

Lingo   *Shareware* is try-before-you-buy software that you can install and use for free. If you like it, you're expected to pay for it. *Freeware* is software that you can use without paying. An increasing number of programs are available for purchase and immediate download—a mechanism called *electronic delivery* to distinguish it from the physical delivery of a CD.

More Info   If you're not sure how to work with compressed files, see the section "Zipping and Unzipping Files," on page 245.

Are you thinking of installing a new program? Don't be in a hurry. A little bit of preparation can help you avoid problems. Before you begin the installation routine, follow these tips:

- **Read the instructions!**   You don't have to pore over every page in the manual, but at least check the opening section to see if your system meets the minimum requirements and if you need to do anything first (like turning off your antivirus program or shutting down your firewall temporarily). You may also discover that the new program is incompatible with another program you use regularly, in which case you may decide not to set up the newcomer.

    Tip   Look for a file called Readme. If you download software from the Internet, the Readme file often contains helpful installation tips and warnings.

- **Check for updates.**   This is especially important for software that you buy in a retail package, which may have been sitting on the shelf for months, and could even be more than a year old. Find the manufacturer's Web address on the box or in the manual. When you visit that site, look for a link called Support or Downloads; that's where you're most likely to find a *patch* or *update* for your program.

    Lingo   *Patches* are small software programs designed to fix bugs in a program you've already installed. *Updates* may provide newer features or functionality or supply a newer driver if one is required.

■ **Be selective about new software.**   A badly written program can slow down your system, cause compatibility problems, and interfere with the operation of other programs. I always like to check out a new program first before purchasing it—and definitely before installing it! Doing a quick search for the program name on Google (*http://www.google.com*) sometimes turns up horror stories and cautionary tales that convince me not to install the new program after all!

■ **Use System Restore to create a restore point first.**   If the program you're about to install turns out to be incompatible with something else on your computer, you can uninstall it and then use System Restore to put everything back the way it was originally.

More Info   For step-by-step instructions on saving and restoring your system configuration, see the sections "Set Up System Restore Checkpoints," on page 98, and "Rolling Back to a Previous Configuration," on page 116.

If the installation process doesn't begin automatically when you insert the program CD, you can get things going manually by following these steps:

1   Click Start and choose Control Panel.

2   Double-click Add Or Remove Programs.

3   Click Add New Programs on the left of the Add Or Remove Programs dialog box, as shown here.

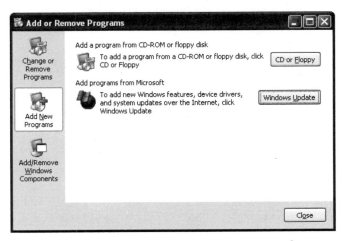

4   Click CD Or Floppy.

5   Follow the wizard's prompts to install your program.

If the CD you inserted contains a Setup or Install program, Windows runs it automatically. If the wizard can't find such a file, it prompts you to search for the correct file. Browse the CD until you find the file.

Is running the Setup program really necessary? Can't you just copy the files from the CD to your hard disk, or from one computer to another? Nice try, but that shortcut works for only the simplest Windows programs. For the overwhelming majority of programs, you need to run the Setup routine to make sure that every detail in the installation process is handled properly. When you run Setup, it copies program files to the correct locations on your hard disk, with different files going in several different folders; it also records technical settings in the Windows registry that tell Windows how the new program works and creates shortcuts that you can use to start the program. If you skip any of these steps, the new program won't work properly.

Every Setup program is a little different, but most follow the same basic principles. A wizard guides you through the installation process, occasionally asking you to supply some information or choose an option. The Microsoft Office XP Setup Wizard, for instance, asks you to enter your name and your initials, and then displays the options shown in Figure 3-1.

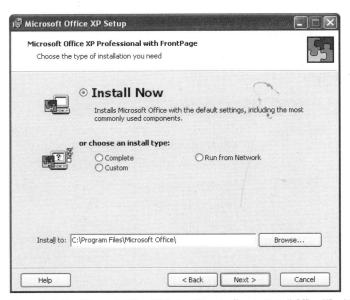

Figure 3-1 The Microsoft Office XP Setup Wizard offers to install Office XP with default settings, or you can choose from a variety of custom options.

It's sometimes tempting to blast through the installation process, clicking Next at each screen without reading the instructions. Most of the time, though, I choose the Custom installation option (if it's available). By looking carefully at each of the choices instead of just settling for the default settings, I sometimes run across an easier way to work with the program, or an incredibly useful feature that I didn't know about.

Tip   When you run a Setup program, one option lets you choose where Windows should copy the program files. *Always* accept the default setting for this location, which is typically a subfolder in the Program Files folder.

Create Shortcuts to Your Favorite Programs

One way to start a program is to double-click the icon for its *executable file*. To begin working with Microsoft Word, for instance, you *could* open the My Computer window, double click the icon for your drive C icon, then the Program Files folder, then the Microsoft Office folder, and finally the Office10 folder. Then you'd scroll to the bottom of the folder until you find Winword.exe and double-click it.

Yikes! Your index finger will wear out in no time if you have to do that much clicking every time you want to start a program.

Lingo   *Executable files* are those that contain the code that actually runs ("executes") a program. These file names usually end with the extension .exe.

Fortunately, there's a much faster, smarter way to start a program. Use a *shortcut* to get to that executable file. When you double-click the shortcut, it has the same effect as if you were double-clicking the file the shortcut points to. You can move the shortcut to a new location (drop it on the Start button, for instance, to add it to the top of the Start menu). You can also make a copy of a shortcut and move it to a different location; the copy works exactly like the one you just created using the wizard. How can you tell a shortcut from the target file to which it's linked? Look for a small arrow in the lower left corner of the icon, as in the examples here (the target file is on the left, the shortcut on the right):

You can have as many shortcuts as you want to a single program, and you can put those shortcuts anywhere you want them, without disturbing the file they point to (called the *target*). When you install a new program, the setup program usually adds one or more shortcuts to the All Programs menu. Some setup programs also put shortcuts on the desktop, at the top of the Start menu, and on the Quick Launch toolbar, just to the right of the Start button.

If you find a program you want to use regularly and it doesn't already have a shortcut, you can make your own, using the Create Shortcut Wizard:

1 Right-click an empty space on the desktop, click New, and then select Shortcut.

2 In the Create Shortcut Wizard, click Browse to locate the file you want the shortcut to point to, and click OK to fill that file name in the location box, as shown below.

Tip   You can type the name of the file, including its full path, if you know it. But it's usually easier to browse for the file instead. Plus, doing this guards against your making a typographical error that would prevent Windows XP from recognizing the file.

---

3 Click Next to continue.

4 In the Type A Name For This Shortcut text box, enter the name you want to appear under the shortcut icon.

5 Click Finish.

That's all it takes to create a shortcut.

To see what's inside a shortcut, right-click the shortcut icon and choose Properties. As you can see from Figure 3-2, the Properties dialog box has a Shortcut tab, which contains information about the target file and some handy boxes that you can use to make the shortcut even easier to work with.

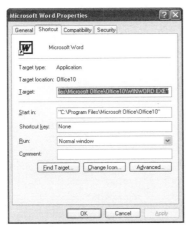

Figure 3-2 Use the Properties dialog box to customize a shortcut.

The area at the top of the Shortcut tab tells you about the file the shortcut points to. In this case, it's an Application (in other words, a program); the Target Location tells you the name of the folder where the target file can be found, and the Target text box has the full name and path of the file.

Tip   It's OK to delete a shortcut icon. Nothing happens to your original file; it stays safe and sound, right where it always was.

The bottom of this dialog box has the most interesting and useful options, as follows:

▪ Enter the name of a folder in the Start In text box, and Windows takes you to that location when you double-click the program shortcut. If you find a program that keeps prompting you to save its files in some obscure location, try typing *%Userprofile%***My Documents** here (be sure to include both percent signs). This forces the program to always start in your My Documents folder.

Tip   A percent sign at the beginning and end of a term identifies it as a *system variable* to Windows. When you type ***%Userprofile%*** (or enter it in a dialog box), Windows checks your logon name to see who you are and then opens the group of folders that hold all your personal files, and it's a heck of a lot easier to type than **C:\Documents and Settings\Edbott.**

■   Would you like your program to start up when you press a specific combination of keys? Click in the Shortcut Key text box and then press the key combination you want to use to start (or switch to) the program. You need to use a letter or number plus at least two of the following three keys: Ctrl, Alt, and Shift. So if you want to make Windows Calculator easy to start, try assigning the shortcut Ctrl+Alt+C. This trick only works with program shortcuts on the desktop, on the Start menu, or on the All Programs menu.

Tip   You can easily add a shortcut key to a program shortcut on the All Programs menu. Click Start, choose All Programs, and find the menu item, just as if you were going to start the program. But instead of clicking it with the left mouse button, right-click and choose Properties. While in the Properties dialog box for the shortcut, try clicking the question mark in the top right corner and then clicking a feature text box to display helpful hints.

■   Use the three options on the drop-down Run list to control how the program starts. You can force it to start up using the full screen, or in a window. If you want the program to be available but stay out of the way until it's needed, choose the Minimized option.

■   You can also add a comment to a shortcut. This is the text that pops up when you let the mouse pointer rest over a shortcut.

Tip   If you have Windows Explorer open and you can see the executable file for your program, you can skip the wizard and create a shortcut directly. Point to the file icon, hold down the *right* mouse button, and drag the icon onto the desktop (or any convenient location). When you let go of the mouse button, a small menu appears; choose Create Shortcuts Here, and you're done! If you don't like the name of the shortcut, you can rename it.

Want to find the file that a shortcut points to? In the Properties dialog box for the shortcut, click Find Target. This opens a Windows Explorer window showing the contents of the folder that contains the target file, with the file itself already selected.

Your Old Program Won't Run Right? Try This Fix

If you're new to Windows XP but not to Windows, you may have an old program or two that you just can't live without. If a program was originally written for an older version of Windows, such as Windows 95 or Windows 98, it might have problems running under Windows XP. So do you have to throw it away? Not necessarily. In some cases, you can trick the program into thinking it's running under that old Windows version and it will work just fine. Here's how:

1   Right-click the shortcut for the program you want to run and choose Properties.

2   On the Properties dialog box, click the Compatibility tab.

3   Select the Run This Program In Compatibility Mode For check box.

4   From the drop-down list, choose the version of Windows that the program worked with previously—for most programs, this will be either Windows 95 or Windows 98/Windows Millennium Edition (Windows Me).

5   When you're finished, the results should look like what's shown in Figure 3-3. Click OK to save your changes.

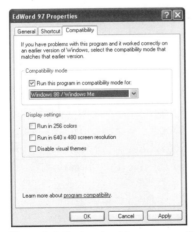

Figure 3-3 If a favorite old program won't work under Windows XP, try setting these compatibility options.

Caution   Some old programs absolutely should not be run with Windows XP. This is especially true of antivirus programs, system utilities, disk defragmenters, and other programs designed to work directly with Windows. Windows XP usually will give you back an error message when you try to use the old program; don't try to get around it or you could end up scrambling your system!

Consider this trick a last-ditch effort. Selecting the Compatibility Mode check box can cause problems with a program that doesn't need to run in a previous Windows environment. The only time you should use this trick is when you have a program that used to run under your old version of Windows and has minor problems under Windows XP. Before you try it, check with the company that developed the software in the first place. A quick search of the Web might turn up a patch that you can download, or it might explain why the program doesn't run properly.

What to Do When a Program Freezes

If you've used Windows for any length of time, you know how frustrating and annoying it is when a program suddenly stops responding. You can pound the keyboard and click the mouse until your fingertips are numb, but the program just ignores you. What do you do next? The good news is that, in Windows XP, a hung program rarely crashes the rest of your computer. If you can figure out how to close the program, you can get back to work. Try these three tactics (in the order shown here) to get unstuck:

- **Wait a minute (or two or three minutes).**   Sometimes the program hasn't really crashed at all—it's just taking its own sweet time to accomplish a task in the background. Go get a cup of coffee, make a phone call, or play a game of FreeCell. You might be pleasantly surprised to discover that the program springs back to life. If that doesn't work, then...

- **Try to shut down the crashed program.**   Right-click its taskbar button and choose Close from the shortcut menu. If the program is truly hung up, this probably won't work, but it's worth a try. If you're lucky, you'll see the dialog box shown here, which forces the program to shut down immediately. (You'll lose any unsaved data—sorry!)

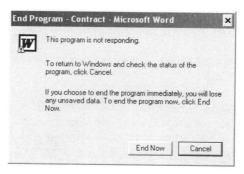

■ **Use Task Manager to shut down the program.** This is one of the most powerful secret weapons Windows XP has. Press Ctrl+Alt+Delete to bring up the dialog box shown in Figure 3-4. The Applications tab lists every program currently running on your PC. If you see the words "Not Responding" to the right of the program that's giving you fits, you know that Windows agrees with you that it's time to pull the plug. Click the hung program and then click End Task.

Figure 3-4 When a program stops responding, click End Task to close it.

After you forcibly shut down a program that has stopped responding, Windows might offer to send an error report to Microsoft, using a dialog box like the one shown here:

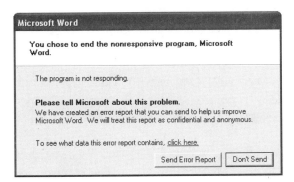

Should you send the report or not? That decision is completely up to you. I suggest that you click Send Error Report if this is a problem that you haven't seen before. (You must be connected to the Internet to send the report.) If this is an error that you see regularly and you've already reported the problem, though, click Don't Send and save yourself a few seconds. Either way, though, don't expect to get a response. The error-reporting procedure isn't designed to solve your particular problem; instead, its purpose is to give Microsoft's engineers a heads-up when lots of people are experiencing similar problems. With enough reports, chances are that someone will figure out why the problem is occurring and write a software patch that fixes it.

More Info   For advice on what to do when your computer crashes (not just a single program), see the section "Troubleshooting 101: How to Figure Out What's Wrong," on page 102.

Choose the Program That Works with a File Type

You don't always have to start a program by clicking a shortcut in the Start menu or on the desktop. If you saved the latest draft of the Great American Novel in your My Documents folder, all you have to do is double-click the icon for the saved document. When you double-click a data file, such as a Microsoft Word document or a digital picture file, Windows searches its list of *file associations* to see if it knows how to open that type of file. If it finds a program that's assigned to open the type of file you double-clicked, it starts that program (or switches to it, if the program is already running) and loads the data file.

Most of the time, this process happens automatically. When you install a new program, the setup routine records the associations between file types and programs. So, when you install Microsoft Office, for example, the setup routine tells Windows that it should open Microsoft Word whenever you double-click a document file whose name ends with the *extension* .doc.

Lingo   An *extension* is the part of a file name that comes after the last period in the name. Most of the time, these extensions are three letters long, although a file name extension can be any length. Windows uses the extension to keep track of which program opens that type of file.

But what happens when you want to open a file with a different program than the one that Windows has associated with that file type? That depends on whether you want to use the alternative program just this one time, or whether you want to change the default association, so that the new program you select always opens that type of file.

Let's start with the temporary solution. Say you've taken some pictures with your digital camera and saved them in your My Pictures folder. The pictures are stored as files in the *JPEG* format, with the extension .jpg at the end of each file name.

Lingo   *JPEG* is the name of a widely used standard for storing graphics files. It's short for the name of the organization that created the standard—the Joint Photographic Experts Group.

Normally, when you double-click one of these files, Windows opens the Windows Picture And Fax Viewer, a handy program that lets you look at the picture and print a copy. But this time, you want to open this picture in your spiffy new photo-editing program, so you can crop and touch up the picture. Here's how to get the picture file into the right program:

1 Right-click the file icon and choose Open With.

2 If more than one program is associated with the type of file you've selected, a list similar to the one shown in Figure 3-5 appears. If the program you want is on this list, choose it. If it's not, click Choose Program. (If only one program is associated with the file type you selected, you won't see a list of program choices, and you can move on to the next step.)

Figure 3-5 Use the Open With menu to choose which program you want to use when opening a file.

3 In the Open With dialog box, Windows lists Recommended Programs, which are already associated with the file type you selected, and Other Programs, as shown below.

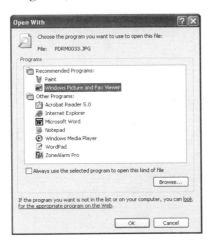

You can choose from the following two options:

● If the name of the program you want to use is in the Other Programs list, select it and click OK.

● If your program isn't in this list, click Browse, find the executable file for that program, select it, and click Open. Then click OK in the Open With dialog box.

4   Right-click the file icon and once again choose Open With. This time, the program you just added should be on the list.

You need to go through this rigmarole only once for a given program. Windows remembers your choice the next time you right-click a file of that type and includes the program on the Open With menu.

What if you want to change the program that runs when you double-click a file icon? That's actually a simple process. Go through the same steps just outlined. In the Open With dialog box, after choosing the program you want to use, select the check box at the bottom, Always Use The Selected Program To Open This Kind Of File. After you click OK, you can double-click the file icon to start up the new program.

Tip   Programs that work with graphics files and those that organize and play digital music are notorious for taking over file types that previously belonged to another program. If this happens to you, and you decide you want those file types to be associated with the old program, your easiest course of action is just to reinstall the older program. Sometimes, too, you can poke around in the menus and dialog boxes and find an option that lets you reclaim file associations after another program grabs them. With Windows Media Player, for instance, you can choose Options from the Tools menu, and then from the File Types tab click check boxes to select the file types you want that program to handle.

Change Programs That Run Automatically at Startup

You probably use some programs every day; others you use only once in a while. For those you can't live without, wouldn't it be handy to have them start up automatically, every time you log on to your computer? You can accomplish this easily, by adding a shortcut to the Startup group on the All Programs menu. Likewise, if you find that you're not using a program that runs automatically each time you start Windows, you can remove it from the Startup group, speeding up your logon time and freeing up some memory.

One thing to note is that Windows actually has two Startup groups. One belongs only to you, and shortcuts you add here run only when you log on to Windows. The other Startup group is in the All Users folder, and as you might guess, it includes program shortcuts that run whenever any user logs on to the computer.

To add or remove a program shortcut in the Startup folder, follow these directions:

1 Right-click the Start button and choose Open from the shortcut menu. (To add a shortcut to the Startup folder for everyone that logs on to your computer, choose Open All Users from this menu instead.)

2 Double-click the Programs folder, and then double-click the Startup folder.

3 Drag a program shortcut into the folder to start that program automatically when you log on, or use the Create Shortcut Wizard to add a new shortcut.

To remove a program from the Startup folder, you can use the same procedure, deleting an existing shortcut instead of adding a new one. Even easier, you can delete these shortcuts right from the Start menu:

1 Click Start and choose All Programs.

2 Click Startup to show a list of all programs that start up automatically on your computer.

3 Right-click the icon for any shortcut you want to remove, and choose Delete from the shortcut menu.

Using the Startup menu is the simplest way to load a program every time you turn on your computer, but Windows has many other places where it can load programs so that they start up when you do. These places include locations buried deep in the Windows registry, where only experts dare to tread.

If you discover that a program is starting up automatically, and it isn't in your Startup folder, you can figure out where it's coming from by using the Windows System Configuration Utility. To work with this program, click Start and choose Run. In the Run dialog box, type **msconfig** and press Enter. When the System Configuration Utility opens, click the Startup tab and you'll see a dialog box like the one shown in Figure 3-6.

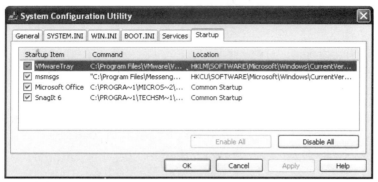

Figure 3-6 This utility displays names and other details for all programs starting automatically on your computer.

If you want to get rid of a program that's in this list, your absolute best bet is to find the option in that program that disables it. For instance, if you use Norton AntiVirus 2002, you can open its Options dialog box and select or clear the Start Auto-Protect When Windows Starts Up box. This is always the best way to get rid of a pesky program.

But if you absolutely can't figure out how to disable that program, use the System Configuration Utility and clear the check box just to the left of the program that's giving you problems. The next time you start your computer, you'll get a harmless error message, but the program won't be there anymore.

Remove Programs the Right Way

You installed a new program. You tried it. You hated it. Now how do you get it off your computer? Don't just delete the shortcuts on the Start menu and the desktop. That still leaves all the program files and settings cluttering up your computer. And whatever you do, *don't* just go into your Program Files folder and start deleting files or folders that look like they belong to that program! That creates even more of a mess and is practically guaranteed to give you headaches, like random error messages and crashes.

The *right* way to uninstall a program is to let Windows do it for you. If you used a setup program to install the program, there's a good chance that the program's author designed an uninstall routine as well. The really considerate ones add an Uninstall This Program shortcut on the All Programs menu, in the same folder that contains your other shortcuts for that program. If your unwanted program doesn't include an uninstall shortcut, click Start and open Control Panel; then double-click Add Or Remove Programs.

Tip Before you remove a program, always open Help And Support first and create a System Restore checkpoint. If anything goes wrong with your uninstallation, you can put things back the way they were by using the Restore My Computer To An Earlier Time option.

On the left side of the Add Or Remove Programs dialog box, click the Change Or Remove Programs icon. When you do, you'll see a list of every program installed on your computer, as in the example shown in Figure 3-7.

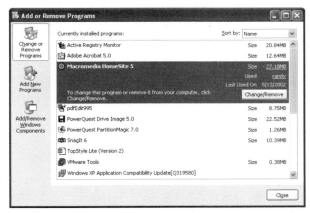

Figure 3-7 This list lets you see which programs you've installed on your computer and remove those you no longer need.

The details in this dialog box tell you a little bit about each program—how much space it's using, how often you use it, and when you last used it, for instance. (Some programs even have a handy hyperlink that takes you to the manufacturer's support site, so you can look for patches or explanations when you run into problems.)

To remove a program, click the Change/Remove button to the right of the listing for that program and follow the prompts.

Tip What do you do if you already deleted some files and the uninstall program gives you an error message? As odd as it sounds, the correct thing to do is to *reinstall* the program. (Don't worry; you don't have to use it again.) After you install it properly, the uninstall routine should work again.

When you remove a program, Windows may ask a few questions, such as whether you want to remove files that don't seem to be in use anymore. Usually, it's completely safe to remove any files that Windows identifies as unnecessary. If you're worried, though, just say no. Having the extra files stored on your hard disk won't hurt anything.

Key Points

- Whenever you install a new program, be sure to run the Setup program to do the job properly.

- Always check for updates when installing a new program. This is especially important for software that wasn't originally written for Windows XP.

- Set a System Checkpoint before installing or uninstalling a program. If anything goes wrong, you can roll your system configuration back to the way it was and get things working right again in a jiffy.

- Create shortcuts for the programs you use most often and add them to the Start menu, the Quick Launch toolbar, the desktop, and any other place where you can find them when you want to use the program.

- Set up keyboard shortcuts for your favorite programs to make them easier to start up.

- Add your most favorite programs, the ones you use every day, to the Startup group so they load automatically when you log on to your computer.

- Learn how to control which program opens files of a particular type.

Chapter 4

Microsoft Windows and Hardware

Is your PC doing everything you want it to do? If it seems to be stuck in a rut, you can expand its horizons by adding some new hardware. Microsoft Windows XP allows you to turn your ho-hum PC into a video editing studio, a digital photo lab, or a desktop printing and publishing shop, just by plugging in a new device. You don't need any special incantations or an advanced engineering degree to get your new hardware to work with Windows, either. Virtually all the new devices you can add to your computer these days use a Windows feature called Plug and Play, which makes it possible for anyone to install a new device and have it working in a matter of minutes. And on those rare occasions when something goes wrong, troubleshooting tools are only a few clicks away.

Hardware Made Easy

With Windows XP, setting up a new piece of hardware doesn't require intricate installation instructions or brain-twisting dialog boxes. In fact, many *devices* literally configure themselves as soon as you plug them in. Most others can be up and running in a matter of minutes if you download the correct software *drivers* and install them correctly.

Lingo   A *device* is a piece of hardware, which may be internal (that is, inside your computer) or external (plugged into a connecting port on your PC). A *driver* is the software that tells Windows how to communicate with a specific piece of hardware. If you don't have the correct driver for a device, Windows can tell that there's an unknown device, but it can't recognize the hardware and therefore can't help you work with it the way you want. A poorly written driver can cause unexplained hardware failures and can even cause your computer to crash.

Hardware comes in all shapes and sizes. Some devices are essential to the operation of your computer, such as your hard disk or video adapter. You can replace these devices with new, improved models, but it's hard to imagine using your computer without them. Other devices, such as network adapters, are not required for your computer to work but are designed to be installed as upgrades. Typically, installing one of these devices requires that you remove the cover from your computer and slip the new device into a *Peripheral Component Interconnect (PCI) slot*. In both of these cases, you install the device once, and it's permanently available for you.

Increasingly, devices are designed to be plugged in when they're needed and removed when they're no longer required. These devices typically connect to *Universal Serial Bus (USB) ports*. Digital cameras, scanners, and handheld personal organizers are just a few of the types of devices that can plug into these ports. This type of device is often referred to as being *hot-pluggable*. The first time you use a device, you must install the necessary driver or drivers. After that, Windows automatically loads the correct drivers and configures the device when you connect it, without requiring that you restart your computer.

Plugs, Ports, and Slots These days, the average PC has a bewildering variety of places where you can connect a new device. Here's a quick guide to help you figure out the difference between all these different plugs, ports, and slots.

USB is short for Universal Serial Bus. These days, just about every PC includes at least two USB ports. To use one of these ports, you plug in a cable with a small rectangular connector, illustrated here, that's about the same width and height as a stick of chewing gum (the other end of the cable plugs into the device). If you buy a new digital camera, scanner, mouse, or just about any hardware addition, chances are it includes a USB connector. Don't worry about running out of USB ports. If you use up all available slots, you can add a USB *hub* that contains extra ports. In theory, you can have as many as 127 USB devices connected to one computer, although the practical limit is much smaller.

Series A USB connector
(plugs into USB device)

Series B USB connector
(plugs into PC or USB hub)

Serial ports were once the most popular way to connect a modem or mouse to your PC, but these connectors are rarely used by new hardware devices, and an increasing number of PCs don't include any serial ports at all. Serial ports come in two varieties: one with 9 pins, the other with 25 holes. (The matching serial connectors, of course, have 9 holes or 25 pins, as shown here.)

25-pin serial connector

9-pin serial connector

Parallel ports are also known as printer ports, because this was once the most common way to connect a printer to a computer. A parallel cable includes a 25-pin connector at one end and a Centronics connector at the other, as shown here. Parallel connections have been largely replaced by USB alternatives.

Plug this connector into your PC

This Centronics connector attaches to a printer

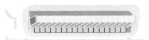

FireWire (also known as IEEE1394) is a high-speed connector used primarily for digital camcorders and, less frequently, for hard drives. FireWire ports are commonly found on Sony PCs and Apple Macintoshes but are rarely found on other types of PCs. You can add FireWire ports to a PC fairly easily with an add-in card. FireWire connectors come in two different sizes—one with 4 pins, used to attach to devices like a video camera; the other with 6 pins, for connections to a PC, as shown here.

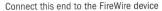

Plug this end into your PC or hub   Connect this end to the FireWire device

PCI slots hold expansion cards inside your computer. This type of hardware is intended to be a more-or-less permanent addition to your computer, such as a network adapter or a TV tuner. To install a PCI card, remove the cover of your PC and carefully insert the card into the slot. If you're uncomfortable with the idea of messing with your computer's innards, ask for professional help.

PC Cards are hardware add-ins that are roughly the size of a credit card. These devices plug into matching slots that are almost always found on laptop computers. Occasionally, you'll see these types of devices referred to as PCMCIA cards. (This abbreviation officially stands for Personal Computer Memory Card Industry Association, but I think it really means People Can't Memorize Computer Industry Acronyms.)

The first time you connect a new device, Windows XP tries to identify the device and locate a compatible driver for it. Windows XP includes a huge collection of hardware drivers, which means that some devices work as soon as you plug them into your computer, with no extra effort on your part. If the driver isn't included with Windows, you'll need to supply the correct driver files when you first install the device.

What to Expect from Plug and Play

When the stars line up right, you can plug in a new device and it just works. Windows XP loads the correct drivers, configures the device for you, and makes it available for your other programs to work with. All this magic is made possible by a feature called Plug and Play, which detects the newly connected hardware device, identifies it, locates a compatible driver, and configures any required device settings.

When you plug in a new piece of hardware, Plug and Play messages keep you informed as to what Windows is doing. For instance, Figure 4-1 shows the message that appears in the notification area, located at the right of the taskbar, when you first plug in a device designed to read the Compact Flash cards typically found in digital cameras. As you can see, Windows can identify the device by name and even recognizes the manufacturer, ImageMate.

Figure 4-1 When you insert a new device, this Plug and Play message appears in the notification area.

Because Windows includes a built-in driver for this device, the configuration process is completely automatic and doesn't require any extra work. After a few seconds, a second message appears in the notification area, announcing that the installation process is complete, as shown here.

What happens if Windows can't locate a correct driver? In that case, after identifying the device, it starts up the Found New Hardware Wizard and asks you to specify where the correct driver files can be found. As I explain in the next section, this process goes a lot more smoothly if you've done your homework first.

Installing a New Device

Are you the impetuous sort? If so, you'll probably be tempted to just plug in your new hardware and see if it works. Most of the time, this slightly reckless strategy works just fine, but every so often it backfires, leaving you with a device that doesn't work properly and can't be easily repaired. Instead of plunging headfirst into the Found New Hardware Wizard, take your time and make sure you do things right. You must be logged on as an administrator to install a new driver. Follow these steps, in order, and you'll avoid the most common pitfalls.

1 Find the correct driver. Ideally, the driver should be digitally signed and certified as compatible with Windows XP. Save the downloaded files to a convenient place, such as the desktop or the My Documents folder. If necessary, unzip the files into their own folder.

> **See Also** For details about how to unzip compressed files, see the section "Zipping and Unzipping Files," on page 245.

2 If the driver files contain their own Setup program, run it now. This step copies the driver files to your hard disk and updates the database of hardware drivers so that Windows can find the files later. If the downloaded drivers don't include a Setup program, skip to the next step.

Tip   Did your new device come with a driver on a CD-ROM or floppy disk? Don't automatically assume that the driver is the newest or best one. Before installing the driver, check the manufacturer's Web site to see if a more recent driver is available.

---

3   Plug in the new device. If the new hardware is an internal device that plugs into a PCI slot, be sure to shut down your computer and disconnect the power before performing the installation. If the device plugs into a USB or FireWire port, you don't need to shut down the computer; just plug in the new device.

4   When you see the Found New Hardware Wizard, choose one of these two options:

   ●   **Install The Software Automatically**   Use this option if you ran a Setup program to install the driver first, or if the driver is on a CD-ROM or floppy disk. Insert the correct CD or floppy disk, if needed, and click Next.

   ●   **Install From A List Or Specific Location**   Choose this option if you downloaded the driver files and didn't run a Setup program first. Click Next to continue.

5   Follow the wizard's prompts to complete the installation. The exact steps vary depending on the choices you make. Pay special attention to the following three options:

   ●   Do you want Windows to search for the driver files automatically and load the one it thinks is best? This option is easiest, but if you know specifically which driver will work with your new device, you might have better luck choosing the option to select the correct driver from a list.

   ●   Is the driver file you're trying to install digitally signed? If so, it should install automatically. If not, you'll see a stern warning message like the one shown on the next page. If you're certain the driver is compatible with Windows XP and that a signed driver is not available, choose the Continue Anyway option. Windows automatically creates a restore point for you, so that you can undo the change if it turns out that the driver causes problems.

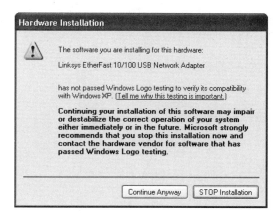

- If more than one driver is compatible with your new device, the wizard might ask you to choose the correct one. If you're not sure which one is correct, cancel the installation and do some more research.

Caution   Don't dismiss the warning about unsigned drivers too quickly. Digitally signed drivers really are safer, because they've been tested for compatibility with Windows XP. An unsigned driver can cause your system to become unstable or even crash. If you choose to install an unsigned driver, Windows automatically creates a restore point. If the new driver causes problems, you can always run the System Restore utility and roll back your system configuration to eliminate it.

Where to Look for Drivers

How do you know whether you have the best driver available for a hardware device? If you're lucky, Windows Update will alert you to a new device driver when you look for updates manually (see Chapter 1 for a description of how to use Windows Update). If you have a specific Web address provided by the manufacturer of the device, you can also check there. You may need to use Device Manager (described in the following section) to determine the version number of the currently installed driver for comparison with the one available for download.

A much longer list appears in the Windows Catalog, a continually updated resource that is available from the Windows XP Help And Support Center. Click Start, choose Help And Support, and then click the Find Compatible Hardware And Software For Windows XP link. The home page lists featured products. To zero in on the specific device you're investigating, enter part of the device name in the Search Windows Catalog box, or click the Hardware tab and browse through the list of compatible devices, which is organized by category.

Figure 4-2 shows a typical page from the Windows Catalog, with a list of compatible products.

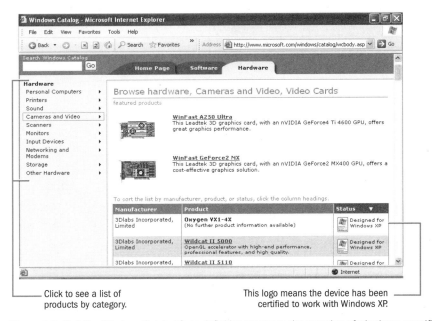

Click to see a list of products by category.

This logo means the device has been certified to work with Windows XP.

Figure 4-2 Visit the Windows Catalog for a definitive answer to the question of whether a specific device is compatible with Windows XP.

The information on this page provides a neat summary of compatibility information for you.

■ The Featured Products at the top of the page are advertisements.

■ The list of products appears initially with certified products at the top of the list, arranged in alphabetical order by manufacturer. You can click any column heading to re-sort the list.

■ Some items in the list include clickable links that take you to the manufacturer's Web site, where you'll find more details. In some cases, that page also includes links to the latest downloadable drivers.

■ The most important item in the list is the Status column. If you see the Designed For Windows XP logo, you know the product has been tested by Microsoft and certified to work properly with Windows XP. In other cases, you may see the words Compatible With Windows XP, which means that a valid driver is available but hasn't been fully tested and certified.

If you're planning to buy a new piece of hardware and you don't see it listed in the Windows Catalog, does that mean it's not compatible with Windows XP? Not necessarily. Many products have perfectly good drivers that work just fine with Windows XP, but for one reason or another, the manufacturer has decided not to list them on this Web page. If that's the case, you can check directly with the hardware manufacturer to see whether a Windows XP–compatible driver is available.

Inspecting Your Hardware with Device Manager

When you look at the computer on your desktop, you probably see just a few pieces: one big box that contains the electronic guts of your computer, plus a keyboard, mouse, and monitor. You might have an extra gizmo or two plugged in, such as a printer or scanner, but basically, the whole thing looks pretty simple. Windows XP, however, sees much more. To Windows, a typical PC might consist of more than 100 individual devices, and the operating system is fully prepared to assist you whenever you need to take inventory of your hardware.

You can see the entire collection of installed hardware and view details for any item on the list by using the aptly named Device Manager. Here's how:

1 Click Start and open Control Panel.

2 Double-click the System icon (if your Control Panel is organized by category, click Performance And Maintenance, and then click System).

3 Select the Hardware tab and then click Device Manager.

Figure 4-3 shows the Device Manager window. The first thing you'll notice is that all your devices are organized by category. So if you want to find your scanner, look under Imaging Devices.

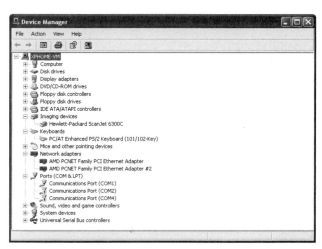

Figure 4-3 Click the plus sign to the left of each category to see the devices included in that category.

Most of the time, looking through Device Manager is about as exciting as reading the phone book. However, if you're having trouble with a device, the information you see here can be helpful indeed. Here's what to look for:

- **Technical information about the installed device and its driver files**   To see these details, right-click the entry for the device and choose Properties from the shortcut menu. This information isn't just gobbledygook (although it can sometimes seem that way). By looking carefully at the details on the Driver tab, for instance, you can figure out where the driver came from, when it was released, and what its version number is, as shown below. Armed with this information, you can then decide whether the driver available for download from the hardware maker's Web site is newer than the one you already have.

- **Problem devices**   When a device isn't working properly, Device Manager indicates the problem by changing the small icon to the left of the device name. A red X over the icon means the device has been disabled. A yellow question mark indicates an unknown device. A yellow exclamation point means the device has another sort of problem, such as a conflict with another installed device. As Figure 4-4 shows, you can enlist Windows to help you find the problem and fix it—right-click the device name, choose Properties, and read the details on the General tab. If a Troubleshoot button is available, click it to see more recommendations that might help you get the device working again.

Figure 4-4 When Device Manager indicates a problem with a device, open the Properties dialog box for that device and click Troubleshoot.

Tip   Is Windows telling you that you have a resource conflict between two devices? This is most likely to happen when one or both devices are old and don't fully support the Plug and Play standard. For an explanation of what each of these resources means, open the Help And Support Center and search for the topic entitled "Configuring Devices." To repair the problem, use Troubleshoot in the Properties dialog box for the device that's reporting the conflict.

■ **Configuration details**   Some devices have settings that you can adjust to improve performance or to solve problems. Network adapters and modems, for instance, are jam-packed with these sorts of options, as illustrated by the example shown below. If you're having trouble getting a device to work properly, a support professional might suggest that you adjust one or more of these settings to fix the problem.

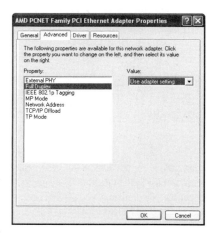

Caution   If you're having a problem, don't start by messing around with the settings in these dialog boxes. Clicking the wrong button or choosing an incompatible
option can cause your device to stop working completely, and in some extreme cases
can even keep your computer from starting properly. Unless you're absolutely sure of
what each option does, resist the urge to poke around with adavnced settings.

Try This!   If you've been using your computer for a while, you might have amassed quite a collection of hardware and drivers without even knowing it. If you ever have a problem with the computer, you may want to know exactly which devices are installed. You can produce a printed report
from Device Manager.

1   Click Start, right-click the My Computer icon, and choose Properties. In the System Prop-
     erties dialog box, click the Hardware tab and then click Device Manager.

2   In the Device Manager window, click the computer icon at the top of the list of devices.

3   From the Action menu, click Print (or click the Printer icon on the toolbar).

4   In the Print dialog box, select the printer you want to use. Under Report Type, choose the
     All Devices And System Summary option.

5   Click Print. Be sure you have enough paper handy! The full report can run 20 pages.

Keep the printout in a safe place along with your Windows XP CD and product ID. Write down
the date when you prepared the report. For drivers you downloaded yourself, make a note on the
report that lists the version number of the driver and from where you downloaded it.

Updating a Device Driver

You've plugged in a new piece of hardware. You've installed the correct driver.
It's working just fine. You're done, right? Yes, indeed—until the manufacturer of
your hardware releases a new version of the driver for that device. Then you
have to decide whether to upgrade to the newer driver or to stick with the one
you have working now. But just because you *can* update a driver doesn't mean
you *should*. If the device in question is working just fine, read the manufacturer's description of what the new driver does and decide for yourself whether
you really need the update.

Tip   Before you make any changes to your system configuration, use the System Restore feature
to create a restore point first (as described in the section "Set Up System Restore Checkpoints,"
on page 98). If the new driver doesn't work properly or causes any problems, you can roll back
to your previous configuration by using System Restore to undo the changes.

If you're lucky, the notice that an updated driver is available shows up when you check Windows Update. In that case, you can download the new driver the same way you would get a patch for Windows, and it installs itself. If the hardware manufacturer chooses not to release the new driver through Windows Update, you might need to install it yourself. To accomplish this task, Windows provides a wizard that is similar to the Found New Hardware Wizard. Here's how to use it:

1 Download the new driver files from the manufacturer's Web site and save them to a convenient place, such as the desktop or the My Documents folder. If necessary, unzip the files into their own folder.

2 Click Start, right-click the My Computer icon and choose Properties. In the System Properties dialog box, click the Hardware tab and then click Device Manager.

3 In the Device Manager window, click the plus sign to the left of the category that contains the device whose driver you want to update and then right-click the name of the device and choose Update Driver.

4 In the Hardware Update Wizard, choose Install From A List Or Specific Location (Advanced), as shown in Figure 4-5. Click Next to continue.

Figure 4-5 If you've downloaded a new driver for your device, choose the Advanced option at the bottom of this dialog box.

5 Select Don't Search. I Will Choose The Driver to Install. Click Next to continue.

6   If the correct driver is not in the list of compatible drivers, as shown in
Figure 4-6, click Have Disk and then click Browse to select the location
where you saved the downloaded files in step 1. Click OK to close
the Install From Disk dialog box and then click Next to continue.

The list of compatible drivers includes important details about
whether the driver you're about to install is signed. Note the green
check mark to the left of the driver name and the wording at the bottom of the dialog box; these highlights let you see at a glance whether
the driver is safe to install.

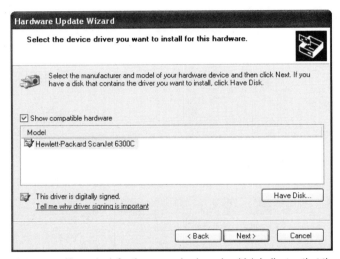

Figure 4-6 Always look for the green check mark, which indicates that the driver you're about to
install is digitally signed by Microsoft.

See Also   *For a refresher course on how Windows Update can help you keep your copy of
Windows XP safe and up-to-date, see the section "Get the Latest Windows Updates," on page 18.
To learn the ins and outs of working with compressed files, see the section "Zipping and Unzipping
Files," on page 245.*

Troubleshooting Hardware Problems

What happens when you plug in a new piece of hardware and it doesn't work
properly? The first thing to try is unplugging and reconnecting the device. If that
doesn't work, you have four options:

■ **Use System Restore to undo the changes**   If you just installed the
device, you can immediately reverse all your changes by opening the
Help And Support Center and choosing the Undo Changes To Your

Computer With System Restore option. Choose the restore point created just before you made the change.

■ **Roll back to your old driver**   If you updated to a new device driver and the update caused more problems than it fixed, you can ask Windows to put back the old driver. From Device Manager, right-click the device in question, choose Properties, select the Driver tab, then click Roll Back Driver.

■ **Disable the device**   If the device isn't working right but also isn't causing any other problems, you might consider disabling it temporarily while you talk with a technical support professional to come up with a more permanent solution. From Device Manager, right-click the device and choose Disable from the shortcut menu. After you fix the problem, you can repeat these steps, this time choosing Enable from the menu.

■ **Uninstall the device**   To remove all traces of the driver you installed, open Device Manager, right-click the device, and choose Uninstall from the shortcut menu. This option is useful if you didn't create a restore point and you don't have a previous driver to roll back to.

Working with Removable Devices (USB and Others)

When you use USB devices, you can physically connect and disconnect the devices at any time. With some types of hardware, this is no problem at all. For instance, if you have a portable Compact Flash card reader that you use to transfer pictures and songs between your PC and a digital camera or portable music player, you can unplug the reader when you're finished with it.

But with some types of hardware, removing a device can cause problems for Windows. You might have a removable hard disk connected to your USB port, for example, or a network card plugged into the PC Card slot on your notebook computer. If a program is currently using files on the disk or is connected to another computer through the network, abruptly unplugging the device could cause you to lose data. To disconnect a device like this safely, you first need to send a message to Windows, letting the operating system know that you're finished working with the device.

The solution for most removable devices is to look in the notification area. Find the Safely Remove Hardware icon and double-click it to display the Safely Remove Hardware dialog box shown on the next page. The list shows all removable devices currently connected to your computer.

Select the device you want to stop using from the list and then click Stop. When you see the message that says it's all right to remove the device, disconnect it.

Key Points

- Windows XP includes drivers for hundreds of devices, and you can download additional drivers from hardware manufacturers.

- Whenever possible, you should insist on digitally signed hardware drivers that have been tested by Microsoft and certified as compatible with Windows XP.

- Thanks to Plug and Play, most hardware devices can literally install themselves, although you might need to specify where the driver files are located.

- Windows XP allows you to see all the hardware installed on and in your computer by using Device Manager.

- Updated device drivers can add new features and fix bugs. Don't automatically assume that a newer driver is better, though!

- Windows XP includes a variety of troubleshooting tools to help you get back to normal if a new piece of hardware causes problems.

- When you use removable devices, it's important to use the Safely Remove Hardware option before physically disconnecting the device.

Chapter 5

Fixing Computer Problems

Microsoft Windows XP is the most reliable version of Windows that Microsoft has ever produced. It's less likely to crash, hang, stall, or otherwise torment you in everyday operation than any previous version of Windows. Unfortunately, Windows XP still isn't perfect, and it can't protect you from defective device drivers, flaky hardware, and buggy programs. So what should you do when you run into problems? In this chapter, I explain how to track down the cause of problems and fix them once and for all.

Be Prepared! Five Habits to Fend Off Trouble

Are you reading this chapter because your computer is misbehaving *right now*, and you want to find out what the problem is? If so, you should skip over this section and go right to the section called "Troubleshooting 101: Figuring Out What's Wrong," on page 102. Be sure to come back and read this section carefully after you get the problem fixed, however. If you follow the advice I list here, chances are excellent that you can recover quickly and fully the next time you have a problem.

If your PC is running perfectly right now, congratulations! Read this section first and make sure you're doing everything you can to prepare yourself for the inevitable problems that will occur someday. Even a few minutes of preventive maintenance weekly can save you hours of anguish later.

Back Up Your Data Regularly

I know, I know—backing up is tedious work and about as much fun as a trip to the dentist. However, if you skip your annual checkup at the dentist's office too many times, eventually your teeth deteriorate and probably fall out. Likewise, if you blithely ignore backing up your important files, eventually you will lose some or all of them. Are you prepared to lose your collection of digital photos? How about the financial records you keep in Quicken or Microsoft Money? Your online address book and all your e-mail messages? Records of your correspondence with businesses and customers? Even if you could replace some of those items, it would take days or weeks, and some of the data would be lost forever.

Despite your best efforts, bad things can happen to your data anytime. Sooner or later, your hard disk *will* crash or you'll inadvertently erase a folder full of files or you'll get clobbered by a brand-new virus that snuck past your defenses. When that day comes, you'll be happy you had your important data files backed up and stored in a safe place. I can't make the process fun, but I can show you how to develop a routine that makes backing up as painless as possible.

Windows XP includes an excellent backup program, but finding it might take some detective work on your part, depending on which edition of Windows XP you have installed.

- If you have Windows XP Professional, the Backup program is installed automatically along with Windows.

- With a retail copy of Windows XP Home Edition, the Backup program is available on the CD, but you have to install it yourself. To do so, pop the Windows CD into your CD-ROM drive and open a Windows Explorer window showing the contents of the CD. Double-click the Valueadd folder, then the Msft folder, and finally the Ntbackup folder. Click the Ntbackup icon to install the Backup program.

- If you purchased a new computer that included a pre-installed copy of Windows XP Home Edition, you might have to ask the computer manufacturer for help in finding the Ntbackup program. This is especially true if your computer came with a "recovery CD," designed to restore the entire contents of your disk drive, rather than a standard Windows XP CD.

Tip   Where should you save your backup file? If you have a Zip drive, use it! Zip disks hold either 100 megabytes (MB) or 250 MB each, and a handful of them should be enough to hold your files. Don't use a standard floppy drive; you would need almost 200 floppy disks to hold the same amount of data that fits on a single Zip disk. If you don't have a Zip drive but you have a CD-RW drive with a program like DirectCD or InCD installed, you can save your backup directly to a CD. If you have only a CD-R drive, save the backup set to a file on your hard drive and then copy it to a CD-R. In either of the latter cases, make sure your total amount of data doesn't add up to more than 650 MB (the maximum amount that fits on a standard data CD).

To start the Backup program, click Start and choose All Programs; then click the Accessories menu, then the System Tools menu, and finally the Backup shortcut. The Backup program uses an easy-to-follow wizard to walk you through the process of backing up.

1   Click Next to skip the Welcome page. By default, the Backup program starts in wizard mode, but this can be turned off by clearing the Always Start In Wizard Mode check box on the Welcome page. If you find yourself unexpectedly in Advanced mode, click the Wizard Mode link to restart the wizard.

2   On the Backup Or Restore page, select Back Up Files And Settings and click Next.

3   On the What To Back Up page, select one of the four options shown in Figure 5-1 and click Next.

- Choose My Documents And Settings if you just want to back up your personal files. This is the option I recommend for most people.

- Choose Everyone's Documents And Settings if your computer has several user accounts and you're responsible for backing up the data files for every user.

- Although the All Information On This Computer option sounds like the perfect way to back up everything on your PC, I don't recommend it unless you have a storage device (such as an external hard disk) that is at least as big as your main hard disk.

- If you need to back up data files stored somewhere other than your My Documents folder, select Let Me Choose What To Back Up.

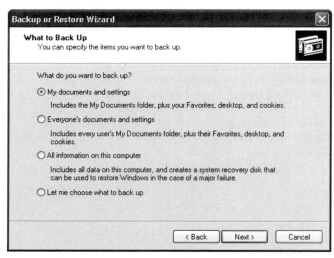

Figure 5-1 Take your choice from this list of backup options—but at a minimum, back up your own documents and settings.

4 On the Backup Type, Destination, And Name page, shown below, choose the place where you want to save your backed-up files and settings. The drop-down list shows all removable drives, or you can click Browse and choose a location on a local or network hard drive. In the Type A Name For This Backup box, enter a descriptive name for the file that will contain your backed-up data, and then click Next to continue.

Note The Select The Backup Type drop-down list option at the top of this dialog box is available only if you have a backup tape drive installed. Most people use the File backup type, choosing a destination on a removable disk or a local or network drive.

5 On the final page, the wizard displays a summary of the settings you chose in the previous pages. If they're correct, click Finish to begin the backup.

Advanced Backup Options When you reach the final page of the Backup Or Restore Wizard, you may be tempted to click Advanced. Most of the time, you can safely bypass these options, and some can actually cause more trouble than they're worth. But in certain circumstances, you may find that these options are useful. When you select Advanced, you see a few extra pages from the Backup Or Restore Wizard, which offer the following options:

- Type Of Backup—If you choose the standard settings, you get a Normal backup, which adds a copy of every file in the locations you've selected to your backup file and then changes the Archive attribute of each file to show that it's been backed up. Using the Advanced options, you can select from four other backup types. The most interesting of these is the Incremental type, which backs up only files that have been changed since the last time they were backed up (when you save a file, the Archive bit is changed to show that it has not been backed up). The Differential and Copy types are for backup experts only. Use the Daily backup type if you want to back up only files that were created or changed today.

- How To Back Up—On this page, you can select the Verify Data After Backup option, which compares the backed-up data to the original data when the backup is complete. Use this option if you are performing a backup where the data is extremely valuable. The Use Hardware Compression option is unavailable unless you're using a tape drive, in which case you should select it. I recommend leaving the Disable Volume Shadow Copy option unselected. This option allows you to back up files that are in use, which ensures that all your files are available on the backup.

- Backup Options—You can choose whether you want to add the backed-up data to your existing backup file or replace the existing backups. Most of the time, you'll want to save a new file; you should consider adding the newly backed-up data to an existing backup if your original was a Normal backup and the new one is an Incremental backup. This step keeps all your data, old and new, together.

- When To Back Up—If you choose Now, the backup runs as soon as you complete the wizard. Select Later and then fill in the blanks to schedule the backup to run at a later date and time. I strongly recommend that you test this option first before relying on it!

When you've finished your backup, store the backup files in a safe place. Ideally, your most important backup files should be stored away from the computer. You could take your backup disk(s) to the office and lock them in a file cabinet, for instance. This would protect your data in the event of a flood, earth-quake, or fire that wiped out your computer and everything around it.

Tip   Make sure you back up at least once a week. Once you learn the ins and outs, the whole process takes no more than about 15 minutes for each gigabyte of data!

To restore backed-up files to your computer, have the disk(s) containing the backed-up files handy and run the Backup program again, this time choosing Restore Files And Settings from the wizard's second page. On the What To Restore page, shown here, you can double-click any item in the left pane (What To Restore).

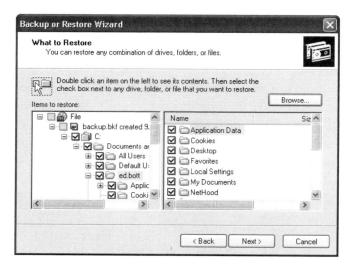

You can then select or clear check boxes to choose specific files and folders to restore, as follows:

- By default, all backed-up files are selected. This is your best choice if you've experienced a severe system crash and you're restoring your data to a new computer or a newly formatted drive.

- Select individual files or folders if you need to recover files that you accidentally deleted or that were damaged in some fashion (by a virus, for instance).

Set Up System Restore Checkpoints

One of the most welcome sanity-saving features in Windows XP is its System Restore capability, which can restore your computer to good working order in minutes after you install a seemingly innocent program or hardware driver that causes your system to crash, hang, or freeze. Here's how it works.

At roughly the same time every day, the System Restore program automatically backs up details of your system configuration and saves the associated files and settings (each such collection is called a *system checkpoint*) in a protected area of the hard disk. Windows creates additional automatic checkpoints every time you install a program or an untested hardware driver, and you can manually take one of these "snapshots" to create a *restore point* anytime you want. If something goes wrong with your computer, start your computer in Safe Mode and run System Restore, choosing the option to roll back your system configuration to one of those earlier restore points, effectively erasing the problem program or defective driver.

Lingo   A *system checkpoint* is a "snapshot" of your system configuration that is created by Windows. A *restore point* contains the exact same type of data, but is created manually when you run the System Restore option.

System Restore works. I've used it to recover from hardware configuration problems that would have taken hours to fix in earlier versions of Windows. In fact, anytime you're about to install a new piece of software or hardware or make any kind of change to your system configuration that could cause problems, I recommend that you create a System Restore checkpoint manually. If anything goes wrong, you can get Windows working again with the greatest of ease.

Let's say you've just purchased a new antivirus program. As you know from reading this chapter, a bug in a system utility or a hardware driver can be the cause of sudden crashes and other problems, so you decide, wisely, to create a restore point before installing the program. The process is so simple, in fact, that you might think you've skipped a step when you first try it! Just perform the following steps:

1   Click Start and choose Help And Support.

2   In the Help And Support Center window, click the Undo Changes To Your Computer With System Restore option. (You'll find it under the Pick A Task heading.)

3   On the Welcome To System Restore page, choose the Create A Restore Point option and click Next

4   On the Create A Restore Point page, shown on the next page, enter a descriptive name for the restore point, such as "Before installing my new antivirus program."

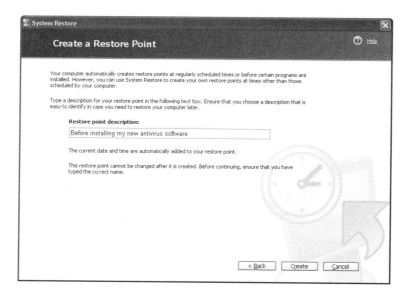

5   Click Create. After a brief bit of activity, you see the Restore Point Created page, which displays the date and time along with the description you entered. Click Close. You're now free to install the program or make any other system changes.

Tip   You don't need to add the date or time when you create a restore point. Windows does this automatically for you. System Restore can also be accessed by clicking Start, All Programs, Accessories, and finally System Tools.

For details on restoring a saved system configuration, see the section "Rolling Back to a Previous Configuration," on page 116.

Check Your Disk for Problems

Hard disks sometimes display warning signs before they fail. You can miss the warning signs unless you check your drives for errors regularly. It's a simple process, and if you do it weekly you might be able to spot the signs of impending disk failure before it happens. If your disk begins to make odd sounds or seems to be taking an overly long time to retrieve data, those could be clues that something bad is about to happen. Use the built-in Windows tools to check the disk for errors. If you notice a sudden rash of disk errors, back up your data immediately and consider replacing the disk.

See Also *For details on how to use Windows XP's built-in disk-checking tools, see the section "Checking for Errors," on page 33.*

Keep Windows Up to Date

Occasionally, a problem with Windows is caused by a bug in Windows itself. This sort of problem is relatively rare, thanks to the thorough testing that each new Windows version undergoes before it's released. But some glitches slip through and can trip up your PC. To avoid being bitten by one of these bugs, make sure you enable Automatic Updates so that you can be alerted right away when new Critical Updates are available. In addition, check the Windows Update site at least once a month for other updates and drivers that apply to your system configuration.

See Also *For step-by-step instructions on how to set up Automatic Updates and check Windows Update manually, see the section "Get the Latest Windows Updates," on page 18.*

Update Your Antivirus Software Regularly

Viruses are the scourge of modern computing, as I explain in detail in Chapter 8, "Protecting Your Privacy and Your Computer's Security." Unfortunately, you can't rely on good habits to keep you safe from infestation. Virus writers have learned to exploit security holes in Windows to craft code that can enter your computer over your network connection, through an innocent-looking e-mail or a malicious Web site. The most virulent cyberpests of recent years, in fact, can attack your PC even if you never do anything more than open an e-mail.

Keeping your PC secure means taking advantage of all the security features that Windows has to offer. It also requires adding one piece of software that isn't included with Windows: a reliable antivirus program. You can take your choice from dozens of capable candidates in this category, but whatever you do, make certain that you keep the software and its database of virus definitions up to date! If your software hasn't been updated in a month or more, you're a sitting duck for the next virus that comes along.

See Also *For an overview of virus protection and other security topics, see Chapter 8, "Protecting Your Privacy and Your Computer's Security."*

Troubleshooting 101: Figuring Out What's Wrong

What do you do when Windows freezes, crashes, locks up, or displays a baffling error message? You could pound on your desk, yell at the computer, and even fling your keyboard against the wall. However, after you work through the initial frustration, you've still got to deal with the problem. When confronted with a Windows mystery, most people just start poking around in dialog boxes, more or less at random, hoping that they'll get lucky and stumble on the fix. There's a much more effective strategy, however—a methodical approach to problem-solving that usually helps you find and fix the overwhelming majority of Windows woes, including system crashes. In this section, I've listed eight steps you can take to troubleshoot any Windows problem. If you go through this checklist one item at a time, you have an excellent chance of finding and fixing whatever's ailing Windows.

Tip   Here's some good news: Any problem you encounter with Windows is likely to be one that other people have encountered as well. That means there's a good chance the solution is out there on the Internet, if you can find it. That's why, throughout this chapter, I emphasize the benefits of using a search engine for troubleshooting.

The three most likely causes of Windows crashes and errors are

- **A bug in a Windows program or device driver**   In fact, a poorly written device driver is the single most likely cause of crashes in Windows. You should always be suspicious of unsigned drivers. When you encounter problems, you should also look closely at software that works directly with the operating system, such as antivirus programs, personal firewalls, CD-burning software, and disk utilities. All of these types of programs install drivers that can interfere with Windows in unpredictable ways and can be responsible for crashes. If you're able to identify a program or driver as the source of your current problems, you need to remove the offending software and contact the manufacturer for an update.

- **A bug in Windows itself**   As I mentioned in the previous section, bugs in Windows are not uncommon (although bugs that cause you to lose data are extremely rare). When such bugs are discovered, Microsoft is diligent about publicizing them in its online Knowledge Base and posting a fix on Windows Update as soon as it's ready. (For more information on using the Knowledge Base, see the section "What to Do When You See an Error Message," on page 112, and the section "Get Answers from the Internet, on page 54.)

■ **Physical problems with hardware**   Some of the most baffling problems aren't caused by Windows at all, but rather by a defective piece of hardware. All sorts of failing components can cause seemingly random and hard-to-trace problems. A bad memory chip, a short circuit on the computer's motherboard, or a poorly built power supply, for instance, can wreak havoc with your computer and your hard disk. When you're troubleshooting, always consider the possibility that a component in your computer may be failing.

Step 1: Isolate the Problem

If your system was working fine last week but is having problems this week, try to identify everything that's changed in the interim. Have you installed any new hardware or software? Did you update a device driver? Did you adjust any settings in Control Panel? Try uninstalling the software, removing the hardware device, or restoring the old driver or settings temporarily, to see if the problem goes away. If you can reproduce the problem with specific steps, you've got a much better chance of knowing when you've found the solution.

Note   Are the crashes and other problems that you're experiencing accompanied by any error messages? If so, write them down carefully; they can be extremely helpful in tracking down a problem. See the section "Decoding Error Messages," on page 112, for more details.

Did your PC start acting up immediately after you made a specific change? If so, you can safely bet that your problem is directly related to that change. In this case, try using System Restore to undo your changes and roll your system configuration back to a point before you started having problems. If you created a manual restore point before making the change, you can choose that from the list of available restore points. Otherwise, choose the most recent system checkpoint that occurred before you made the change.

See Also   You'll find full instructions on using restore points in the section "Rolling Back to a Previous Configuration," on page 116.

Step 2: Use Troubleshooting Tools

In Windows XP, the Help And Support Center includes a number of wizards that can walk you through troubleshooting basics, step by step, for everything from DVDs to universal serial bus (USB) devices. Although some of the suggestions are obvious, this is always a good place to start, if only to make certain that you've covered all the bases. Click Start and choose Help And Support. In the

Help And Support Center, click Index and type **troubleshooting** in the box just above the Index listings. Scroll through the list of Troubleshooting topics until you find one that's right for your situation and then double-click to display it in the contents pane on the right.

Figure 5-2, for instance, shows the Internet Explorer Troubleshooter in action.

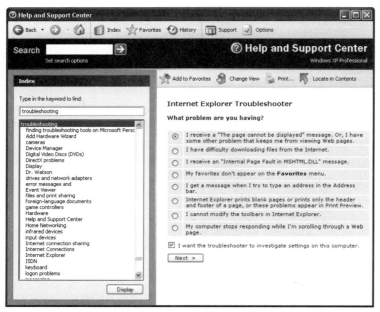

Figure 5-2 If you're puzzled by a problem with Windows, use a troubleshooter to walk through possible solutions step by step.

Each page of the wizard, which appears in the Help And Support Center window, asks a multiple-choice or yes/no question. (Don't worry, you don't need to study and there won't be a grade!) As you work your way through the questions, the wizard narrows down the possible problems and suggests possible solutions.

Step 3: Check Your Hardware

Not all Windows error messages indicate a problem with Windows. Sometimes the problem is a defective piece of hardware or a minor problem with a connection. True story: Several years ago, I called the Help desk at the company where I worked and demanded that they send a support technician to fix my broken printer. The tech arrived a few minutes later, fished around behind the computer, and showed me, to my chagrin, that the cable was unplugged. Oops!

Before you spend too much time troubleshooting Windows settings, check all the obvious hardware connections. Make sure your power is working. Check to see that every cable is securely connected. If you're comfortable taking the cover off your desktop computer, you can shut off the computer, open the case, and check to see that all the add-in cards and memory chips are firmly seated in their slots. If the errors you're encountering seem completely random, that might be a sign of a bad memory chip or a failing power supply. To investigate these sorts of problems, you'll need to enlist professional help.

And don't forget the most obvious step of all: restart the computer. Sometimes that's all it takes to fix a pesky problem.

Step 4: Check Your Hard Disk

Running out of free disk space can cause all sorts of odd symptoms. In fact, if you're addicted to downloading pictures, music files, or movies, you might use up all your free disk space without even realizing it. To check free disk space, open the My Computer window, right-click on the icon for your C drive, and choose Properties. Figure 5-3 shows a disk that contains plenty of free space.

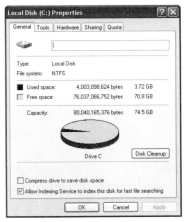

Figure 5-3 Check each drive to make sure you're not running low on free space.

Don't forget to use the Windows disk-checking tools (as described in the section "Checking for Errors," on page 33) to verify that your disk is OK.

Tip Think you might have a hard disk problem? You can do some surprisingly sophisticated tests yourself. Most hard disk makers have diagnostic programs that you can download and run from a floppy disk. Typically, you install these programs to a floppy disk, restart your computer using the floppy disk as a boot disk, and then let the program run its full suite of tests. These utilities can often turn up problems that can't be detected by Windows. To find a program that works with your computer, go to a search engine like Google (*http://www.google.com*) and run a search using the search term *hard disk diagnostic utilities*.

Step 5: Scan for Viruses

Viruses can cause the most bewildering problems of all. Many viruses, in fact, are coded to display meaningless error messages that appear while they're actually doing something more sinister, such as damaging or deleting your data files! If you don't currently have antivirus software installed, use an up-to-date antivirus program to scan for viruses—preferably one that is running from the Web (such as the free Web-based Norton Antivirus scan at *http://www.symantec.com/securitycheck*), from an original CD, or from a *write-protected* bootable floppy disk that was created on a different computer that is certain to be virus-free. If you suspect that a virus snuck onto your computer because your existing antivirus software was using out-of-date definitions, don't assume that your currently installed antivirus program will be able to detect it even after you install the latest updates. Some viruses are sophisticated enough to block or disable antivirus programs.

Tip   How do you *write-protect* a floppy disk? After copying the needed files to the floppy disk, turn the disk over and look for a sliding tab in the top left corner. Move the tab up (so that you see a hole where the tab was previously) to prevent any program—including a virus—from making changes to the disk. Slide it back down to enable changes once again.

See Also   For more information on how to prevent viruses, see Chapter 8, "Protecting Your Privacy and Your Computer's Security."

Step 6: Start Windows in Safe Mode

Just as in previous versions of Windows, you can start Windows XP in a special diagnostic mode called Safe Mode, which loads only drivers and Windows components that are absolutely required. If your system runs properly in Safe Mode, you can bet that the problem is with a program or driver that isn't a part of Windows. On the other hand, if your system's problems persist even in Safe Mode, you probably have a hardware problem or some damage to your operating system files, in which case you need to reinstall Windows. (You'll find full instructions in the section "Using Safe Mode to Repair Windows," on page 118.)

In Safe Mode, try running some programs or performing other tasks that you've determined to be related to the problems you're experiencing. For instance, if you experience a crash every time you start your photo editing program, try running it in Safe Mode.

Step 7: Change Your Video Driver

Believe it or not, video drivers are among the most common causes of computer crashes. When you think about how Windows works, that makes perfect sense.

Every time you do *anything* with Windows, even something as innocent as moving the mouse pointer around, the video driver is responsible for translating your actions into what you see on the screen. So if there's a bug in the video driver, it might appear at any time, and any program could trigger it. Not surprisingly, video drivers are also among the most commonly updated pieces of software. If you're still using the original video driver that came with your computer, the chances are good that a new version of the driver is available, if you know where to look. You may even be able to upgrade your video driver using Windows Update.

You can quickly discover whether your video driver is the cause of your problems by replacing it temporarily with a generic video driver that's included with Windows XP. This generic driver doesn't have any fancy features, but it is guaranteed to work properly with Windows. A tremendously useful troubleshooting tool called the System Configuration Utility can help you do this job automatically:

1   Close all running programs. Click Start and then click Run. In the Open text box, type **msconfig** and press Enter.

2   In the System Configuration Utility dialog box, shown below, click the BOOT.INI tab and select /BASEVIDEO.

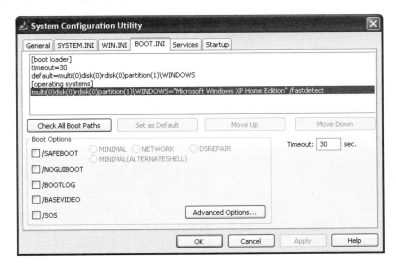

3   Click OK. When prompted by the System Configuration dialog box, click Restart to restart your computer.

4   After your computer restarts, log on as usual.

When you reach the Welcome screen, don't be alarmed if your screen resolution is lower than normal and your color settings are off. That's a direct by-product of using the generic video driver. Ignore any prompts from Windows to "improve" your video settings. Try repeating the same actions that caused your problems earlier. If you no longer experience the errors you were seeing previously, you can conclude that the video driver is the culprit and begin your search for an updated driver.

If this cures the problem, contact the maker of your video adapter for a new driver. After you've finished this troubleshooting step, run the System Configuration Utility again. Choose the Normal Startup option from the General tab, click OK, and restart your computer when prompted.

> **See Also** *Not sure where to find an updated driver? See the section "Where to Look for Drivers," on page 83.*

Step 8: Remove Programs That Start Automatically

Some programs configure themselves to run automatically at startup, without appearing in the taskbar. If you experience mysterious crashes or error messages every time you start Windows, the problem might be caused by one of these programs. To see the entire list of programs that run automatically and trouble-shoot this sort of problem, use the System Configuration Utility to shut down all automatically starting programs; if that cures the problem, start adding programs back one at a time until you find the guilty party.

> **See Also** *For instructions on how to use the System Configuration utility for this task, see the section "Change Programs That Run Automatically at Startup," on page 72.*

Using Remote Assistance for Hands-On Help

Have you ever called a friend to ask for help with a Windows problem? You know how frustrating the experience can be, trying to describe exactly what you're seeing on the screen, painstakingly reading error messages out loud, and trying to follow along with sometimes confusing instructions. It would be so much easier if the friend were able to sit down in front of your computer. But that's not possible when the two of you are miles away. Or is it?

Thanks to a new feature in Windows XP called Remote Assistance, a friend or technical support professional can connect to your computer over the Internet. The expert on the other end of the connection can see the contents of your screen in a window on his or her computer. With your permission, your helper can take charge, making changes to the Windows registry, uninstalling device drivers, and performing just about any task that you can perform while sitting at your keyboard.

> **Note** In Help screens and dialog boxes for Remote Assistance, Windows XP refers to the person requesting help as the Novice and the one providing assistance as the Expert. These are only labels. You don't have to be a novice to ask for help, nor do you need to be an expert before you can offer help.

To set up a Remote Assistance connection, both parties need to be running Windows XP with an open channel of communication between them—preferably Windows Messenger, although e-mail also works. Of course, both computers need to be connected to the same network, usually the Internet. If either party is using a personal firewall, including the Internet Connection Firewall (ICF) built into Windows XP, the connection will fail. You must temporarily shut down the firewall on both computers to use Remote Assistance.

> **Note** In this section, I assume that both parties are using Windows Messenger, which is by far the easiest and fastest way to make the connection. If either party lacks a Windows Messenger account, it's simple to sign up for one; it only takes a few minutes.

Windows XP includes a slew of security checks at every step of the way when you set up a Remote Assistance connection, all designed to require your full permission before allowing another person to take control of your computer. At each step of the way, one or both parties must confirm that they want to continue. As the person requesting assistance, you start the ball rolling by sending a Remote Assistance invitation. Follow these steps.

1   Click Start and choose Help And Support.

2   Under Ask For Assistance, click Invite A Friend To Connect To Your Computer With Remote Assistance.

3   On the Remote Assistance page, click Invite Someone To Help You.

4   On the next page, shown below, select the method you want to use to contact the other person. The first option in this dialog box lists your Windows Messenger contacts; select a name and click Invite This Person.

    If the other person doesn't have a Windows Messenger account or is not online, enter the person's e-mail address in the Type An E-Mail Address text box and click Invite This Person, as shown on the next page.

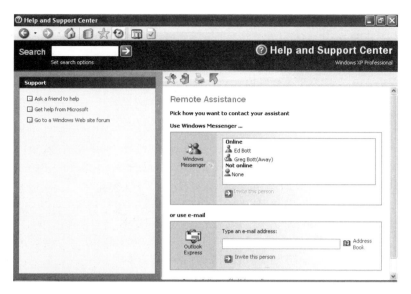

If you sent your invitation by Messenger, the recipient sees your invitation in a conversation window and can choose to accept or decline, as shown below. If you used Microsoft Outlook Express to send the invitation as an attachment to an e-mail message, the recipient should double-click the attachment and type the password you set up when you created the invitation (you can give the other party this password over the phone).

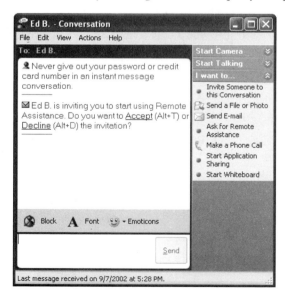

5   When the expert at the other end of the conversation accepts your
invitation, a confirmation dialog box like the one shown below
appears on your computer. Click Yes to complete the connection.

At this point, the expert sees the window shown in Figure 5-4. The contents
of the remote screen appear on the right; the two of you can use the chat window on the left to communicate with one another. Toolbar buttons along the top
of the window let the expert adjust settings for the Remote Assistance window.

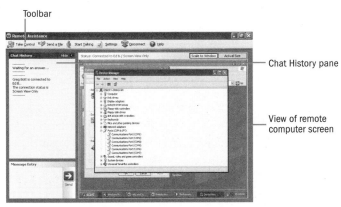

Figure 5-4 The person offering assistance sees the remote screen in this window and can use a variety of tools
to perform tasks.

At this point, the expert can see the remote screen but still can't do anything
with it. If the two of you are talking on the phone or chatting in the window on the
left, you can demonstrate the problem you're seeing. If the expert wants to begin
working with the remote screen, he or she must click Take Control. This produces
yet another confirmation dialog box on your computer, as shown on the next page.

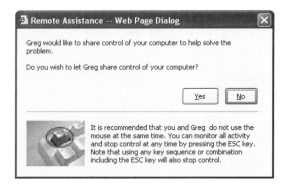

When you click Yes, the expert can begin working with your computer and do almost anything you could do. During this process, you should sit back and avoid touching the keyboard or the mouse. At any time, you can take back control of your computer by pressing the Esc key.

Tip   If the person helping you out is indeed a Windows expert, you can learn a lot about your computer by watching; and if you're carrying on a phone conversation at the same time, you should feel free to ask questions about what the other person is doing!

Decoding Error Messages

Wouldn't it be convenient if, whenever you ran into a problem, Windows could deliver a simple, straightforward explanation of what's wrong? Unfortunately, it might be decades before computers are that smart. In the meantime, we'll have to make do with error messages that vary wildly in terms of helpfulness. Some of these messages are lucid and direct. Others might as well be written in Sanskrit. Even if you can't make sense of the message right away, though, you might still be able to glean valuable information from it.

What to Do When You See an Error Message

When Windows pops up an error message, your first instinct is to click OK and move it out of the way so you can get back to work. Resist that temptation, if at all possible. The exact wording of an error message can be crucial when it comes to solving the underlying problem that produced the error condition! Before you make the message vanish, write down the details. This is especially important in the case of errors that include detailed technical information.

Tip A handy way of capturing detailed error messages is to press Ctrl+C. This copies the text of an error message, which you can paste into Notepad and save for later review. If this shortcut doesn't work, try clicking in the error message box and then pressing Alt+Print Screen. This copies the contents of the active window (the error message dialog box) to the Windows Clipboard. You can then paste it into WordPad or Microsoft Paint and either print it to your printer or save it to a file.

If you see the same error message repeatedly, you might be able to use the text of the message to find the cause of the problem. Use a key phrase from the message to search the Microsoft Knowledge Base. The more specific the message, the more likely you are to find a relevant answer in the Knowledge Base. For instance, a message that includes a specific error number or code is much more likely to lead you to a helpful result than one that simply says, "Your program has encountered an error."

The Knowledge Base is an online treasure trove of articles created by Microsoft technical professionals and used by support professionals to help customers. For access to the most current articles, visit *http://support.microsoft.com* and click Search The Knowledge Base under Welcome To Microsoft Help And Support.

If the error message was generated by a third-party program rather than by Windows, you might want to cast your net a bit wider and search for help on the Internet at large. Although you can choose from many search engines, my favorite by far is Google (*http://www.google.com*).

Tip When using Google, be sure to search the Google Groups page as well as the Web. This archive contains a complete collection of postings to Usenet discussion groups. Many times, you can find detailed discussions of specific errors from someone who has hardware or software that are the same as yours. In cases like these, Google makes it possible to find the needle in the haystack.

Deciphering the Blue Screen of Death

The most dreaded of all Windows error messages is called a Stop error, but Windows experts know it by its more colorful nickname, the Blue Screen of Death, or BSOD. It appears when a serious error occurs and forces Windows to stop completely, without any warning. If you have any programs running, they stop. Any open files that haven't been saved are lost. The only thing you see is a blue screen with several lines of white text.

Figure 5-5 shows a typical Stop error. Much of the text on this page is irrelevant, but a handful of details are crucial. The specific error includes a name and a code that can help you narrow down the cause. A group of four *parameters* after the error code contains technical information that might be helpful as well. Finally, the screen includes the name of the program or driver where the error was detected.

Figure 5-5 When you encounter the Blue Screen of Death, make special note of these details.

Tip   Don't automatically assume that the driver listed at the bottom of a Stop error screen is faulty. In many cases, this program or driver is an innocent bystander, and the real problem occurred elsewhere. Nonetheless, making a note of this detail might help you narrow down the problem. (You'll have to write down the details yourself, as you can't use Alt+Print Screen here.)

A BSOD strikes terror into the heart of even the most hardened Windows user, because of its suddenness and finality. Although it's never pleasant to run into one of these nasty errors, you can comfort yourself with the knowledge of a few facts.

■ Stop errors are almost always caused by hardware problems, faulty device drivers, or bugs in a system utility such as a personal firewall or antivirus program.

■ Searching for the specific error code in the Knowledge Base often turns up detailed answers to your problem.

■ When you find and replace the faulty driver, program, or device, the errors are almost certain to disappear for good.

Tip   Normally, Windows restarts automatically after displaying a Stop error. That can be frustrating if you're trying to write down the details of the error. To change this behavior so that Windows pauses and leaves the blue screen error up indefinitely, open Control Panel, double-click the System icon (in the Performance And Maintenance category), and click the Advanced tab. Under the Startup And Recovery heading, click Settings. Clear the Automatically Restart check box under System Failure and click OK.

Examining Errors in the Event Viewer

Windows XP keeps a running record of errors and informational messages about your system in three different log files. When you're troubleshooting a problem, these logs can be a rich source of information; searching the Knowledge Base using details from the System log, for instance, might help explain errors that seem completely random.

To view the contents of these logs, open Control Panel, double-click the Administrative Tools icon (in the Performance And Maintenance group), and double-click Event Viewer. The Event Viewer window, shown below, consists of two panes. On the left, you choose which of the three logs you want to view; the contents of the selected log appear on the right.

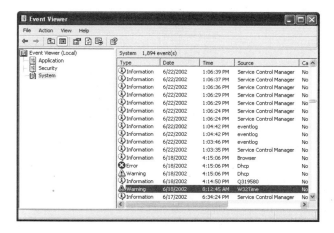

Most of the time, you'll want to look in the System log (for messages about Windows and its services) and the Applications log (for messages produced by Windows programs).

> **Note** The third log, the Security log, is empty by default. If you use Windows XP Home Edition, you can't audit security events. Turning this feature on in Windows XP Professional requires that you use an advanced tool called the System Policy Editor, which is intended for use by experts only and is beyond the scope of this book.

Most of the events in the logs are simply informational entries, denoted by an icon with the letter "i" in blue on a white background. A red X indicates an error, and a yellow exclamation point indicates a warning. For any event, you can double-click the log entry to see more details. Figure 5-6, for instance, shows the details that were recorded in the System log after a Stop error forced the computer to restart.

Figure 5-6 Double-click any item in the Event Viewer window to see details about that log entry.

Although the results are often highly technical, the information might still be useful to help you search for solutions.

Rolling Back to a Previous Configuration

Earlier in this chapter, I told you how to use System Restore to save your system configuration so that you can undo any harmful changes. If your computer is acting up and you're ready to use System Restore to travel back in time to a point where your PC worked properly, follow these instructions.

1 Shut down all running programs.

2 Open the Help And Support Center and, under Pick A Task, click the Undo Changes To Your Computer With System Restore option.

3 On the Welcome To System Restore screen, shown on the next page, choose Restore My Computer To An Earlier Time and click Next.

> **Note**   The third choice, Undo My Last Restoration, is available only after you've used System Restore to return to a previous configuration. If you've never done this before, you see only two options.

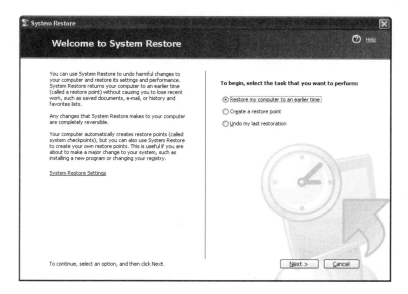

4   On the Select A Restore Point page, choose the date that you want to go back to from the calendar on the left, and then click the restore point entry from the list on the right, as in Figure 5-7. Click Next.

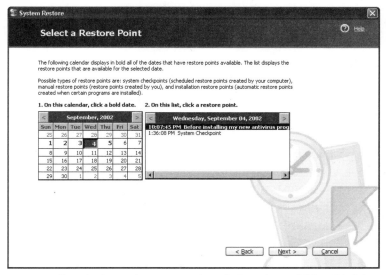

Figure 5-7 To undo changes to your computer, select a restore point from this list.

Tip How do you use System Restore if Windows won't start at all? If you can boot into Safe Mode (as described later in this section), you can run System Restore from there.

---

5 The next page gives you one last chance to confirm your restore point selection. It also reminds you that using System Restore doesn't remove any data files, and you can revert to the current configuration. Follow the prompts to finish the restore operation. When you're finished, Windows restarts and your system should be working again.

Tip When System Restore has completed its work, any programs you installed after the date and time of the selected restore point will no longer work. Before restoring your system to a previous point, I recommend uninstalling any programs that you've installed since that restore point was created. Although this step isn't required, it can prevent problems. If you forget to do this, don't worry—just reinstall the program.

How to Recover After Your Computer Crashes

How do you feel after a computer crash? Do you hold your breath when your computer starts, crossing your fingers and fervently hoping that nothing too serious went wrong? Those are perfectly natural feelings. In this section, let me suggest some steps you can take to lower your stress level and increase the odds that everything will work the way it's supposed to.

Using Safe Mode to Repair Windows

What should you do when Windows refuses to start up in its normal mode? As I described previously in the section "Troubleshooting 101: Figuring Out What Went Wrong," you can start Windows in Safe Mode to run tests and make repairs. Safe Mode usually works even when your computer won't allow you to start Windows in normal mode. When you log on in Safe Mode, you'll probably notice that the Windows desktop looks significantly different from what you're accustomed to in day-to-day operation. For starters, the words "Safe Mode" are emblazoned in all four corners of the screen. In addition, your screen resolution, colors, and desktop icons might look different (usually much worse). Don't worry; these changes are a normal part of the Safe Mode experience.

Try This! To start Windows in Safe Mode, follow these steps.

1 Shut your computer down completely and wait for about a minute. This precaution ensures that nothing is resident in your computer's memory.

2 Press the power switch to start your computer.

3 As soon as you see your computer's startup messages appear on the screen, begin tapping the F8 key about once per second (tap, *one thousand one*, tap, *one thousand two*, tap, *one thousand three*...).

4 When you see the Windows Advanced Options Menu, shown below, select Safe Mode and press Enter. (If you need access to your network or to the Internet, choose Safe Mode With Networking instead.)

```
Windows Advanced Options Menu
Please select an option:

    Safe Mode
    Safe Mode with Networking
    Safe Mode with Command Prompt

    Enable Boot Logging
    Enable VGA Mode
    Last Known Good Configuration (your most recent settings that worked)
    Directory Services Restore Mode (Windows domain controllers only)
    Debugging Mode

    Start Windows Normally
    Reboot
    Return to OS Choices Menu

Use the up and down arrow keys to move the highlight to your choice.
```

5 On the following screen, select the operating system you want to start and press Enter. For most people, this menu consists of only one choice. If you have more than one choice, select your version of Microsoft Windows XP.

6 After a flurry of text messages that list each Windows component as it loads and a brief display of the Windows logo, you should reach the Welcome screen. Click your user name to log on.

In Safe Mode, you can perform all sorts of repair operations, including the following:

■ You can remove, replace, or update device drivers.

■ You can uninstall software.

- You can make changes to the registry, if advised to do so by a support professional.

- You can run System Restore and roll back your system configuration to a previous point where it worked properly.

When you've finished your testing or repairs, click Start, choose Shut Down, and restart your system in normal mode. And remember to breathe!

Restoring the Last Known Good Configuration

One of the simplest mistakes you can make is to install the wrong driver for a piece of hardware. The effects, unfortunately, can be extreme, including preventing you from starting Windows at all. If you're unable to start Windows immediately after making a change to your system, you can use an emergency repair option to replace the new, incorrect configuration with the previous configuration.

Note Restoring the Last Known Good Configuration doesn't repair, remove, or replace any files. All it does is undo the most recent set of changes to the Windows registry.

To use this option, follow the same procedures that I described in the previous section as if you were going to start your computer in Safe Mode. When you reach the Windows Advanced Options Menu, choose Last Known Good Configuration.

Repairing Windows

In extreme cases, you might find yourself unable to start Windows at all because one or more operating system files are damaged. If you find yourself in this pickle, the solution might be simpler than you think. You can repair your Windows XP installation by rerunning the Windows Setup program. This option is quick and not that difficult, although you need to be careful that you don't choose the wrong repair option.

Insert the Windows XP CD into your CD-ROM drive and restart your computer. If you see a Press Any Key To Boot From CD prompt, tap the spacebar. The Windows Setup program runs automatically. When you reach the Welcome to Windows Setup screen, don't choose the option to repair your system with the Recovery Console! That option takes you to a highly technical command-line environment. (A technical support professional or a friendly Windows expert may be able to walk you through making repairs in the Recovery Console, but don't go there alone.) Instead, press Enter to continue the Windows Setup program. After you accept the license agreement, Windows searches your hard disk for an existing installation of Windows. If it finds such an installation, it offers a menu that includes a repair option. Press *R* to perform the repair.

Key Points

- The best way to prepare for problems is to make sure you always have backup copies of important data files.

- System Restore, a new feature in Windows XP, allows you to save system files and settings so that you can undo changes that cause problems and go back to a point when your system worked perfectly.

- Whenever you encounter a problem with Windows, your first goal should be to isolate the problem. If you can reproduce the problem with specific steps, you can test possible solutions more effectively.

- The Windows Help And Support Center is filled with excellent troubleshooting tools.

- Video drivers are among the most common causes of computer crashes. Sometimes, simply updating a video driver can make your problems vanish immediately.

- Do you have an expert friend who uses Windows XP? With the help of a feature called Remote Assistance, you can enlist your friend's aid in identifying and solving even the peskiest problem.

- Don't be intimidated by technical error messages. Write down or do a screen capture of the details and plug key phrases into the search box in the Microsoft Knowledge Base or a good search engine such as Google. You might find the answers, written in plain English.

- When Windows won't start in normal mode, try to start in Safe Mode instead. This special diagnostic mode lets you make repairs and investigate problems.

- Using the Windows XP CD, you can repair your existing Windows installation.

Chapter 6

Connecting to the Internet and Browsing the Web

Microsoft Windows XP and the Internet were made for each other.

Microsoft Internet Explorer is an integral part of the Windows XP operating system, and all the pieces that you need to connect to your Internet service provider (ISP) are included with Windows. No matter where you go in Windows, the incredible richness of the Web is never more than a click or two away. Thanks to some well-designed wizards, it shouldn't take more than a minute or two to get a single PC or a home full of computers connected to the Internet. In this chapter, I assume you already know your way around the World Wide Web and can open a Web page. I'll show you some tricks that can help you keep track of all that information and find your favorite sites when you're ready to return.

Using a Modem to Get on the Internet

In Windows XP, setting up a dial-up Internet connection takes just a few clicks of the mouse, thanks to an efficient wizard. Fine-tuning that connection can take a little extra effort, though. Is your dial-up connection your primary means of access to the Internet? If so, you'll probably want to configure it so it dials automatically when it's needed and hangs up after a suitable period of inactivity. If you pay by the minute for Internet access, you'll want to be even more careful to set brief time-outs that keep your bill from soaring.

On the other hand, you'll want to set things up differently if you normally use a broadband connection and your dial-up connection is just a backup that you use when traveling or when the cable or digital subscriber line (DSL) connection stops working temporarily.

Installing a Modem

Thanks to Plug and Play (PnP) support, installing a new modem requires virtually no effort at all, except perhaps to click OK in a dialog box or two. If Windows doesn't detect the new modem when you plug it in (this is most likely to happen with an older modem that connects through a serial port), try opening Control Panel and running the Add Hardware Wizard. In Category view, you can find this wizard by opening the Printers And Other Hardware category and looking for the Add Hardware link in the task pane at the left of the window.

After your modem is installed, you can make any necessary adjustments by going back to the Printers And Other Hardware category in Control Panel and double-clicking Phone And Modem Options. The Phone And Modem Options dialog box opens, as shown below.

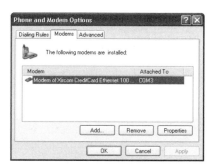

This dialog box tells you the port that the modem is using (in this case, COM3, which is a serial port). If you have any problems getting the modem to work, click Properties and then click Troubleshoot on the General tab of the Properties dialog box.

Making Connections

After your modem is properly installed, use the New Connection Wizard to create a connection that contains all the settings for your dial-up connection. Before you start, make sure you've gathered all the information you'll need from your ISP, including your logon name and password, the phone number that you need to dial for access, and any other technical details.

1 Click Start, open Control Panel, click Network And Internet Connections, and then click Network Connections. (If you're using the Classic view of Control Panel, just double-click Network Connections.)

2 In the task pane at the left of the Network Connections folder, click Create A New Connection. (If the task pane is not visible, click Folders in the Folder toolbar to toggle the task pane, or simply choose New Connection from the File menu.)

3 Click Next in the Welcome page of the New Connection Wizard.

4 On the Network Connection Type page, choose Connect To The Internet and click Next.

5 On the Getting Ready page, shown below, choose Set Up My Connection Manually and click Next.

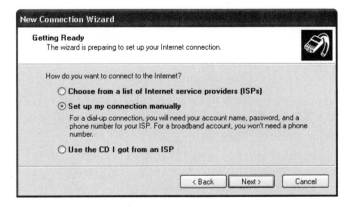

6 On the Internet Connection page, choose Connect Using A Dial-Up Modem and click Next.

7 In the ISP Name text box on the Connection Name page, enter the name that you want to use to identify this connection, as shown on the next page.

Tip   If you travel to different cities and need to create different connections for each city, be sure that the descriptive name you use for the connection icon includes the city name.

---

8   On the Phone Number To Dial page, enter the phone number that you need to dial to connect with your ISP. Include any necessary prefixes or area codes. Click Next.

9   On the Connection Availability page, choose whether to allow the connection you're creating to be used by just you, or others logging on to the computer with their own user name and password.

10   On the Internet Account Information page, fill in the User Name and Password fields. In addition, set the three options at the bottom of the dialog box shown in Figure 6-1, as follows:

- **Use This Account Name And Password When Anyone Connects To The Internet From This Computer**   Leave this option selected. Clear this check box only if you don't want other users to log on to your computer and dial up your ISP. (If you selected the My Use Only option on the Connection Availability page in step 9, this check box will be dimmed.)

- **Make This The Default Internet Connection**   Leave this option selected if this is your primary Internet connection. Clear this check box if you normally have a broadband connection and use this dial-up connection only when traveling or when the cable or DSL connection isn't working.

- **Turn On Internet Connection Firewall For This Connection** Leave this option selected unless you have a different firewall program installed or your firewall is part of a hardware solution.

Figure 6-1 Enter your password here, and Windows saves it for later use.

11 On the final page of the wizard, click Finish.

Tip   Every dial-up connection you create appears in the Network Connections folder. For easier access to dial-up connections, choose the option on the final page of the New Connection Wizard to create a shortcut on the desktop. You can also drag any shortcut out of the Network Connections folder and onto Start, the desktop, or the Quick Launch toolbar, where it creates a shortcut. In addition, you can customize the Start menu so that the Network Connections folder is available in the column on the right, as I explain in the section "Streamline Your Start Menu," on page 210.

Dialing and Disconnecting Automatically

To use your new dial-up connection, double-click it in the Network Connections folder. When you do, you can see the dialog box, as shown on the next page, which includes the user name and password you entered earlier. Click Dial to connect to the Internet.

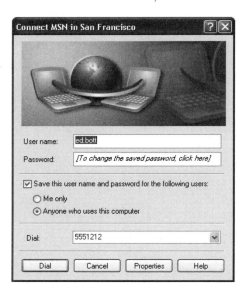

Would you prefer Windows to connect to the Internet automatically whenever you click a Web page or try to check your e-mail? This option makes sense in the following circumstances:

- Your dial-up account is your only means of Internet access.

- You have a dedicated phone line for the Internet, so you don't need to worry about accidentally breaking into a phone call that's currently in progress.

- You pay a flat rate for Internet access rather than by the minute. (Automatic connections are a bad idea if each one costs you money!)

To set up automatic connections, you need to do two things. First, open the Internet Options dialog box. (You'll find this option in Control Panel and on the Tools menu in Internet Explorer.) Click the Connections tab to display the dialog box shown in Figure 6-2.

Choose Always Dial My Default Connection to tell Windows that you want it to dial automatically when you request data from the Internet. Choose Never Dial A Connection if you want to be in complete control and only make manual connections.

Figure 6-2 Use these options to manage your dial-up connections.

Next, you need to adjust the options for your dial-up connection so that you aren't prompted for a phone number or a password. Right-click the connection in the Network Connections folder and click Properties. On the Options tab of the Properties dialog box, shown below, clear the Prompt For Name And Password and Prompt For Phone Number check boxes, then click OK. From now on, when you double-click the connection or request a Web page, Windows connects to your ISP automatically, without pausing for any input from you.

Tip Use the choices under Redialing Options in this dialog box to tell Windows whether you want to hang up automatically after a period of inactivity and also if you want the connection to redial automatically if you are accidentally disconnected from your ISP.

While you're connected to the Internet, a small icon appears in the notification area. To disconnect from a dial-up connection, right-click the icon and choose Disconnect, or double-click the icon and click Disconnect from the Status dialog box.

Setting Up a Broadband (Cable or DSL) Connection

Dial-up Internet connections plod along at a leisurely pace. Broadband connections, by contrast, are usually so zippy that clicking from page to page on the Web is similar to turning the pages of a magazine. These days, the most common forms of broadband connections are cable modems and DSL connections. The former carries data over the same wire that brings television into your home; the latter uses telephone wiring, although it works at many times the speed of a dial-up connection and doesn't prevent you from talking on the phone as you're surfing the Web.

Windows XP fully supports broadband connections, usually treating them as network devices. You add a network card to your computer and connect it to the cable modem or DSL gateway. Configure your computer using the Network Setup Wizard and you should be good to go.

Caution   Broadband connections might be blazingly fast, but that doesn't stop some diehard system tweakers from trying to squeeze even more speed out of the digital line. If you poke around in certain corners of the Internet, you'll find people who swear that you can dramatically speed up a broadband connection by changing a few numbers in the registry. Don't believe them. In general, Windows XP is already set for optimum performance, and if you try these unsupported tweaks, you're most likely to make your computer run *slower*!

To set up your high-speed Internet connection, open the Network Connections folder in Control Panel and click Create A New Connection. In the New Connection Wizard, follow the same steps as in the previous section for setting up a dial-up connection but choose one of the two broadband options shown below.

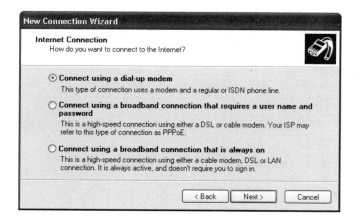

Most people choose the Connect Using A Broadband Connection That Is Always On option. If your ISP requires you to log on for high-speed access, follow the prompts to save your user name and password, just as you would when setting up a dial-up connection.

Sharing Your Internet Connection

If you have two or more computers in your home, it's downright silly to expect each one to access the Internet independently. That would require potentially expensive hardware for each one, and you would find yourselves fighting constantly over who gets to use the phone line or the broadband connection. To preserve domestic tranquility, take your one Internet connection and share it with all the other computers on the local network. You'll need a little extra hardware, but all the software you need is included in Windows XP. Use one of the following configurations:

- **Add a *router* or *residential gateway* to your network.** This piece of hardware connects to your Internet access device, such as a modem or cable modem, on one side and to your network hub on the other end. (Some routers include a hub of their own so that you can connect the network card in your computers directly to the router.) To your ISP, the router looks like a single computer; it does all the work of communicating with the Internet on behalf of your other computers.

    > **Lingo**   As the name suggests, the job of a *router* is to gather packets of data as they come into a network and send (route) them to the correct destination, using the address on each packet for delivery details. A *residential gateway* is a router designed for use on a home network. It might or might not have any special features.

- **Use Internet Connection Sharing (ICS).**   In this configuration, you designate one of your computers as the ICS *host*. This computer needs to have a network card to connect to other computers and a separate Internet access device—either a modem or a second network card connected to a cable or DSL modem.

Which solution should you choose? A router is by far your best solution. It typically adds security features to your network, and because the router is always on, you don't have to worry about knocking other family members off the Net when you restart your computer, as you would with ICS. The only downside is that a router costs a few dollars (although simple home routers have plummeted in price in recent years). Look at your budget and your network and decide which of these solutions suits you.

Although this technology sounds complicated, the only hard part is making sure all the cables connect to the proper ports.

Setting Up a Router or Residential Gateway

Follow the hardware maker's instructions to connect the router to your network and then connect the rest of the network computers. Test your computer to make sure the Internet connection is working properly and then follow these steps:

1 Click Start and then click My Network Places. (If this option isn't available, open My Computer and click My Network Places under Other Places in the task pane at left.)

2 In the Network Tasks pane, click Set Up A Home Or Small Office Network.

Note   If your computer is part of a Windows domain, this option will not be available.

---

3 Click Next in the Welcome page and in the Before You Continue page.

4 In the Select A Connection Method page, shown below, choose This Computer Connects To The Internet Through Another Computer On My Network Or Through A Residential Gateway and click Next.

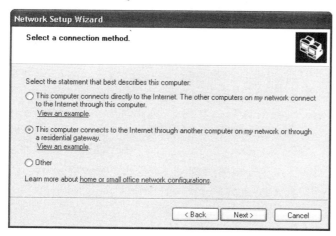

5 In the remaining pages of the wizard, enter a name for your computer and select a workgroup name. (The default settings for each of these pages should be fine.)

6 When you reach the final page, click Finish to apply the changes.

Run the Network Setup Wizard on all other computers on your network, using the Windows XP CD or the floppy disk you created as part of the wizard. Be sure to specify that the other computers on your network also connect through a residential gateway.

Setting Up Internet Connection Sharing

If you've decided to install ICS, make sure that your local network is working and then add your Internet access device and configure it. When these steps are complete, you can let the Network Setup Wizard handle the rest of the details. Sit down at the computer that you plan to use as the ICS host. Follow the steps in the previous section to start the Network Setup Wizard. When you reach the Select A Connection Method page, choose This Computer Connects Directly To The Internet. The Other Computers On My Network Connect To The Internet Through This Computer and click Next.

If you don't have separate connections for your network and your Internet connection, the wizard will inform you that it can't continue. With the right hardware, however, you'll see a page listing the available network adapters, such as the one shown below. Select the one that's connected to the Internet and click Next to continue.

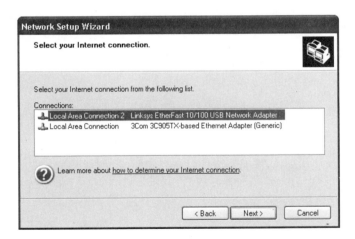

See Also   *If you can't figure out which one is which, see the section "Checking Your Network Configuration," on page 301, for some suggestions on how to tell your Internet connection from your network connection.*

In the remaining pages of the wizard, enter a name for your computer and select a workgroup name. After you complete the wizard, be sure to run it on all other computers on your network, using the Windows XP CD or the floppy disk you created as part of the wizard. Be sure to specify that the other computers on your network connect to the Internet through another computer on your network.

When Internet Connection Sharing is enabled on your network, a new Internet Gateway connection appears in the Network Connections folder for all computers that share the connection through the ICS host. Figure 6-3 shows the dialog box that appears when you double-click this connection. The display shows a schematic diagram of the Internet connection along with statistics about the connection and how much traffic it has handled. The most important part of this dialog box, though, is the button at the bottom. Click Disable to shut down the connection immediately when you're working at a remote computer. This feature can come in handy if the shared connection is one that requires you to pay by the minute. By shutting down the connection when you've finished with it, you can lower your bill dramatically.

Figure 6-3 Click Disable to shut down a shared Internet connection remotely.

If your computer is serving as the ICS host, you might decide you don't want a remote user to be able to shut down your access to the Internet. In that case, follow these steps:

1   Go to Control Panel, open the Network Connections folder, right-click the shared connection (look for the word *shared* in the description to the right of this connection), and choose Properties from the shortcut menu.

2   On the Properties dialog box, click the Advanced tab.

3 Clear the Allow Other Network Users To Control Or Disable The Shared Internet Connection option, as shown below.

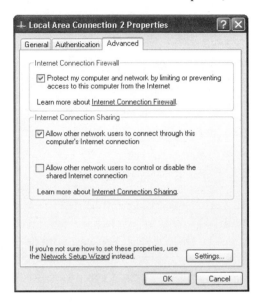

4 Click OK to close the dialog box and apply your changes.

Search Secrets

You can find anything on the Internet, if you know where to look. Microsoft Internet Explorer 6 provides several built-in tools that you can use to extract exactly the information you're looking for from the vast reaches of the Web, as follows:

■ You can type a search term directly into the Address bar. When you do this, Internet Explorer first tries to convert the terms you entered into a Web address (by adding *www* at the beginning and *.com* at the end). If this doesn't work, it sends you to the default search page.

■ You can click Search on the toolbar (or press Ctrl+E) to open the Search Companion. This Explorer bar appears in the left pane of the browser window. You can enter a word, phrase, or question in the Search Companion box, as shown on the next page, and press Enter. The Search results appear in the browser pane on the right. (Note that I've turned off the animated screen character here.)

■ You can also configure the Search pane to use Classic Internet Search, shown below, instead of the Search Companion by clicking Change Preferences, then Change Internet Search Behavior. You can choose different types of searches from this pane. The results of your search request appear in the left pane, and Windows doesn't offer to send your search request to other search engines, as the Search Companion does. You might need to close and restart Internet Explorer to enable the Classic Internet Search pane option the first time.

By default, all these search tools send your request to the default search engine. You can take your choice of other search engines, though; in fact, you can tell Windows that you want all search requests to go to a specific search engine. To do so for the Search Companion, follow these steps:

1   Click Search and choose Change Preferences from the Search pane.

2   Under the heading How Do You Want To Use Search Companion, click Change Internet Search Behavior.

3   In the Internet Search Behavior page, choose whether you want to use Search Companion or Classic Internet Search and then select a default search engine from the list of available choices.

Tip   My favorite search engine by far is Google (*http://www.google.com*), which is available as a choice in the Search Companion preferences. Google's results, based on a massive index of the Internet, seem positively psychic sometimes. Give it a try. If you want to see the other choices as well, feel free to experiment with each search engine choice for a day or two to see if one strikes your fancy as better, more accurate, or more complete than the others. Unfortunately, you can't choose Google with the Classic Internet Search option unless you customize the search settings and choose the option to use one service for all searches.

---

4   Close all Internet Explorer windows and then restart the Web browser to see your changes.

To change preferences when using Classic Internet Search, first follow the steps above to disable the Search Companion. Then, after shutting down and restarting Internet Explorer, do the following.

1   Open the Search pane and click the Customize link at the top of the pane.

2   In the Customize Search Settings dialog box, shown on the next page, select Use Search Assistant.

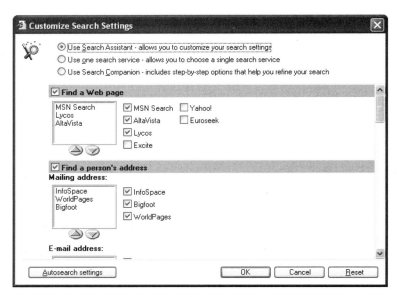

3   Go through each category and select the names of providers you want to use for that category. (You can choose more than one.)

4   In each category, make sure that the first selection is the one you want to use as the default for that category. The remaining choices only come into play if you decide to send your search to other providers after the default search is complete.

5   Clear the check boxes for any categories you don't want to use. For instance, if you never search for addresses on the Internet, clear the Find A Person's Address check box.

6   Click Autosearch Settings and choose the search engine you want to use when you enter terms directly in the address bar, as shown here. (You can choose Google for this one.)

7   Click OK to apply your changes.

Keeping Track of Your Favorite Web Sites

The World Wide Web contains an inconceivably huge number of pages—certainly, the number is in the billions. When you find a page that's especially useful or interesting, do you really want to have to search through those billions of pages to find it again? Of course not. Take advantage of Internet Explorer's Favorites list to save shortcuts to those pages so you can revisit them on demand.

Saving a Favorite Site

To build your list of Favorites, just add a shortcut to the list whenever you're viewing a page that looks like a keeper.

> **Note** Internet Favorites are shortcut files, similar to the shortcuts you use to start programs. To share one of your favorite Web pages with someone else, you can send them a copy of the shortcut. You can also back up your Favorites list by opening the Favorites folder and copying its contents to a floppy disk or a network server. Finally, you can use the Import and Export choices on the File menu in Internet Explorer to save Favorites and cookies in small text files. Although this feature was designed to make it easier to move between Netscape and Internet Explorer, it also works great as a backup tool!

- To add the current page to your Favorites list immediately, press Ctrl+D. The new shortcut uses the title of the current page as its name, and appears in the main Favorites list (not a subfolder). I don't recommend this shortcut, because often the page title isn't enough to properly describe the page.

- To add a Favorite and edit its name and location, choose Add to Favorites from the Favorites menu. In the Add Favorite dialog box, shown below, edit the text in the Name text box and click Create In to choose an existing folder or click Create New to create a new folder on the fly.

Tip   If the Favorites Explorer bar is visible, you can create a new Favorite with the mouse. Click the icon to the left of the Web address in the Address bar and drag it down onto the Favorites bar. Drop it anywhere to create a new shortcut, which you can then rename or drag into a subfolder.

■   To add a Favorite to the desktop, choose Send from the File menu and click Shortcut To Desktop. (Remember that shortcuts are just files and the Favorites folder is just another folder; you can move shortcuts to and from any of these locations any time.)

Organizing Your Favorites Folder

To use the Favorites folder, you can do what most people do: Pull down the Favorites menu and scroll through the shortcuts there. Any folders you've created here appear as *cascading menus*, which fly out to the right or left when you click them. This approach works, although if you create lots of Favorites you'll probably find that this menu is difficult to deal with.

Want a faster, smarter way to get to your Favorite Web pages? Click Favorites on the Internet Explorer toolbar and open the Favorites Explorer bar. As you can see in Figure 6-4, this list appears to the left of the pane that displays the current Web page and lets you click to see and edit all your Favorites.

Figure 6-4 Click a shortcut on the Favorites bar to open the Web page it points to, and click a folder icon to see the shortcuts stored in that folder.

You can drag shortcuts up and down on the Favorites bar to change their order in the list. Right-click and choose Rename to change a shortcut's name, or choose Properties to see a dialog box like the one shown on the next page, which displays the *URL* and even lets you assign a shortcut key to the page. Using the Favorites button (or the keyboard shortcut Ctrl+I), you can also show or hide the Favorites bar anytime you want. If you want more room for the Web page, click the Favorites icon again and make the Explorer bar disappear.

Lingo   *URL* stands for *Uniform Resource Locator,* which is the technical term for the address of a Web site or other location on the Internet.

Editing a single shortcut directly in the Favorites bar is easy. To do more extensive filing and housekeeping, however, you'll want to open a separate window. From the Favorites bar, click Organize, or choose Organize Favorites from the Favorites menu. As you can see in Figure 6-5, the Organize Favorites dialog box shows information about the currently selected item and lets you rename it, delete it, or organize shortcuts in folders.

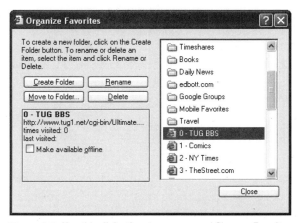

Figure 6-5 Use this dialog box to rename and file your Favorites.

If you find the Organize Favorites dialog box too clumsy, just open the Favorites folder in Windows Explorer. Click Start, choose Run, type **Favorites** in the Open text box, and then press Enter. Rename shortcuts or edit their properties just as you would in any other window.

Creating Shortcuts to Your *Favorite* Favorites

You might have hundreds of shortcuts in your Favorites folder, but I'll bet you can pick out a dozen sites you visit constantly. For those Favorites that really deserve the name, use the Links bar. This is a built-in toolbar that appears alongside the toolbar in the Internet Explorer window and shows individual icons for any shortcuts contained in it. To add a shortcut to the Links bar, drag it from the Address bar directly to the Links bar, or drag it into the Links subfolder in the Favorites folder. I recommend that you rename shortcuts in the Links bar using the shortest names you can come up with; this makes the most of the limited space on this toolbar.

> **Tip**   Don't bother trying to delete the Links folder. Windows automatically re-creates it the next time you start Internet Explorer. You can, however, remove the standard shortcuts (to MSN, Hotmail, and other sites) that Microsoft puts in this folder.

What to Do When a Web Page Won't Work

You click a link and you wait. And you wait. And then you wait some more. How long should you wait for a Web page to load? There's no good answer to that question. The actual time it takes between when you click a link and when the page pops into your browser depends on a number of factors, many of them out of your control. The speed of your Internet connection and the speed of the server at the other end are most important—if you have a super-zippy cable modem but the server you're connecting to is on a slow dial-up link, your connection creeps along at dial-up speeds. Congestion in the data pipeline between you and the Web server also affects your connection.

If a page appears to be hung and won't load at all, try clicking Stop (the red X on the toolbar) and then click Refresh just to its right, as shown here. If that doesn't work, try closing the browser window and reopening it.

Tip   Windows XP includes an excellent troubleshooter that you can use to help you step through possible solutions to problems with your Internet connection. To use it, open the Start menu, click Help And Support, type **Internet Explorer troubleshooter** in the Search text box, and click the green arrow.

If you can still load other pages at normal speed and the problem appears to be with just one site, you can usually assume that the problem is at the other end of the connection. If you can't load any Web pages, on the other hand, the problem is in your Internet connection. If it doesn't clear up by itself in a few minutes, contact your ISP and ask if they're experiencing any problems.

And if none of that works, just wait.

Filling In Forms and Remembering Passwords

Internet Explorer doesn't have a mind-reading module, but it is capable of remembering things you type when working with Web pages, thanks to a feature called AutoComplete. Using AutoComplete, Internet Explorer can remember Web addresses, search terms, logon names, phone numbers, and even passwords you've previously entered on a given page. With the click of a mouse, you can recall the saved values instead of having to retype them. If you decide this feature is a worthwhile timesaver, you might want to make a few changes to make it more useful. On the other hand, if you're concerned about security, you should consider the risks involved in saving this sort of data and decide whether you want to disable this feature completely.

Here's how AutoComplete works.

Every time you click in a text box on a Web page, you see a drop-down list box showing values you previously entered in that form, as shown below. (If the list doesn't appear, press the Down arrow key.) The list can hold an essentially unlimited number of items, but if you save more than seven, you must scroll to see the remaining entries. When you enter a new value, the term is added to the list. You can also type a letter (or number) or two or three to narrow down the list. When you see the item you want to enter into the text box, click its entry in the list to automatically complete the entry. (See why it's called AutoComplete?)

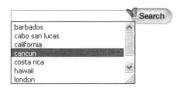

What if you make a typing error when you enter a value in the box and it is added to the list anyway? No problem. Click in the box and press the Down arrow key to display the list. Continue moving down through the list until the entry you want to delete is selected. At that point, press Delete to remove it from the list. You can use this technique with Web forms and passwords alike.

You have every right to be concerned about the security of data you save for use in Web forms, and especially with the wisdom of saving passwords used in Web sites. On the plus side, this data is available only to someone who logs on with your user name and password, and Windows prompts you for your permission before saving data that it recognizes as a password. If you carefully guard these "keys" to your computer and you remember to lock your computer when you step away, your saved data is reasonably safe. But if your computer is in a public place, or if you share the same account with other family members, you should avoid using this feature, especially on sensitive Web sites like the one where you do your banking.

See Also   *For more details about passwords, see the section "Logging On," on page 25.*

To stop saving data associated with Web pages, follow these steps:

1   From Internet Explorer, choose Internet Options from the Tools menu.

2   Click the Content tab and click AutoComplete.

3   In the AutoComplete Settings dialog box shown in Figure 6-6, adjust the settings listed here:

- **Web Addresses**   Controls URLs you type in the Address bar.

- **Forms**   Is for data such as names, addresses, and search terms that you enter in a Web-based form.

- **User Names And Passwords On Forms**   Are stored in pairs in a separate, secure location, and passwords are normally obscured by dots when you enter them. From a security point of view, this option entails the greatest risk.

- **Prompt Me To Save Passwords**   Allows you to stop saving passwords without erasing currently saved name/password pairs. To keep currently saved passwords but not new ones, clear this check box but leave the box above it selected.

Figure 6-6 The AutoComplete feature remembers everything you type in Web forms unless you clear these options.

If you've been saving data on Web pages for some time and you're not sure whether you have any sensitive information stored on your computer, use Clear Forms and Clear Passwords to erase all saved data. From that point on, you can decide on a case-by-case basis whether you want to save a password or not.

Saving a Copy of a Web Page for Later Use

When you visit a Web site that contains useful, valuable, or amusing information, you add it to your Favorites collection, right? But clicking on that saved shortcut doesn't guarantee you'll see the same page. The Web site could go out of business. The Webmaster could remove the page or reorganize the Web site, making it difficult or impossible to find the page you want. The author could rewrite the article and change its content. In any of these scenarios, you risk being disappointed when you visit what you thought would be a great site and find something less.

If you want to make sure you save the information from a Web page, you must save a copy of the page itself. Using Internet Explorer, you have three alternatives. You can save the page itself as a file on your local hard disk so that you can open it anytime in your browser. You can make a copy of the page, send it to yourself as an e-mail message, and then file it in a folder along with your other messages. Or you can try the low-tech solution and just print it out. In this section, I explain all three alternatives.

> **Tip**   At various times, I've used all of the techniques I describe in this section. Saving the infor-
> mation from a Web page is especially important when you find technical information about hard-
> ware or software you own and use regularly. Having quick access to installation instructions and
> troubleshooting information when you need it is much better than having to search the Web for a
> specific bit of information that might no longer be there!

Save It

When you open a Web page in your browser, all you're really doing is loading
a bunch of files stored on a server. It's a relatively simple matter to save those
copies so you have access to the page later. After loading the Web page, choose
Save As from the File menu in Internet Explorer. This opens the Save Web Page
dialog box, shown below. Don't just click Save, though! You have several formats to choose from; make sure you choose the right one.

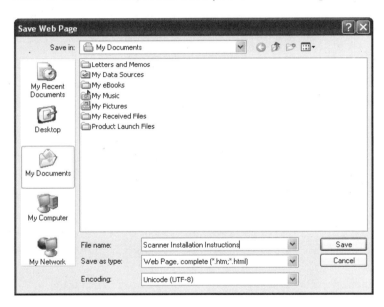

First, choose a destination folder for the saved file. (If you're not sure how
to do this, see Chapter 10, "Organizing Your Files.") Next, click in the File Name
text box and enter the name you want to use for the saved page. Now the most
important step: Select a file format from the drop-down Save As Type list. You
have these choices:

■   **Web Page, Complete**   Although this sounds like the perfect solution,
I don't recommend it. In this format, the Web page is saved as a file
with the name you specified, and all the supporting files for that page
(such as graphics files and scripts) are saved in a separate folder with

the same name. If you want to send someone a copy of the saved page, you must send them both parts or the page is incomplete.

■ **Web Archive, Single File**   I recommend this option for saving any page that contains graphics and other elements that are important to the content. The saved file contains all the graphics and other supporting files in compressed format. If you want to move it or share it with a friend, you only have to deal with one file. When you double-click the icon for the saved file, the complete page opens in Internet Explorer.

■ **Web Page, HTML Only**   Choose this option if you want to save the formatting on the page but you don't care about any graphics or other elements. When you open this type of saved page, you might see a little red X where the graphics should be, but the information is intact.

■ **Text File**   If the page you're trying to save is simple and all you care about are the words, choose this option. The saved file opens in Notepad and includes no formatting or graphics.

E-Mail It

Did you know that your Web browser and your e-mail program speak the same language? HTML is the basic language of the Web, and it's also the format that Microsoft Outlook Express and Microsoft Outlook use to create and display formatted text and graphics in e-mail messages. So, if you already use one of these e-mail programs, just turn the Web page into e-mail and send it to yourself or to someone else.

From Internet Explorer's File menu, choose Send and then click Page By E-mail. This opens a new message window with the contents of the Web page already pasted into the body of the message. Add an address in the To: box (use your own address if you want to save it in your own Inbox) and click Send. If Outlook Express or Outlook are configured to use rich text or plain text, then an icon with the link attached is pasted into the mail message rather than the contents of the Web page.

Tip   You can also save an e-mail message as a file on your local hard disk. Use the Send, Page By Email menu to create a blank message. Then, in the message window, choose Save As from the File menu. Choose a location to store the file, give it a name, and click Save. When you double-click the saved file, it opens Outlook Express and displays the saved page in an e-mail message window.

Print It

If you don't mind filing your favorite Web page in a *real* file folder—you know, the kind made from trees?—you can print a Web page and keep it handy. In fact, for information like installation instructions for a software program, you can't go wrong by printing the page and storing it right alongside the CD that contains the program's setup files.

To print a Web page, you have three choices. Although these choices appear to do the same thing, you'll find that each option is different, and it pays to learn the difference.

■   Click Print on the Standard toolbar. This sends the print job directly to the printer, without any intermediate steps. Use this option if you have only one printer and you want your printed output as soon as possible, without having to think about any options.

■   Choose Print from the File menu (or press Ctrl+P). This opens the Print dialog box, shown below, where you can choose a printer, select which pages you want to print, and specify how many copies to print. Use this option if you know you only want to print a specific page or if you want to adjust margins or choose a different printer.

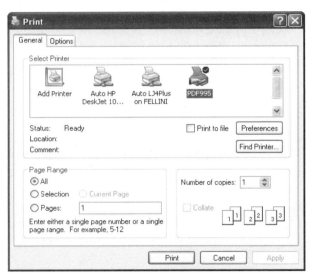

■   Choose Print Preview from the File menu. This option opens a window that shows you exactly how the page you selected appears when you send it to the printer. As you can see in Figure 6-7, this view shows the headers and footers that appear on the printed page and gives you a toolbar that you can use to view each page.

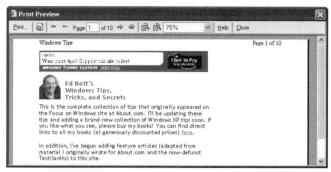

Figure 6-7 Use this window to preview a Web page before printing it.

Try This! I always recommend using the Print Preview menu instead of just clicking Print. Why? Because I can't stand it when I print a Web page and the printer kicks out an extra page that contains a single line of text I don't need! By previewing the printed output first, I can see that page and specify that I don't want it printed. (In the Print dialog box, enter the exact page numbers to print in the Pages text box, under Page Range.) In fact, I recommend that you change Internet Explorer so that clicking Print opens the Print Preview dialog box. Here's how to do it:

1   Right-click anywhere on the toolbar and choose Customize from the shortcut menu.

2   In the Customize Toolbar dialog box, select Print from the Current Toolbar Buttons list.

3   Click Remove.

4   From the Available Toolbar Buttons list, select Print Preview.

5   Click Add.

6   To move the button to a different location on the toolbar, select the Print Preview button and then click Move Up or Move Down in the Customize Toolbar dialog box, shown here.

7   Click Close to save your changes.

From now on, when you click Print Preview from any Web page, you'll get a chance to see what you're about to print before you actually waste any paper. I save hundreds of pages of paper every year with this trick. Faster? Maybe not, but it sure is smarter than the alternative.

Tip   What do you do when you want to print out just a portion of a Web page? Use the mouse pointer to select the part of the page you want to print—text, graphics, or both. Then choose File, Print, and in the Page Range box, choose the Selection option. When you click Print, only the text and graphics you selected appear on the printed page.

Key Points

- To set up your Internet connection, use the New Connection Wizard, which is available from the Network Connections folder.

- By setting the correct options, you can configure a dial-up Internet connection to connect automatically without requiring you to click any buttons.

- On a home network, you only need one Internet connection, which you can share among all computers by using a hardware router or the Internet Connection Sharing (ICS) feature of Windows XP.

- Internet Explorer includes at least three ways to search for information automatically.

- You can set the Search Companion or Search Assistant to use your favorite search engine by default.

- Press Ctrl+D to add the current Web page to your Favorites list immediately.

- For fast access to favorite Web sites, use the Favorites Explorer bar and the Links toolbar.

- Although Internet Explorer includes a dialog box designed to help you organize your Favorites, you'll probably find it easier to make changes to the Favorites folder in Windows Explorer.

- Internet Explorer can remember information you've entered in Web forms, including your user names and passwords, and automatically enter this information for you when you return to a page.

- If you're concerned about the security of saved Web passwords, you can and should disable the AutoComplete feature.

- Use the Web Archive, Single File option to save an entire Web page and all of its graphics in a single file that you can keep or share.

- The Print dialog box and Print Preview window give you more control than Print when you want to print a Web page.

Chapter 7

E-Mail Made Easy

How did we ever get along before the invention of e-mail? If someone in your family had a new baby, you had to wait for them to process the pictures, and then wait a few more days for the postal service to deliver them to your mailbox. Negotiating a big business deal? You had to do it over the phone or send a bunch of faxes. Just want to check in and see how a busy friend is doing? You could play telephone tag for weeks.

It's no exaggeration to say that the ability to send and receive e-mail has changed our lives in ways large and small. It's easy to dash off a quick note to a friend or ask a business associate a question. When you receive e-mail, you can answer it on your schedule, without worrying about coordinating your calendar with someone else. And the ability to send file attachments means you can share work and good news with just a few clicks of your mouse.

Microsoft Windows XP includes a full-featured e-mail program called Microsoft Outlook Express, which allows you to send, receive, and manage e-mail from a dizzying variety of sources. In this chapter, I'll show you how to use Outlook Express to retrieve your mail, compose new messages, and automatically organize your cluttered Inbox. And if you can't wait a few minutes for e-mail, try Microsoft Windows Messenger, which lets you send instant messages across the building or halfway around the world.

Setting Up Your E-Mail Accounts

When you move into a new neighborhood, you must notify the post office that
you've moved in and tell them you're ready to have your mail delivered. When
you set up a new computer, you go through the same process with Outlook
Express. The difference is that Outlook Express allows you to have an unlimited
number of e-mail addresses and have mail from all these addresses delivered
into your Outlook Express Inbox. In this section, you learn how to set up each
of several common types of e-mail accounts.

Set Up Internet E-Mail (SMTP/POP3)

Most Internet service providers (ISPs) include one or more e-mail accounts as
part of their service agreement. If you have a dial-up account with your local
phone company or with a nationwide ISP such as Earthlink or AT&T, you get
e-mail with the package. If you sign up for a high-speed Internet account with
your cable company or get digital subscriber line (DSL) service from your phone
company, they give you an e-mail address too. Most of the time, having this type
of Internet e-mail account means that you send and receive e-mail using two
types of servers: an SMTP server for your outgoing mail and a POP3 server for
your incoming mail.

> **Lingo** SMTP stands for *Simple Mail Transfer Protocol*, which defines the way that e-mail servers
> pass messages between one another. *POP3* is short for *Post Office Protocol, version 3*, which is
> the standard your e-mail program uses to fetch mail from your account on a server.

Don't let those acronyms intimidate you. The techies at your ISP are the
only ones who have to worry about what they really mean. Your job—setting up
Outlook Express so it connects to each server properly—is simple and straightforward. Before you get started, you'll need to gather some information from
your ISP—your full e-mail address, your logon name and password (these are
not the same as those you use to log on to Windows), and the names of the
SMTP and POP3 servers.

> **Note** If you receive your e-mail through an account with America Online (AOL), MSN, or Hot-
> mail, the instructions in this section don't apply to you. Skip ahead a few pages to the sections
> that cover these e-mail alternatives specifically.

When you run Outlook Express for the first time, use the Internet Connection
Wizard to set up your primary e-mail account. If you skip this step, or if you want
to set up an additional e-mail account after you've been using Outlook Express for
a while, you can restart the wizard. The wizard is fairly straightforward, but you

can spare yourself some headaches if you perform a few additional steps, as I explain here. (If you've already begun the wizard, you can skip straight to step 3.)

1   From the main Outlook Express window, choose Accounts from the Tools menu.

2   Click Add and choose Mail.

3   On the Your Name page, enter the name you want other people to see when they receive a message from you, as shown below. Click Next to continue.

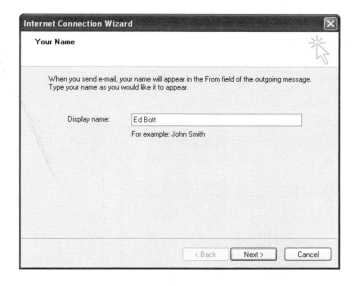

Tip   Although you'll usually want to enter your full name on the Your Name page, you might want to change it for certain accounts. For instance, if you have an MSN account that you use for personal mail and a different account at your business that you use to reply to customers, you might want to add your business name, in parentheses, after your name. When you receive a reply to one of these messages, you'll know at a glance that it's a business-related message, because the other person's e-mail program picks up the name you entered and uses it in the To field.

4   On the Internet E-mail Address page, enter your e-mail address, complete with @ sign and domain name, as shown on the next page. This is the address that other people use to reply to you, so it's important that you enter this information accurately. Click Next to continue.

5 On the E-mail Server Names page, POP3 is already selected in the drop-down list box at the top of the page. Enter the server names for your incoming mail (POP3) and outgoing mail (SMTP) servers in the respective boxes, as shown below. Click Next to continue.

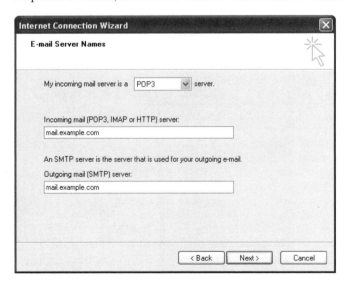

Note   Many ISPs use the same server name for both POP3 and SMTP servers, often in the format mail.*domain*.com, where *domain* is your ISP's domain name. At other ISPs, you might find that the server names offer a clue as to which is which: smtp.*domain*.com and pop.*domain*.com, for instance. The important thing is to enter these names exactly as they're provided for you.

6 On the Internet Mail Logon page, enter the account name and password that your ISP provided to you, as shown below. The Remember Password check box is already selected. Clear this box if you want Outlook Express to prompt you for your password every time you start up. Click Next to continue and then click Finish to close the wizard.

Caution Do not select the Log On Using Secure Password Authorization (SPA) box. This option was used for MSN accounts several years ago, but it is no longer used by MSN—or, for that matter, by any ISP that I'm aware of.

You're now ready to begin sending and receiving e-mail through this account.

Using MSN and Hotmail

If your e-mail address ends with msn.com or hotmail.com, you need to follow slightly different procedures to check your mail. Hotmail provides free e-mail accounts to anyone; if you pay MSN for dial-up or broadband Internet access, you also get one or more msn.com addresses. Both services were originally designed so that you managed all your e-mail through Microsoft Internet Explorer. However, you can set up Outlook Express to send and receive your mail as well. In fact, you can switch between your Web browser and Outlook Express to manage your Hotmail or MSN messages. Using this feature you can check your personal Hotmail account from the office using Internet Explorer, send a few quick replies, and see all the messages in Outlook Express when you return home.

Hotmail and MSN accounts behave a bit differently from SMTP/POP3 accounts. For one thing, all your folders are actually stored on Microsoft's servers. You keep copies of those folders on your local computer, and Outlook Express *synchronizes* the messages on the server with those on your PC.

See Also   *For an explanation of how this process works, see the section "Checking Your E-Mail," on page 159.*

In addition, you can't use Outlook Express *message rules* to sort messages automatically and filter out spam and junk e-mail. Instead, you have to visit the MSN or Hotmail Web site, log on to your account, and set these options there.

Lingo   *Message rules* allow you to set up conditions that Outlook Express checks each time a new message arrives. If the message is from a specific source, such as your bank or stockbroker, you can automatically move it to a folder of your choosing. If it appears to be junk mail or spam, based on your rules, you can delete it automatically without having it clutter up your Inbox.

You can have as many MSN or Hotmail accounts as you want and add any or all of them to Outlook Express. Each such account gets its own set of folders in the Outlook Express Folder List. After setting up your account on the Hotmail or MSN Web page, use the Internet Connection Wizard to add the account to Outlook Express. Follow the same steps as I outlined in the previous section for setting up an SMTP/POP3 account. When you reach the Internet E-mail Address page, enter your Hotmail or MSN address (in the format *yourname*@hotmail.com), and click Next. This opens the E-mail Server Names page, where *HTTP* is already selected in the drop-down list box at the top of the page. If your e-mail address ends with msn.com, then you will need to make the HTTP selection from the drop-down list box. Use the drop-down list to choose Hotmail or MSN, depending on which type of account you have, and click Next to continue.

Lingo   *HTTP* stands for *Hypertext Transfer Protocol*, the technical term for the language that Web browsers use to communicate with Web servers on the Internet. Because Hotmail and MSN accounts are designed for Web access, they use HTTP instead of SMTP and POP3.

As you can see from Figure 7-1, the server information is automatically filled in for you and cannot be changed.

Supply your password and click Next to complete the wizard. Your Hotmail or MSN account is now ready for use.

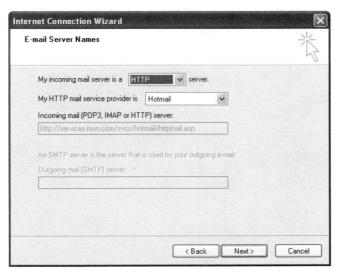

Figure 7-1 When you choose a Hotmail account, Outlook Express fills in server details automatically.

Tip   If you have more than one Hotmail or MSN account, you can rename its entry in the Folder List to make it easier to see which is which. Right-click the account name and choose Rename from the shortcut menu.

Make AOL and Outlook Express Work Together

If you have an AOL e-mail account, AOL expects you to use your AOL software to read your e-mail. You cannot configure Outlook Express to send and receive messages from an AOL account using the standard account setup options. However, you can use a third-party program called eNetBot Mail to bridge the gap between your AOL account and Outlook Express. It's available from *http://www.enetbot.com* in a free trial version. After 30 days, you must pay $20 to continue using it.

Fine-Tuning Your E-Mail Account Options

After you've used the wizard to create an e-mail account, you can change it at any time. You need to do so if your ISP changes your password or moves to different servers. However, you might also want to use these options to perform some tasks that aren't available through the wizard. To edit an existing e-mail account, go to the main Outlook Express window and choose Accounts from the Tools menu. Click the Mail tab to see all accounts you've established, including Internet accounts and Web-based Hotmail or MSN accounts.

To make changes, select an account from the list and click Properties. A partial list of the things you can do with an Internet e-mail account follows:

- **Change the account name**   Click the General tab and enter a descriptive name at the top of the dialog box. The default name is the name of your POP3 mail server, as shown below, but you can change this to something easier to understand, such as "Ed's Earthlink account."

- **Change your reply address**   You might want people who reply to your messages to send those replies to a different address than the one you sent it from. For instance, you might use your Hotmail account to send messages when you're away from home temporarily, but you still want people to send replies to your home e-mail address. On the General tab, fill in the Reply Address text box with the address you prefer.

- **Change server names**   If your ISP changes e-mail servers, enter the new addresses on the Servers tab.

- **Change your account name or password**   Fill in the blanks on the Servers tab, under the Incoming Mail Server heading.

- **Leave messages on the server**   This option is essential if you check the same e-mail account from two different computers. Normally, Outlook Express removes messages from the mail server when you retrieve them. (This is an essential practice, to avoid running afoul of your ISP's limits on e-mail storage.) But if you get mail from the same account using two computers and you leave this setting in place, you'll wind up with some of your messages on one computer and some on the other. The solution is to decide which computer is your main computer where you want all messages to be stored.

Then, on the other computer, click the Advanced tab and select the Leave A Copy Of Messages On Server box, as shown below. With this setting enabled, you can download all messages from your main computer, even if you already read some of them from your other computer.

Caution   The Security and Advanced tabs contain a number of options that you absolutely, positively should not mess with unless you fully understand the consequences. In particular, don't change port numbers or use the This Server Requires A Secure Connection (SSL) options. Doing so makes it impossible for you to retrieve mail from a normal server.

Checking Your E-Mail

By default, Outlook Express checks for new messages every 30 minutes. It does this automatically, as long as Outlook Express is running and you're connected to the Internet. If you have a cable modem, DSL, or another "always on" Internet connection, this is a convenient feature. When you sit down in front of your computer, your mail is already there waiting for you.

However, that 30-minute interval might not be right for you. If you use Outlook Express for business and you're at your computer all day long, maybe you want to check your e-mail every 5 or 10 minutes. On the other hand, if you have a dial-up connection, you might decide that you never want Outlook Express to check for messages on its own so that you can send and receive messages manually exactly when you want. To set these options, go to the main Outlook Express window and choose Options from the Tools menu. On the General tab of the Options dialog box shown below, look at the group of settings under Send/Receive Messages.

To disable automatic checks completely, clear the Check For New Messages Every box. To change the interval for automatic checkups, leave that box selected and either enter a new number (in minutes) or use the up and down arrows to adjust the number of minutes. You can select any number between 1 (check my e-mail every minute) and 480 (check every eight hours).

If you have a dial-up Internet account, you probably want some say over whether Outlook Express automatically takes over your phone line when it's time to check for new messages. You can exert this control by choosing one of the three settings beneath If My Computer Is Not Connected At This Time. The default setting, Do Not Connect, prevents Outlook Express from connecting to the Internet on its own. Choose one of the other options if you want it to dial up even when you're not around.

To manually check for messages, click Send/Recv on the Outlook Express toolbar, or press Ctrl+M. If you have several accounts and you want to check a single account, pull down the Tools menu, choose Send And Receive, and select the name of the account you want to check from the bottom of the menu.

With Internet e-mail accounts, clicking Send/Recv sends any messages in your Outbox to the SMTP server and then retrieves any waiting messages from the POP3 server, deleting those incoming messages from the server after they've arrived safely on your computer. In other words, the e-mail server acts like a post office box, where you pick up and drop off your electronic mail; the server only stores your incoming messages temporarily until you pick them up.

With Hotmail or MSN accounts, however, things work differently. Your messages arrive at Microsoft's servers and stay there, even after you connect to the server and retrieve your e-mail. Instead of *transferring* messages to your computer, clicking Send/Recv *synchronizes* the collection of messages in Outlook Express so that they match the ones on the server. When you synchronize, Outlook Express copies new messages from the server to your computer. If you delete messages from a Hotmail or MSN folder in Outlook Express, they are deleted from the server the next time you synchronize that folder, and vice versa. The advantage, of course, is that you can read your saved e-mail from any computer, just by opening Internet Explorer and logging on to your Hotmail or MSN account. When you're offline, you can still work with your Hotmail or MSN account using the synchronized messages in Outlook Express.

> **Tip**   Hotmail and MSN impose severe storage restrictions on free accounts. Your total account is limited to 2 megabytes (MB) of storage in all folders, and messages are deleted automatically if you exceed this amount. You can overcome these restrictions and gain additional storage by paying Microsoft for an upgraded account. You can also get in the habit of cleaning out your Hotmail and MSN folders regularly. Every week or so, open Outlook Express and look through the contents of your Hotmail or MSN folders; delete the messages you no longer need and then select the messages you want to keep, dragging them into a folder in the Local Folders section of Outlook Express. This removes the messages from the Microsoft server and copies them to your computer, where your only limitation is the amount of free disk space available!

When you're online, you can synchronize with a folder by displaying that folder in the Outlook Express window. You can also synchronize automatically, at the intervals defined in the Options dialog box, or manually, by clicking Send/ Recv. You can control automatic synchronization on a folder-by-folder basis for each Hotmail or MSN account in Outlook Express. To access the synchronization settings, click the MSN or Hotmail icon in the Folder List, as in Figure 7-2.

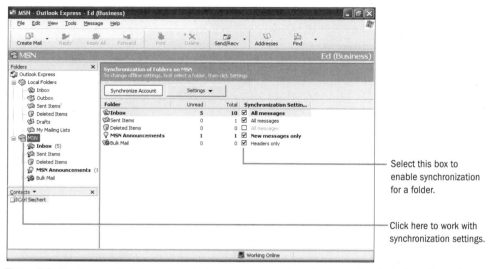

Figure 7-2 Use these settings to control which messages are automatically synchronized with a Hotmail or MSN account.

For each folder, select or clear the check box to enable or disable synchro-nization. You can also specify for each folder whether you want all messages, only headers, or only new messages to be downloaded automatically to your computer. To do so, first select a folder, and then click Settings. For instance, on a slow dial-up Internet account you might decide you want all messages in your Inbox to be automatically synchronized, but you only want to see headers (the name of the sender and the subject) rather than the full body of each message for the Bulk Mail folder, which is designed to intercept suspected junk mail.

Composing a New Message

Composing a new message in Outlook Express is simple, especially if you just want to send a few sentences to a friend or family member. If you're willing to spend a little more time, you can add pictures and other formatting so that your message looks like a Web page. To get started, click Create Mail on the Outlook Express toolbar, or press Ctrl+N, or choose File, New, Mail Message. This opens a blank e-mail window, ready for you to begin adding details to the message.

Tip If you're replying to a message, you can start a new message with addresses and subject already entered. Select the message from the message list or from an open message window. Click Reply (to send your new message to the sender only), Reply All (to send the message to everyone who received the original message), or Forward (to send a copy of the message to someone who didn't receive the original).

Figure 7-3 shows a message that's all ready to send.

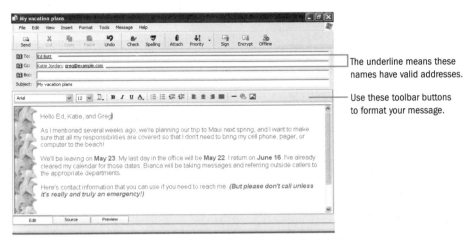

The underline means these names have valid addresses.

Use these toolbar buttons to format your message.

Figure 7-3 This e-mail message is ready to go—all you have to do is click Send.

Here's how to use each section of the message window:

■ **Address the message** In the To: field, enter the e-mail address of the person to whom you're sending the message. You must enter at least one address. You can also enter additional addresses on the To: line, separating them with semicolons. Or you can add addresses in the Cc: (courtesy copy) field instead. If any of the names are in your Address Book, you can click To: or Cc: to open an Address book window, in which you can select names and add them directly to the To:, Cc:, or Bcc: fields in your message.

> **Tip** The Bcc: (blind courtesy copy) field allows you to send a copy of a message to someone without revealing that person's e-mail address to any of the other recipients. This feature is especially useful if you want to send a message to a large list of people but you want them to reply only to you. In that case, address the message to yourself and put all the recipients' addresses on the Bcc: line. By default, the Bcc: field is hidden. To make it available, choose All Headers from the View menu.

If you're replying to a message using Reply or Reply To All, the recipient fields are automatically filled in with those from the original message. You can add an address by entering it directly or from the Address Book, and you can remove addresses by selecting the name or e-mail address entry and pressing Delete. For instructions on how to add to and edit the contents of your address book, see the section "Managing Your Address Book," on page 165.

■ **Enter your subject** Having a clear and direct subject line makes it more likely that your recipients will read your message.

■ **Choose your message format**   Outlook Express gives you the choice of composing your message in plain text or *rich text* (*HTML*). Using plain text means that recipients see the words you wrote, without any special fonts, colors, or formatting such as italics and boldface. With a Hypertext Markup Language (HTML) message (the default setting), you can customize the appearance of text, add background colors, and even insert pictures.

> **Tip**   If your recipients use Outlook Express or Microsoft Outlook, they will have no trouble reading your rich text messages. However, if they use other e-mail programs that don't support HTML, it's likely they will see the *HTML code* of your message instead of the message itself, making it nearly impossible to decipher what you meant to say. If you are sending a message to a mailing list, be sure to ask which formats are acceptable; most list managers prefer plain text messages.

■ **Enter your text**   Use the buttons on the formatting toolbar to change fonts, indent blocks of text, and even add lines and pictures. If you use the plain text feature of Outlook Express, these toolbar buttons will appear dimmed.

> **Tip**   In the message shown in Figure 7-3, I used Outlook Express *stationery* to automatically add background graphics, select a default font, and create custom margins. You can do the same by starting from the Message menu, choosing New Message Using, and then selecting one of the sample stationeries included with Outlook Express. You can download additional stationery from thousands of sites on the Internet. Do a Web search using *Outlook Express stationery* as the search term.

■ **Check your spelling**   This option is available only if you have installed another Microsoft program that includes spelling-checker capabilities, such as Microsoft Works or Microsoft Office. Click Spelling or press F7 to see and, if necessary, fix each possible spelling error in your message, as shown below.

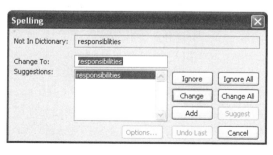

- **Attach files, if you want**   See the section "What to Do With File Attachments," on page 168, for more details.

- **Send it**   Click Send to move the message to your Outbox, where Outlook Express sends it the next time you connect to your SMTP server.

Note   When you create an e-mail message, the exact order of steps is not important. You can compose the message first and add addresses later, if you prefer. The order in which I listed the steps above is from top to bottom in the message window.

Tip   If you find yourself constantly typing your name, e-mail address, and other details at the end of every message, consider adding a signature to Outlook Express. A *signature* is a block of text that automatically appears at the end of every new message you create. To begin creating a signature, choose Options from the Tools menu in Outlook Express and then click the Signatures tab.

Managing Your Address Book

How do you keep track of all your friends, family members, business associates, online merchants, and everyone else you exchange e-mail with? Windows includes a handy program called Address Book that's specifically designed to help you match names and e-mail addresses. To open Address Book, click Addresses on the Outlook Express toolbar. As you can see from Figure 7-4, the Address Book keeps each entry in a list, which you can display using the same choices as in Windows Explorer.

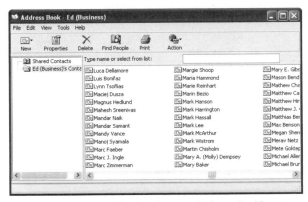

Figure 7-4 Use Address Book to keep track of e-mail addresses and other details for people and companies.

You can add new records to the Address Book at any time; you can also edit existing ones by double-clicking any entry in the Address Book. The most important details (at least as far as Outlook Express is concerned) are kept on the Name tab, where you enter the Display field (the name that's actually shown in the To: or Cc: box when you address a message) and add entries to the E-mail Addresses list, as shown below.

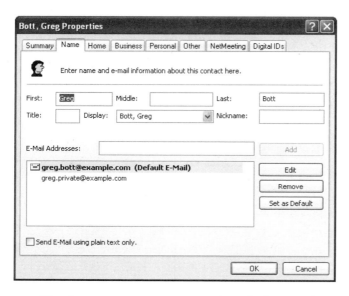

The faster, smarter way to work with the Windows Address Book, though, is to let Outlook Express do the work for you. Whenever you reply to a message that someone else sends you, Outlook Express automatically adds the recipient's address to your Address Book. In addition, you can add any address on an incoming message to your Address Book by right-clicking the name and choosing Add To Address Book from the shortcut menu. (This trick works on addresses in the From:, To:, and Cc: fields.)

Note   Although you can add multiple e-mail addresses to each record in your Address Book, only the default address is used when you address a new e-mail message. To use one of the alternate addresses, you have to create a new Address Book record with that address as the default or enter the address manually.

Try This! In addition to adding individual names to your Address Book, you can also create distribution lists, which consist of multiple e-mail addresses. If you're the secretary for a community group or you're working with a team at the office, you can use distribution lists to quickly and reliably send a message to a group of people without fear that you'll mistype an address or leave someone's name off the list. Here's how to create a new distribution list:

1 From the main Outlook Express window, click Addresses.

2 From the File menu, choose New Group.

3 On the Group tab of the Properties dialog box, enter the name you want to use for your group in the Group Name text box. Although you can use up to 199 characters, you should keep this name short enough to remember it.

4 Click Select Members and begin picking names from the list at the left side of your Address Book, as shown. You can pick one name at a time, clicking Select to add it to the Members list on the right; or hold down Ctrl and select multiple names, clicking Select after you've finished your selections. Click OK when the list is complete.

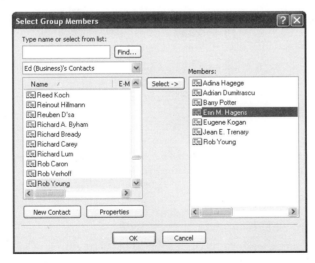

5 In the Group Properties dialog box , check the Group Name and the Group Members list. If you need to add any names that were not in your Address Book, do so using the Name and E-Mail text boxes at the bottom of the dialog box.

6 Click OK to save your new distribution list.

Distribution lists appear in the Address Book window as boldface entries, and all such groups appear under your name in the tree pane at the left of the Address Book window. When composing a message, you can add the distribution list just as if it were a single e-mail address. When you click Send, Outlook Express converts the group name to individual e-mail addresses so that all copies of your message are delivered properly.

What to Do with File Attachments

E-mail messages can consist of much more than words. You can *attach* one or more files to a message, and the recipient can save, view, or edit those files directly. File attachments represent a great way to exchange pictures, collaborate on work projects, and share information. Your biggest challenge in working with attachments is to avoid inadvertently transmitting viruses. (See the section "Protect Yourself from Viruses," on page 182, for more information.) It's also important to avoid overwhelming your ISP and message recipients by sending files that are too big.

Caution   Some ISPs have restrictions on the size and type of attachments on e-mail messages. If you regularly exchange file attachments with a friend or family member, both of you should check with your ISPs and find out if any restrictions might affect you.

Sending a File by E-Mail

Create a new message as usual. Then use either of the following techniques: Click Attach or choose File Attachment from the Insert menu. Either way, you open a dialog box that allows you to browse for the file (or files) you want to attach to your message. After making your selection, click Attach.

You can also drag files from the desktop or from a Windows Explorer window and drop them in a message you've created. You can drop the files anywhere in the message window and Outlook Express attaches them to the message properly.

See Also   *When sending pictures as attachments, Windows gives you some special tools for shrinking files to save space. See the section "E-Mailing Photos to Friends and Family," on page 274, for details.*

Opening and Saving File Attachments

When you receive one or more attachments to a message, what do you do? You have two choices:

- Open the attachment directly by double-clicking the file name in the message window or in the preview pane. Go ahead and try this tactic if your sister sends you a digital snapshot of her adorable new baby and you just can't wait to see the picture.

■ Save the attached files so you can work with them later. You can save attachments from a message window or from the preview pane.

Caution   Make sure you have antivirus software installed and keep it up to date! Let me emphasize how important both of these steps are. If you forget to update your antivirus program for a few weeks, you're a sitting duck when a new virus starts to make the rounds. If you have no antivirus software at all, your unprotected computer is almost certain to catch a virus, despite all your other precautions.

To work with attachments in a message window, double-click the message and look at the Attach: field, just above the message body. You can double-click a file to open it, or right-click a file and choose Save As to save just a single file, or choose Save All to select all attachments and save them to a single location, as shown below.

To work with attachments in the preview pane, click the paper clip icon just above and to the right of the message. The drop-down list shows all attachments in the message. Click any item in the list to open that file, or choose Save Attachments to display a list of files from which you can choose some or all to save, as shown on the next page.

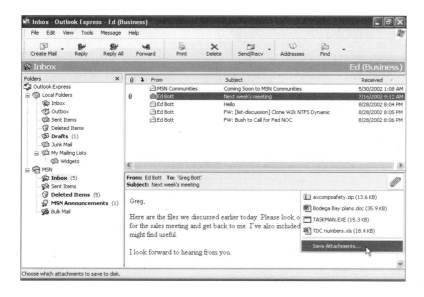

Organizing Your E-Mail

How many e-mail messages do you receive every day? Even if your daily delivery is a measly 10 new messages each day, that can add up over time. And if you work for a company that uses e-mail extensively, you might receive 100 or more messages every single day. If you leave all those messages in your Inbox, eventually it becomes stuffed with hundreds or even thousands of individual items, making it nearly impossible for you to find what you're looking for when you need it. The solution? Sort your messages into folders, either manually or automatically, using *message rules*.

Filing Messages in Folders

When you first begin using Outlook Express, you have five folders to work with. In the Folder List, these appear under the Local Folders icon. As you might guess from the name, these folders are stored locally on your computer. You can't rename, move, or delete these folders. When you retrieve e-mail messages from a POP3 server using your Internet e-mail account, the downloaded messages are stored here. You can also move messages from your Web-based e-mail accounts, such as those on MSN and Hotmail, so that they're always available on your computer and aren't automatically deleted from the server when you reach your storage limits.

The default Local Folders collection consists of the five folders shown in Table 7-1.

Table 7-1 Default Local Folders

Folder Name	What It's Used For
Inbox	All incoming messages from Internet e-mail accounts land in this folder.
Outbox	When you compose a message and click Send, it goes here, where it's ready to be sent the next time you connect to your outgoing e-mail server
Sent Items	Whenever you send a message using your Internet e-mail account, Outlook Express stores a copy here. You can disable this behavior by choosing Options from the Tools menu, going to the Send tab, and clearing the Save Copy Of Sent Messages In The 'Sent Items' Folder check box.
Deleted Items	This folder is the e-mail equivalent of the Recycle Bin. When you delete messages from another local folder, the deleted message moves to this folder.
Drafts	This folder stores copies of messages you're currently working on before you click Send.

Tip   While you're working on a new message, you might decide to save it instead of sending it right away. (This "cooling off" period is especially useful when you're writing about emotional topics.) To save a message so you can think it over, choose Save from the Outlook Express File menu. The message goes into your Drafts folder. You can close the message window and return to the message whenever you're ready by viewing the contents of the Drafts folder. When it's finally ready, click Send to move it to your Outbox and send it on its way.

Over time, the number of messages in your Inbox can grow to enormous proportions, making it difficult to find important messages you've received. The solution is to add folders to help you organize particular types of mail.

Organizing your e-mail messages into folders is a matter of personal style. If you like to keep all your old messages as a personal archive, you can make good use of separate folders to store incoming mailing lists, messages from family members, messages about specific projects, receipts, and shipping information from online merchants—the possibilities are endless. If you're not a packrat, you might choose to discard most messages after you've read them and create a single new folder, Saved Messages, to store the small number of messages you decide to hang onto. The choice is completely yours.

To create a new folder, click File to display the File menu, click Folder, and then click New. You can also right-click any existing folder and choose New Folder from the shortcut menu. In the Create Folder dialog box, enter a name for the new folder you want to create and then select the existing folder where you want the new folder to appear, as shown in Figure 7-5.

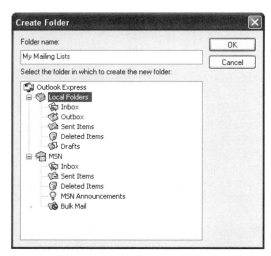

Figure 7-5 The new folder will appear at the same level as the existing five folders after clicking OK.

Note   If you right-click an existing folder before selecting New Folder, your new folder is created on the level below that folder unless you choose a different folder before clicking OK.

After creating a folder, you can move or copy messages into it by dragging messages out of their old folder and into the new one. Using the right-click shortcut menus, you can rename a folder or delete it. You can move it to a different place by dragging it within the Local Folders tree. You can also create subfolders within any existing folder, including those you created. If you subscribe to lots of mailing lists, for instance, you might want to create a My Mailing Lists folder, as shown in Figure 7-5, and then create one new subfolder for each of the lists to which you subscribe.

Sort Messages Automatically with Message Rules

Mailing lists are a blessing and a curse. If you collect widgets, you can probably find a group of like-minded widget collectors who've already started their own widget collectors society, complete with a mailing list that members use to share their experiences with one another. If the group is big enough and active enough, the resulting e-mail can flood your inbox with dozens of messages a day. What to do? You can use message rules to sort those incoming messages into the correct folder automatically. With just a handful of message rules, in fact, you can reclaim control of your Inbox and let Outlook Express sort most of your messages for you.

All message rules work by examining messages as they arrive in your Inbox. A message rule has two parts:

■ The *conditions* define what Outlook Express looks for in the message. You can create message rules that work by finding specific e-mail addresses in the To: or From: lines, words that appear in the subject line, or text in the message body itself, for instance.

■ The *actions* define what Outlook Express does when it encounters a message that matches your conditions. You can move the message to another folder, highlight it using a color, or delete it, for example.

To create a rule, you use a simple wizard. Figure 7-6 shows a completed rule that moves messages sent from a specific mailing list into a folder.

Figure 7-6 As you select conditions in step 1 and actions in step 2, the details of your message rule appear in the third box.

Here's how to create this and similar rules:

1 From the Tools menu, choose Message Rules and then click Mail. If you're about to create your first message rule, the New Mail Rule dialog box appears. If you already have one or more existing rules, click New in the Mail Rules dialog box to open the New Mail Rule Wizard.

2 Under Select The Conditions For Your Rule, select check boxes that match the conditions you want Outlook Express to look for. In the case shown in Figure 7-6, Where the Subject Line Contains Specific Words was chosen.

3   Under Select The Actions For Your Rule, click the option that matches
what you want Outlook Express to do. Move It To The Specified
Folder was chosen in Figure 7-6. You can also select the Stop Processing More Rules action, if you don't want any of your other rules to do
anything to this message.

4   In the Rule Description list box, click any of the underlined values to
enter specific text, a folder name, or other required details, as shown
below.

Apply this rule after the message arrives
Where the Subject line <u>contains specific words</u>
Move it to the <u>specified</u> folder
    and Stop processing more rules

In this example, clicking the underlined value Contains Specific
Words displays the Type Specific Words dialog box, shown below,
where you can enter one or more words or phrases. You can enter a
phrase that always appears in the subject line for a mailing list. You can
also make this rule work by specifying text that appears in the message
body or using the name of the mailing list sender. Be sure to fill in all
the blanks.

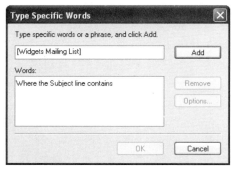

5   Enter a descriptive name for the rule in the Name Of The Rule text box
and click OK to save your rule.

Caution   Message rules are powerful, but they can also be confusing. Like all computer software, Outlook Express is extremely literal when it comes to enforcing your
wishes. If you make a typing error in a rule, your message rule might not work the way
you expect it to. Also, if you have two or more rules in your list, Outlook Express
applies them in the order in which they appear. If your first rule moves a message out
of the Inbox, the second rule won't have a chance to inspect the message!

Tip In the Message Rules dialog box, you can use Move Up and Move Down to change the order of rules.

It's always a good idea to test messages after creating them. Make sure you have a message in your Inbox that matches the conditions of the rule you just created. Open the Message Rules dialog box and select the box to the left of the message you want to test and then click Apply Now. If it doesn't work as you expected, select the rule from the Message Rules list, click Modify, and take another look at your conditions and actions to see what's not working.

See Also *Message rules are a great way to block spam, too. Read more about this subject in the section "Block Spam and Junk E-Mail," on page 187.*

Changing the Outlook Express Layout

To make it easier to work with folders, you can rearrange the parts of the Outlook Express window. These options are available by clicking the Layout option from the View menu. Figure 7-7 shows the dialog box that allows you to specify which elements are visible and which are hidden. Try selecting and deselecting the different layout check boxes, and then click Apply. You can see the changes without having to close the dialog box.

Figure 7-7 Use these options to customize the layout of your Outlook Express window.

Here's a brief description of what each option does:

- **Contacts**   Shows or hides the list of names at the lower left corner of the Outlook Express window. This is a handy way to access your Address Book without having to open a separate window.

- **Outlook Bar**   Uses large or small icons to represent folders. This option vaguely resembles Microsoft Outlook but requires extra effort to customize. If you use it, you probably want to hide the Folder List.

- **Views Bar**   If you have created any custom views (using the View menu), you can add a list of available views to the top of the Outlook Express window.

- **Folder Bar**   This is the thin gray bar that appears below the toolbar. Hide it if you want some extra space.

- **Folder List**   This list is essential if you have multiple accounts or you use folders to organize your e-mail.

- **Status Bar**   This is the small text bar at the bottom of the Outlook Express window that displays information messages. Hide it if you want a little bit of extra room for messages.

- **Toolbar**   Show or hide the toolbar that appears at the top of the Outlook Express window by selecting or clearing this button.

- **Preview Pane**   Show or hide the preview pane, which lets you view the contents of messages without opening them first.

Tip   Some people prefer not to use the preview pane at all, because of the risk that they'll download an offensive image or message sent as spam. With the preview pane hidden, you can delete suspicious messages without reading them.

You can also add or remove buttons on the toolbar that appears at the top of the Outlook Express window. To do so, click Customize Toolbar. You also have the option to make the toolbar buttons smaller so that they take up less space in the Outlook Express window. You can also access the customize options by right-clicking the toolbar.

Using Windows Messenger

Sometimes e-mail just isn't immediate enough. In that case, you might want to send an instant message with Windows Messenger. If the person at the other end of the line is available, you can carry on a direct conversation by typing your messages in the Windows Messenger window, as shown in Figure 7-8.

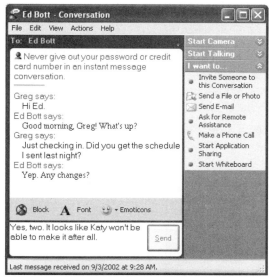

Figure 7-8 Use Windows Messenger when you want to carry on a conversation without waiting for messages to pass through mail servers.

Before you can sign on to Windows Messenger, you have to sign up for a Microsoft .NET Passport. When you first sign on to Windows Messenger, a wizard walks you through this process. All you need is an e-mail address and a password, which you create yourself.

After signing on to Windows Messenger, you see a dialog box that shows all currently available contacts. If the people you want to contact aren't listed, click Add A Contact to add their names and e-mail addresses. (It's a good idea to check with them first to make sure they've signed up for Windows Messenger or MSN Messenger, the compatible service used by people running versions of Windows other than Windows XP.)

Note Do some of your friends use AOL Messenger instead of Windows Messenger? Sorry, the two programs and services can't communicate with one another. You'll have to install the AOL product, or your friend will have to use Windows/MSN Messenger, before you can carry on a conversation.

Key Points

■ To set up an Internet e-mail account, you need some details, including your logon name, password, and the names of your ISP's SMTP and POP3 servers.

■ You can check mail using a free Hotmail or MSN account using Outlook Express.

■ With Internet e-mail accounts, mail is downloaded to your computer. With Web-based accounts, Outlook Express synchronizes the contents of folders on your computer and on the Web-based mail servers.

■ If you have an AOL e-mail account, you need special software to send and receive e-mail with Outlook Express.

■ Normally, Outlook Express checks for new messages every half-hour, although you can change this interval to be more or less frequent.

■ You can send e-mail using plain text or create Web-style messages using rich text (HTML) format, with fancy fonts and even pictures.

■ When you receive a file attachment, always be alert that it doesn't contain a computer virus.

■ Outlook Express makes it easy to organize your messages using folders.

■ You can set up message rules that allow Outlook Express to automatically file messages for you as they come into your Inbox.

■ If e-mail isn't immediate enough, you can use Windows Messenger to instantly contact friends and family members who are online.

Chapter 8

Protecting Your Privacy and Your Computer's Security

When you walk through the streets of any big city—New York, London, Paris, Cairo—you can stare in wonder at the sights around you. However, you also need to watch for pickpockets, muggers, and speeding taxis. Wandering around the Internet requires the same sort of vigilance. The Web is filled with wonderful information and dazzling sites to see, but danger lurks around many corners. If you remain vigilant and practice common sense, you can protect yourself from viruses, hackers, and other risks. In this chapter, I'll show you how to protect yourself from the not-so-nice parts of the Internet. I'll also explain what cookies really do and show you how you can protect your privacy when using your Web browser.

What You (and Your Family) Need to Know

Your Internet connection isn't a one-way street. Every piece of e-mail and every Web page represents a potential avenue that an unscrupulous person can use to attack your computer. I'm not trying to alarm you unduly, but having a healthy respect for the darker corners of the Internet is a smart way to approach your computer. When you know the risks, you can take sensible precautions.

What should you watch out for? My short list of threats includes the following:

- **Hackers and other intruders**   Right at this moment, thousands of unsavory characters around the world are probing and poking at computers on the Internet, looking for computers whose owners have been careless about security. When they find one, they can sneak in, rummage through private files, and even plant a program that they can use to attack other computers. Windows XP includes a *personal firewall* program that you can use to keep cybervandals from breaking and entering into your computer.

> **Lingo**   A *firewall* is any sort of hardware or software designed to protect a computer or network from unauthorized and unsafe connections. Corporate networks often include specialized computers that do nothing but block would-be attackers. Windows XP includes a *personal firewall* called Internet Connection Firewall (ICF), which I discuss later in this chapter.

- **Viruses and other hostile programs**   Several times a year, a new virus sweeps around the world and makes headlines on the nightly news. Even after the hysteria passes, however, viruses remain in circulation. New and old viruses can strike your computer at any time, unless you protect yourself, as I explain in the next section.

- **Threats to your personal privacy**   When you browse the Web, you give away little pieces of information about yourself. In addition, some details about you can persist on your computer in the form of small text files called *cookies*. You've probably read alarming articles about cookies. Later in this chapter, I explain what cookies can and can't do, and I show you how to configure your Microsoft Internet Explorer settings so that you take complete control of private information.

- **Risks to your bank account**   The Web represents the biggest shopping mall in the world. Before you type in your credit card number and click Buy, however, make sure you're doing so over a secure Web connection, where all the details that pass between your computer and the

Web server are *encrypted* for your protection. How can you spot a secure connection? Look in the Address bar and make sure the Web site address begins with *https://*—the *s* stands for *secure*. Also look in the lower right corner of the Internet Explorer window for a small padlock icon like the one shown here.

If you're not sure about the secure connection, double-click the padlock icon. This opens the dialog box shown in Figure 8-1, which shows details about the Web site and the certificate used to encrypt the data. If there's a problem with the certificate, Windows warns you with an error message.

Caution   If you don't see the padlock icon, don't enter *any* sensitive information, such as a Social Security number or credit card details. And be aware that the secure connection only protects your information while it's in transit. If you allow the company at the other end of the connection to receive your data, you also need to trust that they'll safeguard it properly. If you're not comfortable giving your information to a company, don't click the Send button.

Figure 8-1 The details of a digital certificate can help you decide whether to send confidential data over a secure connection.

Lingo   *Encryption* uses digital technology to protect the details of data as it travels between two computers. It relies on *digital certificates*, which are maintained by companies like VeriSign, to guarantee that the merchants you're dealing with are who they say they are. Only the party at the other end of the secure connection can *decrypt* the data. Anyone who intercepts encrypted data as it travels over the Internet sees nothing but gobbledygook.

Protect Yourself from Viruses

Some of the most widely distributed programs in the world can't be found in any computer store. Unfortunately, *viruses, worms, Trojan horses*, and other hostile programs are ever-present on the Internet, and each year these nasty programs seem to get a little more dangerous and a lot craftier at attacking your computer.

Lingo   *Viruses* are programs that take over (or *infect*) other programs. *Worms* are viruses that spread from computer to computer, using e-mail messages or network connections. *Trojan horses* are programs that appear to be innocent but actually do something else, such as allow another person to take over your computer from across the Internet and use it to attack other computers, without your knowledge. Many widely distributed viruses in recent years have had all three of these characteristics.

If you let your guard down and your computer is infected by a virus, the effects can be disastrous. Viruses can delete data files and cause other programs to stop working properly. Cleaning up the infection is time-consuming, and recovering the data files can be difficult or even impossible. Worst of all, as long as you're infected, the virus tries to spread itself to your friends, family members, and business associates, and if those innocent bystanders haven't taken the proper precautions, they can become infected, too.

Don't assume that you're safe just because you never open a file attachment. Viruses can execute themselves automatically, using unpatched security holes in Internet Explorer or Microsoft Outlook Express, when you do nothing more than view them in the preview pane. This is why it's so important to use Windows Update to install the latest security patches.

See Also   For step-by-step instructions on how to set up *Automatic Updates* and check *Windows Update* manually, see the section *"Get the Latest Windows Updates,"* on page 18.

Antivirus Essentials

Obviously, your first priority should be to block viruses from ever reaching your computer. In addition, you should teach everyone who uses your computer (including yourself!) how to avoid becoming a virus victim. Protecting yourself and your computer involves a three-part strategy.

■   **Install antivirus software and keep it up to date.**   Although Windows XP can prevent some types of hostile acts by viruses, it does not include any built-in protection against dangerous programs. You must add this protection yourself. Simply installing antivirus software isn't enough! You also need to make sure that the software updates itself with details of the latest viruses, so that you can be certain you're protected from new viruses as soon as they appear. Most virus programs can automatically update themselves over the Internet. Be sure to set this feature up as soon as you install the program.

Note   You can choose from dozens of antivirus programs for Windows. Whichever one you choose, look for two things: a certification logo from ICSA Labs, which indicates that it has passed some stringent tests and actually works; and a guarantee that the version you're buying is compatible with Windows XP.

■   **Block suspicious e-mail attachments.**   Many, if not most, viruses today spread from one computer to another by attaching themselves to an e-mail message. The best place to stop this type of virus is at the e-mail server. Check with your Internet service provider and see if they offer this service. Even better, set up an account with Hotmail or MSN; all messages that pass through these e-mail servers are automatically checked for viruses using McAfee.com antivirus software.

You can also configure Outlook Express to block all e-mail attachments that could be dangerous. To do so, open Outlook Express and click Options from the Tools menu. On the Security tab of the Options dialog box, shown below, select Do Not Allow Attachments To Be Saved Or Opened That Could Potentially Be A Virus. Click OK to save your changes (and make sure you repeat this procedure for every user account on your computer).

Tip   When the option to block unsafe attachments is enabled, you might find your-self unable to open some legitimate attachments. What do you do in that case? If you're 100% certain the attachment is safe, click Options on the Tools menu in Out-look Express and clear the Do Not Allow Attachments To Be Saved Or Opened That Could Potentially Be A Virus option. Close the dialog box, open or save the file attach-ment, and then immediately re-enable the protection.

■   **Practice safe computing.**   Viruses can attack from a variety of sources. In addition to attaching themselves to e-mail messages, hostile programs can arrive in the body of an e-mail message, as a link on a Web page, or in a file downloaded from a Web server. A download that looks like an innocent game or screen saver, for instance, can actually be a virus or Trojan horse in disguise. Train yourself and everyone who uses your computer (especially children) to be extremely careful when using the Internet. Never download files from unknown Web sites or click links in e-mail messages that come from suspicious sources.

Whenever you download a program from the Internet or save a file that's attached to an e-mail message, Windows warns you that you're about to do something that could be dangerous. The dialog box shown in Figure 8-2 gives you a chance to stop and think before deciding to save the file. If you have any doubts at all, stop and do some research to see if the file could be dangerous. And never, ever download any files unless your antivirus software is up-to-date!

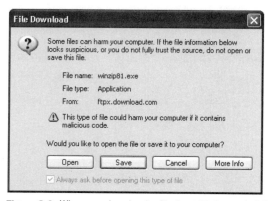

Figure 8-2 When you download a file from the Internet, Windows warns you that it could be dangerous.

Spotting Virus Hoaxes Every week, I receive at least one and sometimes several messages in my e-mail Inbox warning me of the outbreak of a deadly new computer virus. These messages all have a few things in common. Each one claims that the original warning came from an unnamed expert or from a big company like Microsoft or IBM. The description of what the virus can do is always dire—it will scramble your hard disk beyond repair and delete data files with reckless abandon. Every one of these warnings ends with an urgent plea to forward the message to everyone in your address book.

Oh, and one more thing—every single one is a hoax.

Virus hoaxes have been around as long as computer viruses. They're generally spread by naïve but well-meaning computer users who truly believe that they're doing a favor by spreading the word. Most of the time, the hoax messages cause no harm, but a handful of recent virus hoaxes convinced unwitting Windows users to delete perfectly normal operating system files that were mistakenly reported to be dangerous viruses.

What should you do if a friend sends you an e-mail message warning you of a new computer virus? For starters, be skeptical, especially if the message is sensationalistic and doesn't include links to information from any reputable authorities. When in doubt, check it out. A handful of Web sites serve as clearinghouses for information on genuine viruses and virus hoaxes. If you receive a warning and you're not sure it's real, search the Web for more details. Three sites that I recommend enthusiastically are Symantec's authoritative Online Virus and Hoax Encyclopedia (*http://www.symantec.com/avcenter/vinfodb.html*); Ron Rosenberger's amusing and educational Vmyths.com (*http://www.vmyths.com*); and Hoaxbusters (*http://hoaxbusters.ciac.org*), maintained by a division of the U.S. Department of Energy. A few minutes at any of these sites usually turns up a definitive answer about the e-mail you just received.

Also, if a friend or family member forwards you a virus hoax, don't pass it on! Instead, write back to the sender, explain what you've learned here, and steer them to one of these sites for the straight dope.

Avoiding Unsafe File Attachments

Unfortunately, not all file attachments consist of good news. Over the past few years, computer viruses have become an epidemic, and most of them spread by attaching themselves to e-mail messages. How can you tell a virus from a legitimate attachment? The short answer is, you can't—at least, you can't be sure whether an attachment is safe or dangerous just by looking at it. That's why it's so important to install a good antivirus program and keep it up-to-date. However, you can rely on some telltale signs to spot attachments that are suspicious.

- ■ **The message appears to come from someone you know but is unexpected.**   The authors of these nasty viruses know that you're likely to open an attachment if it appears to come from someone you know, so they make sure that the From: address on the message comes from a real address on the infected computer.

- ■ **The text of the message urges you to open the attachment.**   The message might claim that the attachment is a cool new game or a picture of a sexy celebrity. Some even pretend to be antivirus updates. Don't fall for these tricks!

- ■ **The file is a program or other executable file.**   When you get right down to it, a virus is just another program, although its effects are anything but ordinary. Some viruses claim to be innocent programs, such as games. If you receive any sort of *executable file* attached to an e-mail message, be suspicious. It might not be what it seems.

Lingo   *Executable files* are those that can perform activities like a program. In Windows, dozens of file types are potentially executable, not just the *.exe* extension at the end of a program's file name. Some common extensions used with executable files include *.bat, .pif, .vbs, .scr,* and *.com.* The best way to guard against sneaky executable files is to enable the attachment blocking features in Outlook Express.

- ■ **The file name has two extensions, not one.**   Some viruses work by pretending to be an innocent picture or text file, with a file name extension of .jpg or .txt. Then they tack on a second extension that is used to run the virus. Because Windows Explorer hides file extensions, this fools some older Windows versions. However, Outlook Express isn't duped by this trick. If you look at the attachment and see two periods and two three-letter extensions at the end of the name, as shown in the example on the next page, don't open it!

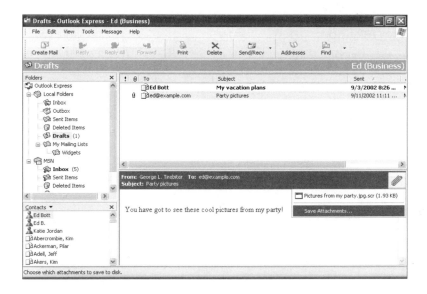

Block Spam and Junk E-Mail

Everyone who's had an e-mail address for any length of time knows that *spam*—unsolicited commercial e-mail—is a royal pain in the Inbox. When your e-mail address lands on a spam list, the flood of messages begins, and it only gets worse with time. Spammers offer bogus products, get-rich-quick-schemes, and shockingly explicit pornography, and they're as persistent and annoying as a room full of mosquitoes.

How can you block spam and junk e-mail? Unfortunately, there's no magic solution, but by taking the following simple steps, you can reduce the flood to a trickle:

1 **Guard your e-mail address as if it were gold.** Spammers use all sorts of tricks to capture legitimate e-mail addresses for their sleazy lists. Never give your "real" e-mail address to someone unless you know for certain that they're trustworthy. Set up a free Hotmail account and use that address when you visit a Web site that requires you to supply an address when registering. Later, if the site turns out to be legitimate, you can switch the e-mail address to your preferred account. Never, ever post your private e-mail address on a Web site or in an Internet discussion group, either.

2 **Take advantage of spam-filtering tools if your Internet service provider (ISP) offers them.** Some mail providers install software on their servers; when it works properly, it detects messages that appear to be junk mail and give you the option to delete the messages automatically or divert them to a different folder, so that you can pick out the legitimate messages that are mistakenly tagged as junk mail. Hotmail is particularly effective at this task; see the sidebar at the end of this section for step-by-step instructions on how to set up junk-mail filtering for your Hotmail or MSN account.

3 **Use message rules wisely.** Most people who try to use message rules in Outlook Express to block spam go about it all wrong. The criminals, irresponsible businesses, and social misfits who send out this junk are constantly refining their techniques for sneaking past your defenses. If you try to use rules to block them, you'll be frustrated. Instead, I recommend that you identify the mail you *want* to read, such as messages from friends, family, and mailing lists you belong to. Use rules to sort those messages into folders or leave them in the Inbox, and then set up one final rule that dumps all other messages into a Junk Mail folder. Figure 8-3 shows my message rules; note that the rules at the top take precedence over those at the bottom. All of the messages from people or groups I know are sorted first; anything that's left over is either junk mail or from someone I haven't added to my other rules yet.

Figure 8-3 Use message rules to identify messages you want to read.

Every day or two, I go through the Junk Mail folder. If a legitimate message ended up there, I go in and tweak my message rules so that future messages from that person go to the right folder.

See Also For step-by-step instructions on creating message rules in Outlook Express, see the section "Sort Messages Automatically with Message Rules," on page 170x.

---

4   **Never, ever respond to spam!**   One of the sneakiest tricks that spam artists use is to provide a link or an address that they promise will take you off their mailing list. When you use this option, however, you actually confirm to them that your e-mail address is good. That means you're likely to get more junk mail, not less! Only use these so-called opt-out links if you know the message is from a legitimate company that will respect your wishes.

Filtering Junk from a Hotmail Account
Sooner or later, every Hotmail user complains about the ever-increasing volume of junk mail flooding into their account. How can you stem the tide? Let Microsoft do the dirty work by setting up junk-mail filters in your Hotmail account.

Even if you read your Hotmail or MSN messages in Outlook Express, you must make these changes from the Web-based Hotmail/MSN interface. Here's how:

1   Using Internet Explorer, log on to your Hotmail account.

2   Click Options.

3   Under Mail Handling, click Junk Mail Filter.

4   From the list of four options, choose High or Exclusive. The High setting means that the Hotmail servers will try to identify junk mail based on its content and origination. The Exclusive setting is much more restrictive, blocking all messages unless they come from an address in your Address Book or on your Safe List. Click OK to continue.

5   Click Junk Mail Deletion and choose one of the two available options. Immediate Deletion zaps the messages before they ever reach your Inbox. (Use this option with care!) Delayed Deletion moves suspected junk messages to a Junk Mail folder so that you can sort through and find any worthwhile messages that were incorrectly tagged as spam. Click OK to continue.

6   Enter the addresses of any of your trusted contacts using the Safe List link.

After making these changes, your flood of spam should be slowed to no more than a trickle. You should go through the Junk Mail folder periodically. If you find a message that is from a friend or business associate, open the message and click This Is Not Junk Mail.

Keep Hackers Out with a Firewall

Every time you connect to the Internet, you open the door to a world of incredible information and entertainment. Unfortunately, that door swings both ways, and unless you take precautions, you run the risk that an unscrupulous person can break into your computer. Most people have misconceptions about the world of hackers, probably fueled by too many bad movies where teenage hackers with a limitless supply of pizza and Mountain Dew ruthlessly focus on a single computer, tapping keys and scowling until they finally break in.

In the real world, hacking is far more boring. Most attempts to break in to computers are performed by automated software programs run by technically unsophisticated teens looking for unprotected computers that they can break into. These programs, called *port scanners*, load up one Internet address after another, quickly, and try to break in using known security holes. Think of it as the equivalent of someone walking down your street, trying every doorknob in search of one that's unlocked.

You can prevent juvenile delinquents from breaking into your home by locking your doors. You can keep your computer from suffering a similar fate by setting up a *personal firewall*. In this section, I'll show you the ins and outs of the Internet Connection Firewall included with Windows XP.

Tip   Like many features bundled into Windows, the Internet Connection Firewall is a no-frills program. It does its job well, but it doesn't offer a lot of extra features. If you decide that you want bells and whistles with your firewall, you have several choices among third-party products. One widely respected firewall program is ZoneAlarm (*http://www.zonelabs.com*), which is available in a free version as well as a more powerful version available for purchase.

Using Internet Connection Firewall

When you turn on the Internet Connection Firewall, you essentially post a software agent at the gateway to your computer and tell it to act as a bouncer. When you send a request to a server on the Internet (by clicking a Web link or clicking Send/Recv in Outlook Express, for instance), the firewall program makes a note that you asked this server to send you some data. When that data arrives, the firewall checks its list, sees that the data is in response to your request, and lets it through. However, when a teenage hacker tries to probe your ports, the firewall sees that you never requested this connection, and it rejects the request. As you can imagine, this bouncer is extremely effective at turning away intruders.

You don't need any technical experience to begin using the Internet Connection Firewall. In fact, it sets itself up automatically when you use the Network

Setup Wizard. The firewall is on by default when you set up a dial-up Internet connection or a broadband connection for a single computer. If you use Internet Connection Sharing (ICS), the Network Setup Wizard enables the firewall on the shared connection to the Internet but leaves it off on the local connection on the ICS host and on all other local computers. (If the firewall were left on for the local connection, it would block all communications between local computers, defeating the purpose of a network!)

The firewall is turned off when you set up a hardware router or residential gateway and use it for shared Internet access. In this configuration, the hardware device performs the work that the Internet Connection Firewall normally does.

Caution   One specific network configuration causes problems with the Internet Connection Firewall. If you plug your cable modem or digital subscriber line (DSL) line directly into a network hub, right alongside all the computers on your local network, you're asking for trouble. Every computer is directly connected to the Internet and to every other computer, making it impossible to provide security. If you choose this option from the Network Setup Wizard, Windows warns you that the configuration is insecure, and it turns on the Internet Connection Firewall, making your Internet connections safe but effectively shutting down your network. For more information on setting up a network properly, see Chapter 14, "Setting Up and Running a Small Network."

You shouldn't need to do anything manually to enable Internet Connection Firewall. However, you might want to turn it off temporarily when it's blocking a task you're trying to accomplish over your network or the Internet. To view the current Internet Connection Firewall settings, follow these steps.

1   Click Start, choose Control Panel, and double-click the Network Connections icon. (You'll find it in the Network And Internet Connections category.)

2   In the Network Connections folder, look at the icon for your Internet connection. If Internet Connection Firewall is enabled, you'll see a padlock in the upper right corner of the icon, and the word *Firewalled* appears in the descriptive text to the right of the icon, as shown below. Right-click the connection icon and choose Properties.

3 To enable or disable the firewall, click the Advanced tab and select or clear the lone option under the Internet Connection Firewall section, as shown here.

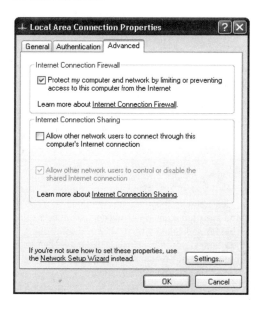

Note If your computer is acting as an Internet Connection Sharing Host, the option to enable the Internet Connection Firewall is unavailable for the local network connection. This makes perfect sense, because turning on the firewall here would shut down all communications with other local computers, including the shared Internet connection. To set up ICS, always use the Network Setup Wizard.

If you disable the Internet Connection Firewall manually, Windows warns you that you're about to lose its protection by displaying the message box below. If you know that the firewall is no longer needed (if you've installed a third-party firewall program like ZoneAlarm, for example), you can safely ignore this message.

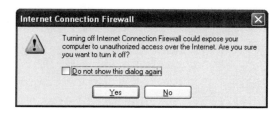

Other Firewall Options

Firewalls, like bouncers, can be ruthlessly effective. In fact, even when you want to allow specific types of connections, you might find them blocked by your firewall. The most common situations occur when you're running a server program and you want to allow other people to connect to it, or when you're running a file transfer or remote control program that uses direct connections. To make these programs work properly, you need to find the *ports* that are being used for the connection and open them.

Lingo   In this context, *ports* are numbered connection requests that a Transmission Control Protocol/Internet Protocol (TCP/IP) network uses to exchange a specific type of data. Some ports are standard. Web servers communicate on port 80 by default, for instance, and your e-mail program uses port 25 to talk to your POP server. Other port numbers are arbitrary and are set up on the fly as needed. Default port numbers that reside in the range between 0 and 1023 are managed by the Internet Assigned Numbers Authority (IANA) and are called *well-known ports*. To see a listing of well-known ports, visit *http://www.iana.org/assignments/port-numbers*.

Most programs that are part of Microsoft Windows, such as Windows Messenger and Remote Assistance, can communicate through the firewall just fine. If you find that communication is being blocked, you might need to tweak these settings manually. To see these settings, open Control Panel and double-click the Network Connections (in the Network And Internet Connections category, if you've set up Control Panel to view icons by category). Right-click your Internet connection and choose Properties. On the Advanced tab, click Settings. (This button is available only if the Internet Connection Firewall is enabled.) Figure 8-4 shows the Advanced Settings dialog box.

Some of the settings in this dialog box are already defined. If you want to run a small Web server, for instance, and allow people to access it over the Internet, just select the Web Server (HTTP) box. On the other hand, if you're using a third-party messaging program or a multiplayer game, you might need to do this manually. And you'll need to play Sherlock Holmes to get all the details you need.

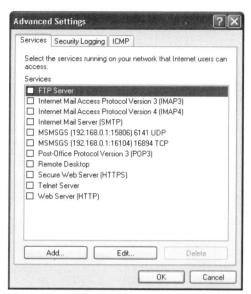

Figure 8-4 To allow programs to work through the firewall, configure settings here.

Your goal is to find out which TCP or UDP ports your program uses. You might need to search the Internet for these details, or pore through the software program's manuals, or call the company that makes the software and ask. The popular game Rainbow Six, for instance, uses TCP ports 2346, 2347, and 2348 to communicate, whereas AOL Instant Messenger from America Online uses TCP ports 443 and 563. You'll also need to know the name or IP address of your computer. Armed with this information, you can set up a custom service and tell the Internet Connection Firewall to allow packets through when they come in on those ports.

Lingo *TCP* stands for *Transmission Control Protocol*. *UDP* is short for *User Datagram Protocol*. Both are network standards used for whizzing packets of data from one computer to another over the Internet. *HTTP* stands for *Hypertext Transfer Protocol*, the protocol used to carry requests from Web servers back to the requesting browser.

Tip To find out the IP address of your computer's Internet connection, double-click its icon in the Network Connections folder and look on the Support tab. To learn your computer's name, double-click System in Control Panel (in the Performance And Maintenance category), click the Computer Name tab, and look at the Full Computer Name entry.

To configure a custom service on your network, perform the following steps:

1 In the Advanced Settings dialog box, click Add.

2 In the Description Of Service text box, enter a name for the service. (This text appears in the listing in the Advanced Settings dialog box.)

3 In the Name Or IP Address text box, enter your computer's name or IP address.

4 Enter the first port number in both the External and Internal text boxes and select TCP or UDP, whichever is appropriate, as shown here.

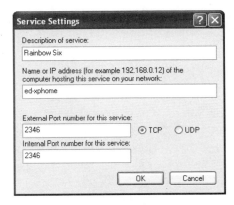

5 Click OK to save the custom service.

6 If the service uses more than one port, repeat steps 1-5, using a variation of the service name and the correct port number.

7 Select the check box to the left of each newly created service and click OK.

The Truth About Cookies

Depending on who's telling the story, *browser cookies* are either an incredible timesaving tool or the greatest threat to your privacy since X-Ray Specs. As with so many topics that concern Windows, of course, the truth is somewhere in between. Used properly, cookies are a useful way to save time and make everyday Web browsing easier. Used improperly, they pose a risk of revealing information about you and about your Web browsing habits—information that you might prefer to remain private.

Internet Explorer 6, which is included with Windows XP, offers the capability to block or allow cookies. You can use predefined groups of settings, or you can create your own custom settings. Before you even think about adjusting these privacy settings, however, let's figure out exactly what cookies are and how they work.

What Cookies Can and Can't Do

A *cookie* is a small text file that is stored on your computer and is recalled when you return to the Web site that is associated with that cookie. Why on earth would a Web site need a cookie?

Lingo   Where does the term *cookie* come from? Although it sounds like it came from a J.R.R. Tolkien novel, the history of the term is actually much more mundane. Computer scientists have used the word for years to describe pieces of data held by intermediaries. When the early designers of Web browsers needed to build this feature into their creations, this term was a natural.

Well, think about the Web sites you visit every day. Maybe you check the headlines and weather on MSN.com each morning, and then you visit your favorite Web merchants to see if they have any special offers for you. At each of these sites, the cookie helps to remind the Web site of who you are. When you first visited MSN, for instance, you entered your Zip code, which was stored in a cookie. Each time you return to MSN.com, the Web site checks for that cookie, finds your Zip code, and shows you local news and weather, as shown below.

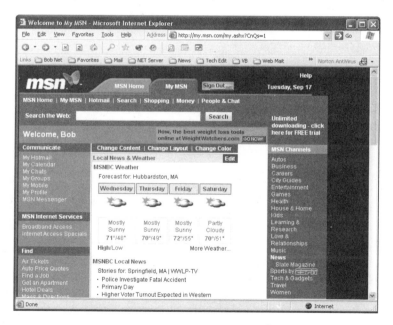

Likewise, a cookie at a merchant's site remembers your customer ID, which you entered when you first visited the site. Knowing who you are, the merchant can look in its database, see that you like classic rock and science fiction, and tailor its front page to show you new offerings in those categories.

So far, so good. In fact, both of these examples demonstrate the benefits of cookies effectively. Now let's consider an example of a cookie that is not so benign. When you visit your favorite forum for football fans, you barely notice the advertisement at the top of the page. Although it appears in the same browser window as your football forum, the ad actually comes from a completely different Web server, example.com, run by Example Advertising, a giant company that specializes in online advertising and places ads on thousands of Web sites all over the world. Unbeknownst to you, that site plants a cookie on your computer, assigning you a unique identification number. Now, every time you visit a Web page that includes an ad from Example Advertising, the server makes a note in the file for the computer whose cookie uses ID number 234005681. Over time, Example Advertising learns that you're a football fan, that you like classic rock and science fiction, and that you've been looking at travel sites for destinations in Mexico. From this dossier, which is all based on a cookie, Example Advertising can start tailoring the advertisements it shows you, offering things that match your browsing habits.

The big advertising agency still doesn't know who you are, of course. All they have is the unique ID number that was assigned to you when you first visited a site with one of their ads on it. But what if they displayed an ad that offered you a chance to win a new car or a trip to Cancún? All you have to do is click the ad and enter your name and address. Of course, as soon as you do that, Example Advertising can match your name with ID number 234005681. They know what part of the country you live in, and they can target your interests even more closely.

If it seems like this cookie is a way for someone to keep tabs on you as you go from site to site on the Web, you're right. Some people don't mind having a shadow on the Web. Others see it as an affront to their privacy. Whichever camp you fall in, you can take charge with a few clicks of the mouse, as I'll explain shortly.

But first, let me point out what cookies *cannot* do:

- A cookie cannot run a program or carry a virus. Cookies consist of text, not program code.

- A cookie cannot search your disk for information. It cannot uncover your e-mail address or learn anything about you except for details you choose to enter.

- A cookie cannot give information to any Web server other than the one directly associated with it. If you visit a specific site, it can retrieve only information from its own cookies.

Taming the Cookie Monster

In previous versions of Windows and Internet Explorer, you had only the most rudimentary control over cookies. With Internet Explorer 6, however, you can exercise fine-grained control over cookies, choosing which ones you want to keep and which you want to reject. To use this feature, choose Internet Options from the Tools menu in Internet Explorer, or double-click the Internet Options icon in the Network And Internet Connections category of Control Panel. Click the Privacy tab to see the full array of privacy options, as shown in Figure 8-5.

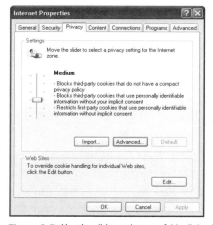

Figure 8-5 Use the slider at the top of this dialog box to choose one of the preset privacy options or construct your own.

To understand the options available to you, it's important to understand the two flavors of cookies in Internet Explorer:

- **First-party cookies**   are those that are placed by a site you visit directly. If you type **www.example.com** in the Address bar, the cookie from the example.com Web site is considered a first-party cookie.

- **Third-party cookies**   are placed by servers whose address does not match the URL shown in Internet Explorer's Address bar. Advertisements are the most common form of third-party content on Web pages.

When you move the slider control on the Privacy tab, you control how Internet Explorer handles each type of cookie. In addition, these controls rely on a *compact privacy policy*, which defines how the site in question handles your information. Those that promise not to divulge your personal information without your specific permission are treated differently from those that have no policy or that say they will share your information with other companies.

You can slide the Privacy control up and down, choosing any of six different options, each of which is clearly described in the explanatory text on the dialog box. At one extreme, you can block all cookies completely—a radical solution that makes browsing the Web downright painful. At the other end of the scale is the option to accept all cookies, a devil-may-care choice that I certainly don't recommend! In fact, I don't use any of those ready-made options. Instead, I choose to decide on a site-by-site basis whether I want to accept a cookie.

Try This! I cannot think of any good reason for a third-party company to keep track of information about me, so I prefer to reject all third-party cookies, with no questions asked. For first-party cookies, I like to decide whether to accept or reject cookies whenever I visit a site for the first time. You can do this, too, by customizing your privacy settings.

1 Choose Internet Options from the Tools menu.

2 In the Internet Options dialog box, click the Privacy tab and then click Advanced.

3 In the Advanced Privacy Settings dialog box, select Override Automatic Cookie Handling.

4 Under the First-Party Cookies heading, select Prompt.

5 Under the Third-Party Cookies heading, select Block.

6 Select the Always Allow Session Cookies option, as shown below.

7 Click OK to save your changes.

After setting these options, Internet Explorer quietly rejects all cookies created by third parties. When you visit a site for the first time, Internet Explorer asks you what to do with the request to create a cookie.

Select Allow Cookie or Block Cookie to accept or reject the cookie request. To avoid being bothered the next time you visit this site, choose Apply My Decision To All Cookies From This Web Site before clicking whichever button you choose. Not sure what's in that cookie? Click More Info to see an expanded view, which shows you exactly what's in the cookie in question.

Key Points

■ Any computer that's connected to the Internet is at risk from a variety of sources, including hackers and viruses.

■ The best defense against viruses is to install antivirus software and make sure to update it regularly.

■ If you receive an e-mail message warning you of a new virus, it might be a hoax. Check it out before you forward the message.

■ If you're concerned about viruses that piggyback along with e-mail messages, configure Outlook Express to block potentially dangerous file attachments.

■ Spam, also known as unsolicited commercial e-mail, is difficult to stop, but you can make a dent in the problem by using filters with your e-mail program.

■ Windows XP includes a powerful personal firewall program, Internet Connection Firewall (ICF), which can stop hackers from breaking into your computer.

■ Cookies are generally helpful files that make the Web easier to use, but they can pose some privacy risks.

■ Internet Explorer 6 includes tools that you can use to reduce the risk to your privacy from cookies.

Chapter 9

Making Windows Work Your Way

My physical desktop is piled several feet high with papers, books and magazines, letters, pictures, CDs, and computer equipment. My Microsoft Windows desktop, on the other hand, is as neat as a pin, with every icon arranged just so and not an ounce of clutter. I keep my files meticulously organized and I make my icons easy to find, because that's the way I prefer to work. Whether you're a compulsive cleaner or a slob, Windows XP can adapt to your style. The more you work with Windows, the more you discover its many different ways to open, work with, and arrange programs and files. In this chapter, I show you how to take advantage of that flexibility by customizing the Windows display, the taskbar and Start menu, and various screen elements to your liking. You'll also learn how to add fonts and fine-tune (or squelch) the beeps and squawks that are part of the Windows XP experience.

Choose Your Interface: Windows XP or Windows Classic

Be honest: What did you *really* think the first time you saw the Windows XP user interface? Did you say, "Wow, that's cool..."? Or did you reach for your sunglasses? With its brilliant colors, rounded windows, and oversized icons, it's a dramatic switch from the good ol' Windows 95 or Windows 98 desktop you've probably grown accustomed to over the past few years. Eventually, some people learn to love the new look (especially when they learn how it makes so many tasks easier to accomplish). But others consider the new interface garish and unpleasantly reminiscent of a Saturday morning cartoon. Beauty, it seems, is in the eye of the beholder, especially when it comes to Windows.

Well, never fear. If you prefer classic rock, classic cars, and classic Coke, you can add the Classic Windows visual style to your environment, too. In fact, you can mix and match elements of the new and old interface.

■ You can change the entire Windows *theme* to Windows Classic so that everything in the interface—the windows, sounds, and icons—looks just as it did in your old Windows version.

> **Lingo**   A *theme* in Windows XP is an organized look-and-feel that coordinates the look of windows, dialog boxes, sounds, and icons. You can select a Windows XP theme, download additional themes, or even create your own.

■ You can change the display properties in Windows to show all windows and message boxes in the Classic style.

■ You can display the icons in individual windows by using Classic style in folder windows.

Let's take a look at changing the whole shebang first.

> **See Also**   There's yet another Classic option available to you when you want to make changes to the Start menu. To find out how to switch the Start menu back to Classic style, see the section "Streamline Your Start Menu," on page 210.

Displaying Classic Windows

The pre-XP Windows style was a little less vibrant, a little less rounded, and a bit more businesslike. The sounds were simpler; the icons smaller, and everything a lot flatter. If you prefer that look and you want to change the whole collection of Windows elements, you can change the Windows theme to Windows Classic. It's a surprisingly simple process. Just perform the following steps:

1   Right-click any blank spot on the desktop and choose Properties from the shortcut menu shown here.

> **Note**   As I explained in Chapter 2, this shortcut is the faster, smarter way to get to the Display Properties dialog box. The slow but sure route is to click Start, open Control Panel, open the Appearance And Themes category, and then click Change The Computer's Theme from the list of available tasks.

2   In the Display Properties dialog box, click the Themes tab and choose Windows Classic from the drop-down Theme list.

3   Click OK.

A message box appears, saying "Please Wait," while Windows reconfigures the display. When the Display Properties dialog box reappears, it (and all the desktop behind it) has adopted the new—or rather, old (fashioned)—look.

> **Tip**   You probably noticed that the Themes dialog box has an Apply button as well as OK. What's the difference? In practical terms, nothing. If you click either one, you tell Windows to make the changes you selected on the dialog box. When you click OK, Windows applies your changes and closes the dialog box. Click Apply if you want to see the changes but leave the dialog box open. The Apply button lets you experiment with different settings or adjust several groups of settings without having to continually close and reopen a dialog box.

Changing Only Windows and Message Boxes

OK, so what if you want to get rid of the rounded edges on windows, boxes, and buttons but you want to keep the Windows XP desktop background, sounds, and icons? You can flatten the appearance of those Windows elements without changing the entire theme. To choose Classic-style windows and message boxes, follow these steps:

1   Open the Display Properties dialog box again by right-clicking the desktop and choosing Properties.

2   On the Appearance tab, choose Windows Classic style from the drop-down Windows And Buttons list, as I've done in Figure 9-1.

Figure 9-1 Use the Appearance tab to display Classic-style windows and message boxes.

3 Click OK to make the change.

Tip　You can further customize the look of the Classic-style windows by making different choices from the Color Scheme and Font Size lists on the Appearance tab of the Display Properties dialog box. In fact, with the Windows XP theme in operation, you have a choice of only three colors—Blue, Olive Green, and Silver; when you choose the Windows Classic appearance, however, you have the full list of old-style color choices, including Teal, Eggplant, and (my personal favorite) Desert. You also can click Effects to control the look and behavior of menus, Screen Tips, icons, and key combinations; or you can click Advanced to make individual choices about the appearance of desktop items by changing their color, font, or size.

Saving a Custom Scheme

After you've tinkered with the look and feel of windows, icons, colors, sounds, menu effects, icons, and just about everything else on the Display Properties dialog box, you end up with a theme that isn't Windows XP *or* Windows Classic. In fact, if you return to the Themes tab, you'll see that the choice in the Theme list now reads Modified Theme. If you've decided that this theme is a keeper, you can save it to reuse on the same computer or share with someone else. On the Themes tab, click Save As, give your new theme a descriptive name (the default is My Favorite Theme, but you can probably come up with a better name than that), and click Save.

Make the Taskbar Easier to Work With

If you've used any of the last several incarnations of Windows, you're familiar with the taskbar. In Windows XP, the taskbar performs the same functions as always: it offers a way to start programs, to switch quickly between running programs, and to see messages and other alerts from the operating system and from programs. The taskbar, shown in Figure 9-2, consists of three different areas.

Quick Launch toolbar   Notification area

Taskbar buttons

Figure 9-2 The taskbar is divided into three sections that offer you different ways to access programs.

■ **Quick Launch toolbar**   Displays programs that you use regularly and want to launch with a single click of the mouse button instead of going through the Start menu or selecting the program icon on the desktop.

> **Tip**   If the Quick Launch bar is not visible, you can make it appear by right-clicking any empty space on the taskbar, choosing Toolbars from the shortcut menu, and then selecting the Quick Launch option. You can add your own favorite programs to the Quick Launch area by dragging a program icon from the desktop or the Start menu and dropping it directly on the Quick Launch area.

■ **Taskbar buttons**   Appear for each running program or open window. Clicking a taskbar button for a program or window that isn't currently visible brings that window to the foreground so you can work with it. For most programs or windows, clicking the taskbar button again minimizes the program.

■ **Notification area**   Displays icons for utilities and system programs that are installed on your computer. For instance, when you use a modem to make a dial-up Internet connection, a small status icon appears in the notification area. Pointing to this icon gives you statistics about the connection, and double-clicking the icon gives you access to a dialog box you can use to control the connection. By default, the system clock also appears in the notification area.

> **See Also**   You can customize the notification area so that only those icons that you use regularly appear. Doing so helps keep the taskbar from becoming cluttered with icons you rarely (or never) use. See the section "Getting Rid of Unwanted Icons on the Taskbar," on page 208, for more details.

One annoyance that you've probably experienced firsthand with previous Windows versions occurs when you have a large number of windows open at one time. For the first few windows, at least, the taskbar shows the window title.

However, after you've opened a sixth (or eighth, or tenth) window, the taskbar buttons shrink to the size of an icon, showing no text and providing no clue as to what's in that window.

You can make the taskbar more useful by customizing its appearance. The following sections walk you through these features. Some of the tricks I describe in this section have been around for years, but Windows XP includes one new capability that greatly improves the usability of the taskbar—the capability to group related windows under a single button.

Giving Your Taskbar Some Extra Room

If you have trouble seeing which open window or running program goes with each taskbar button, one simple solution is to increase the height of the taskbar from its normal one line to two lines or even three. You lose a tiny amount of room for program windows, but that's a small price to pay for the benefits you get from making this change. Here's how to make your taskbar taller:

1   Right-click any empty spot on the taskbar and look at the shortcut menu. If you see a check mark to the left of the Lock The Taskbar menu choice, click it to unlock the taskbar.

2   Aim the mouse pointer at the top edge of the taskbar until it turns to a two-headed arrow and then click and drag the top edge up to create an extra row. (Stick with two rows for now. Later, if you decide you need even more room, you can repeat this process.)

3   Right-click an empty spot on the taskbar and select Lock The Taskbar from the shortcut menu.

After you finish this customization, you'll be able to read more text on each taskbar button. Compare the taskbar shown in Figure 9-3 with the single-row version in Figure 9-2. The exact same number of buttons is visible in both versions, but the taller taskbar is much easier to work with. As a bonus, notice that the little icons in the Quick Launch bar and the notification area stack up as well, giving you more room in these areas, too—and the clock shows the current day and date, not just the time!

Figure 9-3 With a two-row taskbar, you can see much more information about running programs.

Sliding the Taskbar Out of the Way

In the previous section, I explained how to steal room from program windows and give it to the taskbar. Do you prefer having as much room as possible for programs and other open windows? No problem. You can give yourself a bit of extra room by configuring the taskbar so that it slides out of the way when it isn't needed.

As in previous versions of Windows, you can configure the Windows XP taskbar to slide down and out of the way when the mouse pointer is in the upper portion of the desktop. To make it reappear, just move the pointer down to the bottom of the screen. To turn on this feature, follow these steps.

1 Right-click any empty area on the taskbar and choose Properties from the shortcut menu. (If you right-click a taskbar button, you display a shortcut menu for that program instead.)

2 In the Taskbar And Start Menu Properties dialog box, select the Auto-Hide The Taskbar option.

3 Click OK to apply the change.

With this change in place, whenever you move the mouse off the taskbar area, it appears to "roll down" to the bottom edge of the desktop. When you move the mouse back to the taskbar area, it rolls back up. It takes some getting used to, but this technique is extremely useful on small screens where every square inch of desktop space is precious.

Note   As noted earlier in this chapter, Windows XP includes a new feature that allows you to lock your taskbar into position—a feature that can prevent the disconcerting problem of having the taskbar float in the middle of the screen or "dock" to one side or to the top of the screen. If your taskbar ends up somewhere other than the bottom of the screen, point to any empty space on the taskbar, click and hold the left mouse button, drag the taskbar down to the bottom of the screen, and then release the mouse button. To lock the taskbar, right-click it and choose Lock The Taskbar from the shortcut menu.

Grouping Taskbar Buttons

As I noted earlier, Windows XP makes it easier to read taskbar buttons by grouping similar buttons together so they take up less room. This feature, which comes into play when you run out of room on the taskbar, collapses buttons to a single button according to the program you use to open them. Thus, if you open five different Microsoft Word documents and run out of room to see each one's button, they'll all appear under a single Microsoft Word taskbar button.

When you click the button, a list rolls up from the button, displaying the title of each document, as shown on the next page.

To turn on this feature, open the Taskbar And Start Menu Properties dialog box by right-clicking the taskbar and choosing Properties. Select the Group Similar Taskbar Buttons option to enable it. Then click OK to close the dialog box and save your change.

Note   If you find out later that you really don't like this grouping feature, clear the Group Similar Taskbar Buttons option to disable grouping. When grouping is not applied, each individual file has its own button in the taskbar. If you rarely work with more than two or three open documents, you might prefer this see-it-all-at-once method.

Getting Rid of Unwanted Icons on the Taskbar

As I mentioned earlier, the notification area is the official name of the far right portion of the taskbar, where you see icons typically associated with system utilities installed on your computer. Right at this moment, for instance, I have seven icons in the notification area on my computer, including one icon for the volume control, another for Windows Messenger, a third that allows me to safely remove hardware plugged into a universal serial bus (USB) port, and four more installed by various utilities, including Norton AntiVirus. As you can imagine, this space can quickly become cluttered, and all those icons can eat up some of the space you need for taskbar buttons.

Unlike previous versions, Windows XP keeps an eye on icons in the notification area and displays only those icons you really use. This feature is on by default. To check that it's enabled on your computer, right-click any empty space on the taskbar and choose Properties. In the Taskbar And Start Menu Properties dialog box, make sure the Hide Inactive Icons option is selected.

At any time, you can take a peek at the hidden icons by clicking Show Hidden Icons in the notification area. When this arrow is pointing left, as shown below, it means you have some icons hidden; when it's pointing to the right, all icons are visible.

Take Control of the Notification Area

Some icons in the notification area are a waste of space, while others are incredibly useful. On my computer, I like to have the Volume icon displayed all the time. This allows me to change the volume quickly and easily, with just a few clicks of the mouse. If you want Windows to hide inactive icons, how can you prevent it from hiding the icons you use all the time? Use the Customize Notifications dialog box, shown in Figure 9-4, to make your preferences known for each icon.

1   Right-click any empty space in the notification area and choose Customize Notifications.

2   In the Name column of the Customize Notifications dialog box, click the item you want to change.

3   In the Behavior column, click to select one of the three available options from the drop-down list. If you want an icon always to be visible, for instance, choose Always Show.

4   Repeat steps 2 and 3 for any additional icons you want to change and then click OK to close the dialog box.

Figure 9-4 The Customize Notifications dialog box allows you to decide how you want icons to appear on the desktop.

To return the display of notification icons to their default settings, click Restore Defaults in the Customize Notifications dialog box.

Streamline Your Start Menu

The Windows XP Start menu is radically different from the one you've become used to in earlier versions of Windows. Instead of one column, it has two. The column on the left is almost completely under your control. You decide which program icons you want to include there—presumably those you use most often. In the column on the right, Windows displays icons that quickly take you to system folders and common storage locations. You can't add your own folders to this list, but you can decide to show or hide some of the entries available here.

To modify the Start menu so that it displays the programs you want, just the way you want them, follow these steps.

1   Right-click Start and choose Properties from the shortcut menu. The Taskbar And Start Menu Properties dialog box appears, with the Start Menu tab displayed, as shown in Figure 9-5.

Figure 9-5 You can customize the Start menu by selecting the programs you want displayed there.

2   Click Customize. In the Customize Start Menu dialog box, make your choices for the following items:

● Choose the size of the icons you want to display for program items. The Large Icons option is selected by default. Choose Small Icons if you want room to add as many programs as possible to the Start menu.

● Indicate how many programs you want Windows to display on the Start menu. By default, Windows "remembers" the six programs you've used most recently, kicking out the oldest one to make room for the latest one you've used. You can choose any number between 0 and 30 here. Click Clear List to remove all existing programs from the menu. (This action doesn't affect the actual programs themselves, however, or the shortcuts available under All Programs on the Start menu.)

Tip   Don't be confused by this option. The programs that Windows adds automatically to the Start menu are those that appear below the thin horizontal line that divides the left column. You can "pin" a program icon to the Start menu either by dragging its icon from the bottom of this list (or from the desktop or the All Programs menu) and dropping it above the line, or right-clicking it and selecting Pin To Start Menu from the shortcut menu. When a program icon is pinned to the Start menu, it stays in that position until you remove it.

● Select the programs you want to use for Web browsing (Internet Explorer is the default) and e-mail (Outlook Express is the default on a clean installation of Windows XP).

3   Click the Advanced tab, shown in Figure 9-6, and adjust any or all of the following options.

Figure 9-6 In the Advanced tab of the Customize Start Menu dialog box, you choose how you want submenus to appear and select the other elements displayed on the Start menu.

● If you want submenus to appear automatically when you point to them with the mouse, click the first option. To cause new programs you install to be highlighted on the Start menu, click the Highlight Newly Installed Programs option.

● In the Start Menu Items panel, scroll through the list and click any items you want to include. You can also click to clear the check mark from any selected items you *don't* want to include on the menu. You can also decide that you want some types of system folders (My Computer, for instance) to appear as a menu rather than as a link (which opens in a new window when clicked).

● Normally, Windows includes a list of your most recently used documents on the Start menu. To stop keeping track of documents you open, clear the List My Most Recently Opened Documents box. To clear the existing list so that Windows can begin keeping track from a clean slate, click Clear List.

4 Click OK to save all your changes to the Start menu. You can immediately click Start to display the menu, complete with all the new changes.

Back to Classics in the Start Menu Earlier in this chapter, I showed you how to change the Windows XP display back to the Classic Windows style. When you do that, the Start menu takes on a different visual style but still has the new, two-column, Windows XP–style arrangement of program shortcuts. If you want to restore the Classic, one-column look of older Windows versions to the Start menu, you can by performing the following steps:

1 Right-click Start and choose Properties.

2 Select the Classic Start Menu option in the Taskbar And Start Menu Properties dialog box.

3 Click OK to apply your changes, or, if you want to choose the display of individual items on the Classic Start menu, click Customize, select the menu options you want to include, and click Add. When you're finished adding (or removing or sorting) the items in the Classic Start menu, click OK to save your changes and return to the Windows XP desktop.

Redecorate Your Desktop

Would you wear the same outfit day after day after day? Of course not. So why stare at the same background every time you start Windows? You can liven up your desktop by using a graphic image as wallpaper. Windows XP uses the Bliss image—an idyllic scene of a deserted pasture—as its default wallpaper. However, you can customize your desktop to reflect a bit of your own personality. In addition to adding a suitable background image, you can change colors and fonts for window titles and hide icons so that they don't obscure your desktop.

Tip The selection of pictures available for you to choose as a background consists of images included with Windows as well as the contents of your My Pictures folder. If you have an image you want to use, just make sure you add it to the My Pictures folder first.

Designing Your Own Wallpaper

You can use any image as your *wallpaper*—the Windows term for an image that covers the desktop surface. Windows XP includes an assortment of high-resolution images, including an eerie moonscape and a refreshing beach tableau, but I recommend using one of your own images instead. You can download suitable pictures from the Web or use one captured with your digital camera. Either way, you'll be truly personalizing your workspace and not just settling for the same image that millions of other people have.

To change the background display, follow these steps.

1   Right-click any empty space on the desktop, choose Properties from the shortcut menu and click the Desktop tab.

2   In the Background list box, click different selections to see which ones you like. As soon as you click your choice, the background is displayed in the preview screen at the top of the tab.

3   When you've found the right image, examine the preview window. If the image doesn't fill the area, click the Position down arrow and choose one of the three options.

●   If you've selected an image that's exactly the same size as your screen, or just a bit smaller, pick Center.

●   To fill the entire desktop with two or more copies of a small image, use the Tile option. Be prepared for some strange results, however. Tiling works best with images that were specifically designed for this option.

●   Use the Stretch option to take an image that's a little too big or a little too small for your screen and resize it to fill the entire desktop space. Feel free to experiment with this setting, but don't be surprised if the image becomes distorted to the point of looking downright strange. All three options are shown in the illustration below.

Center   Tile   Stretch

4 Click Apply to see the image as your desktop background. If you don't like the results, start over. If the results are acceptable, click OK to close the dialog box.

Get Rid of Clutter

When you first begin using Windows XP, clutter might not be an issue. If you're using only a few programs and saving your files in their respective folders (you *are* organizing your files, aren't you?), you probably don't have a lot of icons and unused shortcuts sitting around on your desktop.

But after you work with Windows XP for a few weeks and then several months, you might find that programs you install and files you download leave shortcuts all over the desktop. Oh sure, you promise that you'll clean them off later. But eventually, your desktop is so full of icons that you can't find a thing.

Time to clean up that mess! Or, more accurately, it's time to instruct Windows XP to do it for you automatically (so next time you won't even need to think about it). Here are the steps:

1 Click Start and open Control Panel.

2 Click the Appearance And Themes category and double-click the Display icon.

3 Go to the Desktop tab in the Display Properties dialog box and click Customize Desktop. The Desktop Items dialog box appears.

4 In the Desktop Cleanup frame, click the Run Desktop Cleanup Wizard Every 60 Days option.

5 To straighten your desktop right now, click Clean Desktop Now.

6 The Desktop Cleanup Wizard starts. Click Next.

> **Tip** For a faster, smarter way to start the Desktop Cleanup Wizard, right-click the desktop, choose Arrange Icons By on the shortcut menu, and then choose Run Desktop Cleanup Wizard. You can do this any time—no need to wait until the next 60-day cleanup!

7 The wizard checks all the shortcuts on your desktop and displays a list of those you have not used recently. The list tells you when the shortcut was last used and gives you the option of keeping the shortcut instead of clearing it away, as shown in Figure 9-7. Select the check box to the left of any item to clean it up and then leave the box unselected to keep that shortcut on the desktop. Click Next.

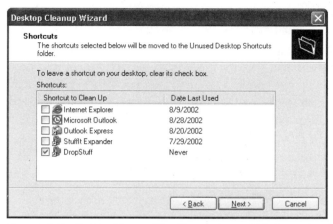

Figure 9-7 The Desktop Cleanup Wizard lets you know which shortcuts you're not using and offers to move them to another folder.

8 Review the list of shortcuts to be cleaned up. If it's acceptable, click Finish to complete the operation.

Note The Desktop Cleanup Wizard doesn't delete any files or programs on your computer. Instead, it removes any shortcuts you've placed on the desktop to a folder, located on your desktop, named Unused Desktop Shortcuts. You can open that folder and use those shortcuts or place them back on the desktop later if you choose.

Arranging Icons

After you've cleaned up unnecessary desktop icons, you might be left with a fairly large number of icons still on your desktop. If that's the way you want to use the desktop, go right ahead. In that case, you can still enlist the help of Windows XP to arrange those icons. When you right-click any empty space on the desktop and choose Arrange Icons By, you see a shortcut menu that offers a number of icon arrangement choices, as shown here.

For instance, you can automatically reorder all the icons on the desktop by name, size, type, or the last date they were modified. In general, this is a terrible way to arrange icons. If you're using the desktop to launch programs and store files, you probably want to put those icons where they make some sense and are easy to access. So skip the top four choices and use Align to Grid instead. This causes the icons to remain in the same general position, but snaps them neatly into line using an invisible grid of horizontal and vertical lines.

Tip   If you want to hide all the shortcuts and icons and display only the desktop background, click Show Desktop Icons and remove the check mark. Click it again to make your desktop icons reappear. This option is great if you've added a piece of spectacular artwork as your background wallpaper, and you don't want those pesky icons to interfere with your desktop masterpiece.

Hiding (and Restoring) Desktop Icons

In previous versions, Windows placed various icons on the desktop—My Documents, My Computer, and so on—and you had no option to remove them. In Windows XP, you can selectively hide or show these icons. To change the icons displayed on your desktop, right-click any empty space on the desktop and choose Properties. In the Display Properties dialog box, click the Desktop tab, and then click Customize Desktop. On the General tab of the Desktop Items dialog box, clear any of the selections in the Desktop Icons area that you do not want to appear. By default, Windows XP displays only the Recycle Bin icon, although you can choose to display icons for My Documents, My Computer, My Network Places, and Internet Explorer. If any of these icons are visible and you decide you don't want to see them anymore, remove them by clicking the check box to clear the selection.

Change Colors, Fonts, and More

For really fine-grained control over what your desktop looks like, you can be creative and change the color scheme and font sizes you use to display windows, window titles, menus, and more. Here are the steps to use:

1   Right-click the desktop and choose Properties to open the Display Properties dialog box.

2   Click the Appearance tab. On the bottom of this tab, click the Color Scheme down arrow. Depending on the style you've selected for windows and buttons, you might have three or more selections available.

3   Click the color scheme you want and look at the preview window. Like it? If not, select a different color scheme by repeating this step.

4 Change the Font size by clicking the Font Size down arrow. The three font sizes available are Normal (the default), Large Fonts, and Extra Large Fonts. Again, after you make your choice, the preview window shows the change.

> **Caution** The Extra Large Fonts option is excellent for anyone with severe vision impairment, but it severely limits the number of icons and windows you can see. If your vision can be corrected with ordinary glasses, you should stick to the Large Fonts option. Any Windows user with vision, hearing, or mobility needs should explore the tools available in the Accessibility Options section of Control Panel.

5 When you like the changes you've made, click OK to save them.

If you want to change the font—and not just the font size—of individual elements, click Advanced. The Advanced Appearance dialog box appears. Here you can use the drop-down Item list box to choose an item for which you want to change the font. (For example, you might choose Active Title Bar, which displays the title of the window that is currently selected. All other windows use the settings from Inactive Title Bar.) After you select the item, the Font option becomes available, as shown in Figure 9-8.

Figure 9-8 You can change the font displayed for various Windows XP elements by using the Advanced Appearance dialog box.

Click the Font down arrow and choose the font you want from the list that is displayed. If you want to change the font size, click the Size down arrow and make your selection. In addition, you can choose a different font color and use the buttons to make the text boldface or italic. After each change, the new selections are reflected in the preview window. When you like what you see, click OK to save the changes.

Set Up a Screen Saver

Once upon a time, screen savers did exactly what their name implies, preventing on-screen images from being "burned in" to the phosphors of an old Cathode Ray Tube (CRT) monitor. Those days are long gone, however, just like your collection of baseball cards and comic books, because today's monitors are virtually immune to burn-in. Surprisingly, though, Windows screen savers are still among the most popular downloads on the Web.

Why all this fascination with a piece of software that isn't even necessary? Well, your monitor might no longer need protection, but your data does. Screen savers offer three advantages:

- **Privacy**   At home or at the office, when you step away from your desk, anyone who wanders by can peek at whatever is currently visible on your screen. A screen saver replaces the contents of your screen with an interesting image, protecting you from snoops.

- **Security**   In Windows XP, screen savers include an option that allows you to password-protect your screen while the screen saver is running. After the screen saver kicks in, moving the mouse or touching any key pops up a dialog box forcing you to enter your user name and password. Even if someone wants to sneak a peek at what's on your screen, they'll be unable to do so without your password.

- **Entertainment**   Screen savers are just plain fun. Windows XP includes its own collection of screen savers that fill the screen with swooping, whooshing geometric shapes or text messages when you're not actively using your computer.

See Also   *You can find additional screen savers on the Web and in products like Microsoft Plus! for Windows XP, which can turn your computer into an aquarium filled with tropical fish or display your collection of digital photographs from the My Pictures folder. (You'll find more details about Plus! at* http://www.microsoft.com/Windows/Plus.*)*

To set up one of the Windows XP screen savers, right-click any empty space on the desktop, choose Properties, and select the Screen Saver tab from the Display Properties dialog box, shown below. Choose an option from the drop-down Screen Saver list box and look at the preview screen in the top of the dialog box. You can also specify how many minutes you want Windows to wait before allowing the screen saver to take over. Be sure to make this interval long enough that you won't be interrupted when you take a two-minute break, but short enough to activate when you step away from your desk. The default of 10 minutes should be good for most people. If you want to see how the screen saver looks in full-screen size, click Preview. To stop the preview and return to the Screen Saver tab, just move the mouse or press a key.

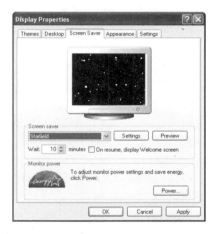

Tip   After you've selected a screen saver, click Settings to see additional options that might be available for your choice. In general, you can choose the speed of the effect as well as certain display characteristics (such as the number of pipes and surface style for the 3D Pipes screen saver). Hold on to your hat if you choose Starfield and leave it at the default Fast setting under Warp Speed!

Finally, if you want to password-protect the screen saver (so no one else can sit down and work with your computer while you're away), select the On Resume, Display Welcome Screen option. (If you are part of a Windows domain, this option will be named On Resume, Password Protect.) Of course, this option is only effective as a security measure if you've added a password to your account, as I recommend in Chapter 2, "How Windows Works (and How to Work with Windows)."

Add New Fonts

Windows XP includes an all-purpose assortment of *TrueType* and *OpenType* fonts that you can use to see a variety of typestyles in documents and on the Web. When you install some new programs, they add fonts to your system. With just a bit of searching on the Web, you can find additional fonts, in all shapes, sizes, and degrees of ornamentation, which you can easily download and install. You can use fun fonts in headlines, staid fonts for business documents, and even fonts that mimic handwriting, when you want your printed document to look as though you wrote it by hand.

Lingo *TrueType* and *OpenType* are the technical terms for standards that define typefaces used in Windows. Although Windows XP can use several other types of fonts, virtually all the fonts you add to your system follow one of these standards. When you search for new fonts on the Web, make sure they are compatible with one of these standards.

To see which fonts are currently installed on your computer, open the Fonts folder. The safe, predictable, somewhat roundabout route to this location is to click Start, open Control Panel, click the Appearances And Themes category, and then click the Fonts icon in the task pane along the left side of the Control Panel window.

The faster, smarter way to get to the Fonts folder is to click Start and choose Run. Then, in the Run dialog box, type **fonts** and press Enter. The Fonts folder looks like just another Windows Explorer window, but it works a little differently. When you double-click the icon for a font, you see details about that font including the font name and a preview of every character available in that font (in a variety of sizes), in a preview window like the one shown here. Click Print to see what the font looks like on paper.

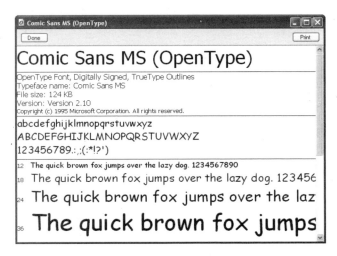

After downloading a new font, you can add it to your collection by dragging the font file into the Fonts folder. If you've downloaded several fonts and you're not sure which files you should drag, use the Add Fonts dialog box instead.

1   Open the Fonts folder and choose Install New Font from the File menu.

2   Using the Folders list box, select the drive and folder containing the fonts you downloaded. (If your new fonts are on a CD or floppy disk, select that location from the drop-down Drives list box.)

3   In the list of fonts, select the ones you want to add (hold down Ctrl to select multiple fonts, or click Select All) and then click OK.

Windows XP adds the fonts you selected to the Fonts folder. The fonts are now available to all programs you run in Windows XP.

Customize Windows Sounds

"I'm sorry, Dave. I'm afraid I can't do that." Ha! We're now well into the 21st century, and diabolical talking computers like the HAL 9000 in *2001: A Space Odyssey* don't exist yet, thankfully. Still, your PC is now powerful enough to make a variety of noises and even read back text from the screen. If the bells, whistles, beeps, and squawks become annoying, you can convert them to melodious chimes and tunes instead.

Choosing a New Sound Scheme

Windows XP allows you to choose sound schemes to assign a whole collection of sound items to various events—starting or exiting Windows, closing a program, and receiving an instant message, to name a few. Here's how to choose a new sound scheme:

1   Display the Control Panel by selecting it from the Start menu.

2   In the Pick a Category window, select Sounds, Speech, and Audio Devices.

3   Select Change The Sound Scheme. The Sounds And Audio Devices Properties dialog box appears, as shown in Figure 9-9.

Figure 9-9   You can choose a new sound scheme or tailor individual sounds in the Sounds And
Audio Devices Properties dialog box.

4   Click the Sound Scheme down arrow and choose a new sound scheme
from the displayed list.

Tip   To preview the sounds in the new scheme, select any item from the Program Events
list and click Play Sound (just to the left of Browse at the bottom of the dialog box).

---

5   Click OK and the new sound scheme is in effect. The next time you
shut down Windows or hear a system beep, the sound should be new
music to your ears.

Selecting Sounds for Individual Events

If you can't find a sound scheme that's just exactly perfect, you can create your
own, or modify an existing scheme, by changing the individual sounds tied to
specific events. Open the Sounds tab of the Sounds and Audio Devices Properties dialog box (as explained in the previous section). Then scroll through the
Program Events list and click the event you want to change. Click the Sounds
down arrow to display a list of sound files or click Browse to display a large collection of sound files in the Browse dialog box, as shown in Figure 9-10.

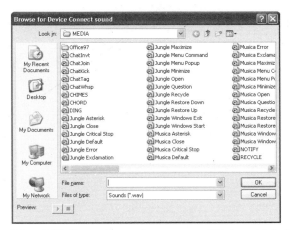

Figure 9-10 You can browse for a new sound file to assign to the event you selected.

Click the sound you want to use and click OK. Back in the Sounds tab, click Play Sound (to the left of Browse) to sample the sound. If you're happy with what you hear, click OK to apply the sound and close the dialog box.

What Else Can I Do with Sound? Once you get the hang of customizing the sounds tied to individual events in Windows XP, you might want to experiment with doing some recording, using speech recognition (programs in Microsoft Office XP support this capability), or adding sounds you download from the Web. As you work in more detail with sound, you'll want to know more about the other tabs in the Sounds And Audio Devices Properties dialog box. Here's what the different tabs enable you to do:

- **Volume** Lets you control the volume of sounds played on your system, display the Volume icon in the notification area, and control the speaker settings on your computer.

- **Sounds** Display available sound schemes and individual event sounds.

- **Audio** Enables you to choose the devices you use for playback, recording, and Musical Instrument Digital Interface (MIDI) playback. If you have a microphone or you use different speakers for different tasks, you might need to enable the devices here.

- **Voice** Enables you to choose and configure the devices you'll use for voice recording.

- **Hardware** Lists the various sound devices supported by Windows XP and gives you the option of troubleshooting hardware problems related to sound devices.

Key Points

- You can switch to the Windows Classic display in several different ways: by changing the display theme, altering only windows and message boxes, changing the Control Panel display, or changing the look of the Start menu.

- The taskbar includes three different areas: the Quick Launch bar, the taskbar buttons, and the notification area.

- You can make the taskbar larger to make buttons easier to read, or hide it automatically to give you more room on the desktop.

- You can hide inactive icons in the notification area to allow more room on the taskbar.

- You can customize your desktop by choosing a new background image (wallpaper).

- Use the Appearance tab in the Display Properties dialog box to set the color scheme and font settings for screen elements in Windows XP.

- Adding a screen saver is a simple matter in the Display Properties dialog box. Click the Screen Saver tab, find the one you want, choose your Settings, if available, and you're good to go.

- You can add new fonts to Windows XP by using the Fonts folder. Any fonts you add this way are available for all your Windows programs.

- Windows XP allows you to choose different sound schemes and assign different sounds to individual program events. To make a sound change, choose Sounds, Speech, and Audio Devices in the Control Panel.

Chapter 10

Organizing Your Files

What makes personal computers so amazing is their phenomenal capacity to store data and recall it with a few clicks of the mouse. You can store photos, music files, letters, memos, and just about anything that can be translated into bits and bytes. Of course, retrieving that information isn't as easy as it sounds. You must remember where you saved that file and what you named it.

That's why it's so important to learn the ins and outs of Windows Explorer, the all-purpose file management tool. By learning how to organize your files, you increase your chances of finding them when you need them. If they get lost, don't worry; the Windows XP Search Companion can track down the missing data as long as you can provide a few details about it.

Where Should You Keep Your Stuff?

Windows XP strongly encourages you to keep your files organized by designating a single location, the My Documents folder, to store all your document files. When you use the Open or Save menus in just about any application, including Notepad, Microsoft Word, Microsoft PowerPoint, and so on, Windows displays the contents of the My Documents folder by default. Although you can save files elsewhere, this is the best place to do so. By developing the habit of using the My Documents folder, you always know where to find your files. In addition, when you back up your personal files, Windows automatically copies all the files stored here without requiring any extra effort on your part.

Note   If you set up multiple user accounts in Windows XP, the My Documents icon appears in the same place for each user; however, it opens a unique folder that holds that user's personal documents. Magic? Not really. The My Documents icon is a *system shortcut* that points to a different location for every user. When you click this icon, Windows checks your logon name, finds the set of folders that contain your personal files (called your *profile*), and then opens the Documents folder stored there. If you log off and someone else logs on with his or her user account and clicks the My Documents icon, Windows repeats this process, finding the Documents folder that belongs to that person's account. If you search through Windows Explorer, you'll discover that the actual folder is named Documents, although its system shortcut appears as My Documents in the My Computer window.

Inside the My Documents folder, Windows includes a pair of folders to help you become organized.

- My Pictures is set aside for images, photos, animations, and icons you create in various graphics, drawing, or animation programs. When you connect your digital camera to your computer and download the shots you snapped on your latest vacation, they go in the My Pictures folder by default.

- My Music—as you have probably guessed—is the default storage location for music and sound files you create, add, or download. When you use Windows Media Player to copy songs from a CD to your disk drive, they go here.

Within the My Documents folder, you can create as many subfolders as you want. You can organize your files by project, by date, or by document type. If you prefer, you can also throw everything into the main folder and sort it out later. When you install Windows programs, they sometimes add their own folders as well. In the My Documents folder shown here, for instance, you can see My Data Sources (added by Microsoft Office XP), My eBooks (created by Microsoft Reader), and My Received Files (used by Windows Messenger).

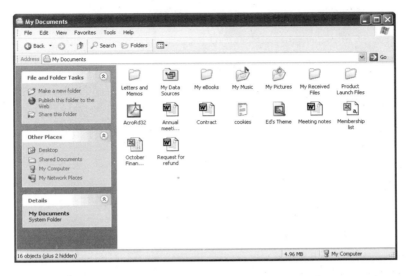

In addition to the My Documents folder, Windows XP also includes a handful of other common locations where you might choose to store files:

■ **Desktop**   You can save data files on the desktop for temporary use. You can also put shortcuts or frequently used files here for easy access. Like My Documents, this is actually a system shortcut, and every user's desktop is stored in his or her personal profile.

■ **My Computer**   Use this folder as the starting point for navigating to specific locations by starting at a specific drive.

■ **Shared Documents**   This folder, which appears in the My Computer folder, is designed for easy access by every user of the local computer. Make the contents of your My Documents folder private and use this location to store files that everyone can read and edit.

■ **My Network Places**   If you've set up a local area network (LAN), the folder appears in the My Computer folder. Use it to browse to shared folders on other computers.

So how do you get to these different folders? When you're opening and saving documents using a Windows program, you can take advantage of clever navigation tools to quickly jump to common locations. Click the My Documents icon in the *Places bar*, for instance, to jump to your personal files when using the Open or Save As dialog box, as shown in Figure 10-1. You can also open the Desktop folder, see a list of shortcuts to recently used documents, or browse through your computer or shared folders on your network.

Places bar

Figure 10-1 Click any of the five icons in the Places bar to jump quickly to commonly used storage locations.

Tip The Places bar is identical in every Windows program, with one noteworthy exception: Programs from the Microsoft Office suite use a dialog box that includes a Places bar whose icons are slightly different. They don't have the Windows XP look and feel, and the selection of icons is different as well. To browse for files by starting with My Computer, for instance, use the drop-down list at the top of the Open or Save As dialog box in any Office program.

To open one of these common storage folders in Windows Explorer, take your choice of several techniques. Feel free to choose whichever is most comfortable for you:

- Double-click the My Documents or My Computer icon on the desktop. If these icons are hidden, see the section "Hiding (and Restoring) Desktop Icons," on page 216, for instructions on how to make them visible again.

- Open My Documents, My Computer, and other common folders by clicking the folder's shortcut atop the right side of the Start menu. Click Start and you'll see a menu similar to the one shown in Figure 10-2.

Note If you've modified the items on your Start menu (a topic I cover in Chapter 9, "Making Windows Work Your Way"), your menu might look a little different from the one shown here.

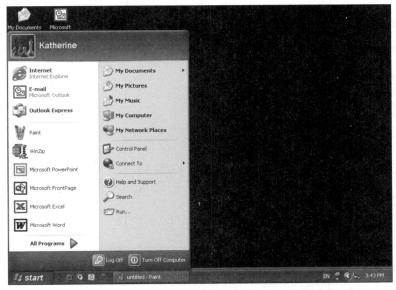

Figure 10-2 The shortcuts at the top of the Start menu's right side lead directly to your most commonly used folders.

■ From any Windows Explorer window, look for shortcuts to common storage locations in the Other Places task pane. The list of shortcuts shown here changes, depending on the folder you're currently browsing.

■ From Windows Explorer, you can also click Folders to see a tree-style list of all the drives and folders on your computer. Although this list can be intimidating, it's easy to use if you remember that the Desktop folder is always at the top, with the My Documents folder directly below it, as shown here. To return to a task pane view, simply click Folders again.

> **Tip** My Documents, My Computer, My Network Places, and Recycle Bin always appear at the top of the list of folders under the Desktop icon. If this list is too hard to read, click the minus sign to the left of any of these folders to collapse the list of subfolders and make navigation a little easier.

Working with Windows Explorer

If you've used versions of Windows previous to Windows XP, you're probably familiar with Windows Explorer, the all-purpose file management utility. To start Windows Explorer in Windows XP, click Start, then click All Programs, open the Accessories menu, and click the Windows Explorer shortcut. This opens the familiar two-pane Windows Explorer window, which displays your files and folders in a tree-like structure on the left and the contents of the currently selected folder on the right.

What you probably don't realize, however, is that this is only one side of the incredibly multifaceted Windows Explorer. When you open the My Computer or My Documents window, you're using Windows Explorer. Control Panel and most of its subfolders appear in Windows Explorer windows. When you open or save a file from a program like Notepad, the dialog boxes you use are nothing more than miniature Windows Explorer windows. In fact, the desktop, Start menu, and taskbar are all part of Windows Explorer as well!

> **Tip** Want to open a Windows Explorer window quickly? Learn these two shortcuts: Right-click the Start menu and choose Open or Explore from the shortcut menu. To use the keyboard instead, hold down the Windows logo key and press E. (That's easy to remember—*E* is short for Explorer.)

Every Windows Explorer window is divided into two panes. The menu bar is always visible, but other elements—the Standard toolbar, the Address bar, and the status bar, for example—can be hidden using options on the View menu. In addition, other programs can add toolbars that are available in Windows Explorer—Norton Antivirus, for instance, tacks on a tiny toolbar with icons you can use to scan specific files or folders for viruses.

> **Tip** If you're satisfied with the arrangement of elements in Windows Explorer and you don't want to accidentally move or hide any of them, choose Toolbars from the View menu and then click Lock The Toolbars. A check mark appears next to this option to let you know it's active

The left side of a Windows Explorer window shows either a task pane, with clickable links to common tasks that apply to the currently selected folder, or a tree-style list of all the disks, folders, and subfolders on your system. To toggle between the task pane and tree-style views, click Folders. The right side displays the contents of the currently selected folder. You can expand or collapse the display of subfolders beneath any folder by clicking the small + or - button to the left of the folder name.

To move from folder to folder, you can use the task pane and the Folders list. It also pays to learn how to use the Address bar and the buttons on the Standard toolbar, as shown in Figure 10-3.

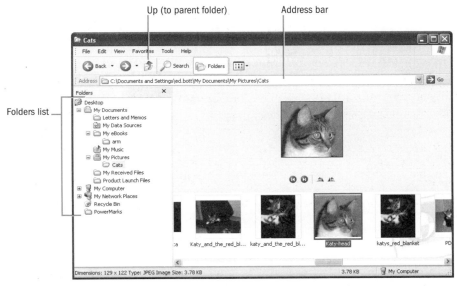

Figure 10-3 Windows Explorer offers a variety of ways to move from folder to folder.

- ■ Click Back to move to the last folder you viewed.

- ■ Click Forward to move to the next folder in a sequence. (This button is available only if you previously clicked Back.)

- ■ Click Up to move to the parent folder of the current folder. (If there is no parent folder, clicking this button displays the Desktop folder.)

- ■ Click the down arrow at the right of the Address bar and select any folder or drive from the drop-down list to display the contents of that location.

- ■ Click in the Address bar, type the folder name, and then press Enter or click Go.

- ■ Click the icon for any folder or drive in the Folders list.

Changing Your View

Different file-management tasks demand different views of the icons in a Windows Explorer window. To sort through a long list of files, it's often useful to see details about those files—when they were created, how much space each file occupies, and when it was last modified, for instance. For pictures, on the other hand, it's far more helpful to see a thumbnail image of each file. Using Views on the Standard toolbar or the View menu, you can set your viewing preferences for any folder. Depending on the contents of the folder, you might have as many as six views to choose from:

- **Thumbnails**   Displays the contents of the folder using oversize squares that display miniature views of the actual contents of some file types (images and Web shortcuts, for instance); if Windows Explorer can't display a preview, it shows a large icon identical to those shown in Tiles view.

- **Tiles**   Lists all files and folders using a large icon and three lines of text that include the file or folder name and other details about the file. This is the default view for the My Computer folder.

> **Tip**   Tiles view is most useful when you combine it with the Show In Groups option, which you select by choosing View, Arrange Icons By.

- **Icons**   Is the default view for most windows. It displays a large file or folder icon with the name underneath. This view is most useful when the number of files in a folder is relatively small.

- **List**   Displays the files or folders with small icons in a vertical list and allows you to see more files than in Icons view.

- **Details**   Shows the files and folders in list form (small icons in a vertical list) and adds the file size, the file type, and the date and time the file or folder was last modified. Click any column heading to instantly sort the list by that heading; click again to sort in reverse order.

> **Note**   The selection of columns in Details view varies according to the data type. You can customize this view and add or remove columns by right-clicking any column heading and choosing items from the list.

In addition, for folders that contain pictures, you might have the option to choose a Filmstrip view. In this view, the left pane shows the Explorer bar (task pane, Folders list, or Search Companion, for instance), while the right pane shows the contents of the folder in a strip of icons that runs along the bottom portion of the right pane, with the currently selected image visible in a large preview area at the top of the pane, as previously shown in Figure 10-3.

Windows Explorer makes the Filmstrip view available only when it detects a folder filled with picture files. However, you can force this option to be available for any folder. Right-click the folder icon and choose Properties. In the Properties dialog box, click the General tab and then select Photo Album or Pictures from the Use This Folder Type As A Template list, as shown here. (You can also use options in this dialog box to use a custom graphic on the yellow background in place of the folder icon in Thumbnails view.)

Customizing Windows Explorer

For most people, the basic operation of Windows Explorer is just fine, especially after you adjust the arrangement of toolbars and icons to match your preferences. A handful of additional options are available when you choose Folder Options from the Tools menu. Depending on your personal taste, you might find that some of these options help you manage files more easily.

Two tabs on the Folder Options dialog box, shown here, control the behavior of Windows Explorer windows.

On the General tab, you can make the following choices:

■ In the Tasks frame, the default option, Show Common Tasks In Folders, displays a task pane in all folder windows when the Folders list is not visible. When you choose Use Windows Classic Folders, the task panes are not used, and hiding the Folders list allows more room for files.

> **See Also**   For more information on selecting other Windows Classic options, see Chapter 9, "Making Windows Work Your Way."

■ Under the Browse Folders frame, Open Each Folder In The Same Window (the default option) allows Windows Explorer to reuse the same window whenever you click a different drive or folder icon. Choosing the Open Each Folder In Its Own Window option pops open a new window each time you click a disk drive or folder icon. Given the potential for clutter, I don't recommend this option.

> **Tip**   When you're viewing a folder window that contains icons for subfolders, you can open a new window by using shortcut menus. If the task pane is visible, right-click the folder and choose Explore. If the Folders list is visible, right-click and choose Open.

■ The options under Click Items As Follows allow you to specify how you want folders to act when you point to or click a folder or file. The default setting requires that you double-click a folder or icon in order to open it. If you choose Single-click To Open An Item (Point To Select), all Windows Explorer windows act like Web pages, with each item appearing as a hyperlink that responds to a single click.

Caution   Using the single-click method might drive you crazy. Trying to select items is more difficult than it sounds, and whenever I try it, I end up inadvertently opening documents and starting programs no matter how careful I am. My advice? Stick with the double-click.

The View tab in the Folder Options dialog box enables you to set a specific view to all folders that you haven't customized. You can also click Reset All Folders, which restores the standard views to every folder. You might want to display all folders and files in List view or Details view, for example. To do this, make sure the folder is currently displayed in the view you want to use. (If it's not, click Cancel to close the dialog box, select the view you want by clicking Views and clicking your choice, and then redisplay the Folder Options dialog box by choosing Folder Options from the Tools menu.) In the View tab, click Apply to All Folders. Windows displays a warning message telling you that the setting will be applied to all folders. Click Yes to make the change or No to cancel it.

The Advanced Settings list in the View tab of the Folder Options dialog box gives you the ability to control the display and behavior of individual characteristics of files, folders, and display items. For example, you can choose to display the contents of system folders, show the full path to a file in the Address bar, or show the entire file path in the window's title bar. If you change the Advanced Settings and want to return to the Windows XP defaults, click Restore Defaults. Clicking OK closes the dialog box and saves the folder option settings you selected.

Working with Hidden Files

If you like to see everything in Windows Explorer, you might want to display any hidden files or folders on your system. By default, Windows XP hides system files and folders. Many programs, including Microsoft Word and Microsoft Excel, also hide temporary files that are created as you work but aren't intended for you to use directly. In some cases, you might want to see all the files in a folder, even those that are hidden. This option is important, for example, if you're planning to manually move all files from one folder to another. If files are hidden, you might leave some behind without even knowing it. To show hidden files, click the View tab in the Folder Options dialog box and select Show Hidden Files And Folders from the Advanced Settings list. Click OK to save your settings. To see system files as well, clear the Hide Protected Operating System File check box. When you choose this option, you see the warning dialog box shown here. Click Yes to continue or No to cancel.

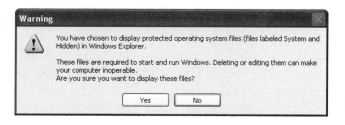

Tip   If you need to display hidden and system files, leave these files visible for only as long as it takes to complete the task at hand. After you're done, reset the option to hide these files. Leaving them visible increases the risk that you'll inadvertently damage or delete an important system file that shouldn't be touched.

Organizing Files

How do you make sense of the mountain of files stored in the My Documents folder? For starters, try to use file names that are short but descriptive. Use a filing and file-naming system that makes sense to you, so you can quickly see from a file's name what's inside. Use folders to keep similar files together and to keep the number of files in any one window to a manageable size.

To manage files, you'll use a variety of tasks: renaming files, moving them between folders, and creating copies. Before you can do anything, however, you must master the process of selecting files. Oh sure, you can rename and move files one at a time, but you'll be much more effective when you learn to work on multiple files at the same time.

- To select a single file, click it.

- To select two or more contiguous files, click the first file, hold down Shift, and click the last file in the list. All the files in the list between the first and last will be highlighted. (If you prefer to use the keyboard exclusively, tap the spacebar to select the first file, and then hold down Shift and use the arrow keys to extend the selection to additional files.)

- To select noncontiguous files, click the first file, press and hold Ctrl, and click the subsequent files. (Using the keyboard, hold down the Ctrl key and move from file to file using arrow keys. Tap the spacebar to select each file.)

Managing Folders

As I noted earlier, the My Documents folder starts out with just two subfolders: one for music, the other for pictures. If you want to become organized, you must create additional subfolders on your own. To add a folder in the current window, click Make A New Folder in the task pane or right-click any empty space and choose New and then Folder. Be sure to rename the folder immediately.

Tip   If you're viewing files in the Open or Save As dialog box, you can create new folders at any time. Use the Create New Folder button, which appears in the top right corner of the dialog box, above the list of files, or right-click in the dialog box and choose New, Folder.

You can rename, move, copy, or delete a folder at any time. If you delete a folder, the folder and its entire contents move to the Recycle Bin (unless you've configured Recycle Bin to delete files immediately).

Copying and Moving Files

When you want to copy files in Windows Explorer, you can choose from a variety of techniques. Depending on the task, I use all of these techniques at various times. Feel free to select the techniques that are most comfortable for you.

Dragging and Dropping Files

The easiest way to reorganize files is by dragging them out of one folder and dropping them in (or on) another. Here's how.

1   Open Windows Explorer and browse to the folder containing the files you want to copy or move.

2   Select the file or files using the methods described in the previous section.

3   Hold down the right mouse button and drag the files to the new location. This location can be the name of a folder in the Folders list, the name of a folder in the Other Places box on the task pane, an open folder window, a folder icon, or a shortcut to a folder.

4   When the selected files are directly over the destination folder and it appears highlighted, release the mouse button. Because you held down the right mouse button, you see a shortcut menu that lets you choose whether to move, copy or create shortcuts to the selected files. Make your choice and Windows performs the action you specified.

Note What happens if you hold down the left mouse button? That depends. If the original folder and the destination are on the same disk drive, dragging the files moves them to the new location, deleting the originals. If the destination is on a disk drive with a different letter, however, dragging the files creates a copy in the new location, leaving the original files untouched. You can reverse this behavior by holding down Ctrl, but it's much, much easier to use the right mouse button and the shortcut menu instead.

Using the Clipboard

With the help of the Windows Clipboard, you can move files in a two-step operation. Start by selecting the files or folders from their original location; then right-click and choose Cut (to move the files) or Copy from the shortcut menu. Next, point to the destination folder (in a folder window, on the Folders list, or using a shortcut), right-click, and choose Paste.

Using a Dialog Box

If you're comfortable with long lists of folders, you can use a dialog box to move or copy files from one place to another. After making your selection, open the Edit menu and choose Copy To Folder or Move To Folder. In the Copy Items (or Move Items) dialog box, shown in Figure 10-4, navigate to the destination folder (click the expand [+] buttons as needed to display subfolders), select the folder, and click Copy (or Move).

Figure 10-4 Use Copy Items if you prefer dialog boxes to dragging-and-dropping files.

Renaming Files

To rename a file or folder in Windows Explorer, click the file once to select it and then click the file name area. (If you prefer, you can choose Rename from the File menu or press F2 to select the file name.) A box appears around the file name and the name itself is available for editing: Type the new name and press Enter.

Try This!   What if you want to rename more than one file? In previous Windows versions, you had to enter commands at an MS-DOS prompt to perform this task. In Windows XP, you can take advantage of a new feature that does this automatically from Windows Explorer. Say, for example, that you have a group of photos that you've moved into a new folder. Each file has a different name, with no rhyme or reason to them. You want them all to have names that match. Here's how to get the job done.

1   Open Windows Explorer, navigate to the folder, and sort the files in the order in which you want them renamed.

2   Press Ctrl+A to select all files in the folder. (This is a universal shortcut for Select All; you can use it almost anywhere in Windows.)

3   Right-click the first file in the list and choose Rename from the shortcut menu.

4   Enter the name that you want to use as the base name for all files in the list. For instance, you might choose Picture.

5   Press Enter. Windows renames all files using the base name you entered in the previous step, adding a number in parentheses for the second and subsequent files.

Finding Lost Files

Over time, you'll probably create hundreds, even thousands of files. No matter how precisely you name your files, no matter how meticulously you organize them in folders, sooner or later you're going to lose track of one. When that happens, you can round up the stray file quickly by using the Search Companion, a new feature in Windows XP. The Search Companion uses an animated puppy to walk you through the process of specifying your search parameters and then finding the missing file. (If you find the puppy annoying, you can replace it with a different character, or you can use a more streamlined and businesslike interface, as I explain shortly.)

Tip   You can make the Search Companion appear by clicking Search on the Start menu or clicking Search on the Standard toolbar in any Windows Explorer window. You can also start a search by pressing F3 or Ctrl+F while you are working with system folders.

To start searching, follow these steps:

1   Open Windows Explorer and click Search. The Search Companion
appears in the left pane, as shown here.

2   Click All Files And Folders. The contents of the Search Companion
pane change to offer you fields in which you can specify one of three
different hints for searching:

●   Enter all or part of the file name if you know it.

●   Type a word or distinctive phrase used in the file.

●   Choose the folder in which you think the file is stored.

In addition, if you know when the file was modified or how large
it is, you can search on those parameters. If you know the specific file
type, you can click More Advanced Options to give Windows Explorer
more information for the search.

3   Click Search to begin looking for the file. The Search Companion displays the status of the search, telling you which folders are being
reviewed. When the search is complete, the Search Companion either
displays the found files in the panel on the right, or informs you that
there are no results to display.

Not a dog lover? No problem. Just above the puppy's head, click Change
Preferences. (You may need to use the scroll bar to the right of the search
choices to see this option.) Next, click With A Different Character to choose
from an assortment of other cartoon characters, including Merlin the wizard and
Earl the surfer.

Better yet, replace Rover with a more generic Search Companion. You can also enable a more powerful interface that lets you enter every search parameter in a single dialog box instead of having to walk through a multi-step wizard. To do this, just above the animated character, click Change Preferences, and then, under How Do You Want To Use Search Companion, click Without An Animated Screen Character. After Rover walks off into the background (no, I'm not kidding), click Change Preferences and then click Change Files And Folders Search Behavior. Choose the Advanced option and click OK.

Deleting Files

To delete one or more files or folders in Windows Explorer, first select them and then press Delete. If you prefer, you can right-click and select Delete from the shortcut menu, or select Delete from the File menu, or click Delete on the Standard toolbar. All these techniques accomplish the same thing. Windows XP displays a warning message asking you whether you want to deposit the file in the Recycle Bin. (The file is not actually erased until you empty the Recycle Bin.) Click Yes to move the file to the Recycle Bin or click No to cancel the operation.

If you want the file or folder to be deleted immediately, without going to the Recycle Bin, select the file or folder and hold down Shift as you right-click. Choose Delete from the shortcut menu and click Yes when prompted to permanently delete the file.

Normally, Windows displays a confirmation dialog box every time you delete a file. Are you sure you want to delete that file? When you get tired of telling Windows "Yes, I'm sure," you can turn off this option. Right-click the Recycle Bin icon and choose Properties. In the Recycle Bin Properties dialog box, shown below, clear the Display Delete Confirmation Dialog option and click OK. From now on, you'll be able to get rid of unwanted files without having to do the two-step each time. You can also use the slider control on this dialog box to reduce the amount of space that the Recycle Bin sets aside. If you have a gargantuan drive, you probably don't need to set aside 10% for files you deleted. For drives that are more than 10 gigabytes (GB) in size, you can safely reduce the size of the Recycle Bin to between 3% and 5%.

Oops! You Deleted a File by Mistake. Now What?

The Recycle Bin can be a lifesaver if your finger is a little too quick on the Delete key. If you erase a file that you really meant to keep, double-click the Recycle Bin (you'll find it on the desktop and in Windows Explorer) and scroll through the list of deleted files until you find the one you want to restore. Select that file and choose Restore This Item from the task pane, or right-click the selection and choose Restore. The selected item goes back to the exact same location where it was when you deleted it, with the same name and other properties.

Compressing Files to Save Space

Big files pose special storage problems. If you have a large collection of high-resolution digital pictures, music files, or video clips, you already know that they can take up huge amounts of storage space. If you're not careful, in fact, these collections can completely use up that hard disk that once seemed so big. In addition, these oversize files are difficult to copy to floppy disks and pose special problems with e-mail. Many ISPs set limits on the size of file attachments, and a digital snapshot can easily exceed those limits. Not to mention the havoc that file attachments create on the recipient's end: Sending even one or two digital pictures as file attachments can fill up the other person's Inbox and prevent them from seeing any further messages. And if they're using a dial-up Internet connection, they won't be too pleased to find that it takes an hour to download your message!

Windows XP includes two built-in features that allow you to *compress* individual files, groups of files, and even entire folders so that they occupy less disk space. On a drive formatted with the NTFS file system, you can use NTFS compression to make more efficient use of your disk drive space. You can also use the Compressed Folders feature to store files more efficiently using the popular Zip format.

Should You Squeeze That File? To use file-compression features safely and effectively, you must have a basic understanding of how the technology works.

For starters, be certain you understand the difference between compression techniques. The standard Zip format is *lossless*. When you expand a file that was compressed using this format, the result is exactly the same as the original file you started with, and not a single detail is lost. The same is true when you check the Compress box for a file or folder stored on an NTFS disk drive.

By contrast, some programs designed to store music and pictures in compressed formats use *lossy* compression techniques. When you copy a music track from a CD and save it to your disk drive in MP3 or Windows Media Audio (WMA) format, for instance, the resulting file takes up a fraction of the space of the original. However, the compressed file has been changed and some of the information is lost. An audiophile who listens to the original CD and the compressed audio file can hear the difference. The same is true with digital pictures—when you convert an original bitmap image to JPEG or GIF formats, the resulting image is less sharp and clear, and nothing you do with the compressed file can restore the missing bits.

Does this mean you should always choose one format or the other? Not at all. If you're planning to listen to music on your computer or portable player, with less than state-of-the-art audio features, you're probably perfectly willing to trade a small loss of quality for the ability to store ten times as much music in the available disk space. In general, you want to use lossless compression in situations where having a perfect copy is more important than saving space. Use lossy techniques when you want to save as much space as possible and you don't mind trading a little bit of quality.

Finally, be aware that not all files can be compressed with equal results. Some files, such as high-resolution pictures and Word documents, are highly compressible. However, if a file is already in a compressed format, such as an MP3 song or a JPEG image, adding it to a Zip archive saves you little or no space.

Compressing Folders and Drives

On a drive that uses NTFS, you can specify that you want a single file, a group of files, or an entire folder to be compressed. When you use this option, Windows handles all the work of compressing the files when you save them and decompressing them when you open a file. For day-to-day use, there's no difference between a compressed file and one stored normally. NTFS compression works best if you have a folder filled with files that use up a lot of space and can be highly compressed, such as high-resolution pictures taken by a state-of-the-art digital camera.

To enable NTFS compression, follow these steps:

1 Open a Windows Explorer window and select a single file, a group of files, or a folder.

2 Right-click and choose Properties from the shortcut menu.

3 On the General tab of the Properties dialog box, click Advanced.

4 Select the Compress Contents To Save Disk Space option, as shown here, and click OK.

Caution   If you use Windows XP Home Edition, you might notice that the Encrypt Contents To Secure Data option is unavailable. That's because this feature is only supported by Windows XP Professional. Even if you use Windows XP Professional, I don't recommend using the encryption option unless you fully understand how encryption works. Used without proper precautions, this option can cause you to lose all access to your data!

5 Click OK to close the Properties dialog box. If you chose to compress an entire folder, you see the Confirm Attribute Changes dialog box. Choose the default option, Apply Changes To This Folder, Subfolders, And Files, and click OK.

Tip   You can spot files that are compressed using NTFS compression at a glance in Windows Explorer, because the file or folder name is blue instead of black.

To remove file compression, repeat the above steps, clearing the Compress Contents To Save Disk Space option in step 4.

Zipping and Unzipping Files

To shrink one or more files so that you can send them as an e-mail attachment or copy them to a disk, use the industry-standard Zip format. Third-party programs like PKZip and WinZip have offered the capability to compress files into special file types called *Zip archives* for years. Windows XP builds this capability directly into Windows Explorer, although the terminology is a bit confusing. Just as other Zip programs do, Windows XP can take one or more files, remove the extra space, and stuff them into a single archive file with the .zip file name extension. Here's how:

1 Open any Windows Explorer window and select the file or files you want to compress.

2 Right-click and choose Send To from the shortcut menu; then click Compressed (zipped) Folder.

Note In this section, I assume you haven't installed any third-party Zip utilities on your computer. If you've set up WinZip or another such utility, it will take over the functions I describe here, and you won't be able to use the built-in Compressed Folders features unless you uninstall the third-party program.

A dialog box displays the progress as Windows compresses the files and creates the new Compressed Folder file (although the process might happen so quickly that you don't even notice it). The new file, which appears in the current folder, has a folder icon with a zipper on it, as shown below. Your original files remain unaltered in their original location.

Cats

You can rename the Compressed Folder file, send it to another person as an e-mail attachment, or move it to a different location. You can add files to the Compressed Folder file by dragging them out of a Windows Explorer window and dropping them onto the Compressed Folder icon. When you double-click this icon, you see the contents of the Compressed Folder (zipped) file in what appears to be a folder window. Although you can view files in a Compressed

Folder file (for instance, you can double-click a picture to preview it), you must *extract* the compressed files and save them in a regular folder to do other tasks, such as editing a document.

In the task pane, click Extract All Files to launch a wizard that lets you specify the location where you want the uncompressed files to appear. The extracted files and folders appear in the same location as the Compressed Folder file, in a real folder with the same name.

Tip   Want some extra protection for your compressed files? To add a password to the file, double-click the Compressed Folder file, select any compressed file, and choose Add A Password from the File menu. The password applies to all files in the Compressed Folder file. When you open a password-protected Compressed Folder file, click Password to enter the password and view the files.

Key Points

- The My Documents folder is the preferred location for storing your personal data files. Windows XP automatically creates the My Pictures and My Music subfolders for you, and you can add other subfolders as you see fit.

- Use Windows Explorer for day-to-day file management tasks.

- You can choose from as many as six different views of a folder.

- Normally, Windows hides temporary files and system files from you. Using the Folder Options dialog box, you can make these files visible.

- To copy or move a file between folders in Windows Explorer, hold down the right mouse button and drag the files to the new location. When you release the mouse button, choose the action you want to take—copy, move, or create a shortcut—from the menu.

- Windows XP includes a new feature that allows you to rename a group of files all at once.

- Windows Explorer allows you to add files to a Compressed (zipped) Folder, reducing the size of files and making them easier to transport. In addition, you can turn on file compression for an entire folder, as long as the drive is formatted with NTFS.

Chapter 11

Managing Music (and More) with Windows Media Player

Microsoft Windows XP includes everything you need to turn your computer into a digital jukebox. You can play CDs directly, using your computer's sound card and speakers for playback. You can also copy songs from your CD collection to a local disk drive and download tunes from the Web. Using Windows Media Player, you can mix and match tunes to play disk jockey, creating custom playlists and even burning your favorite tunes to custom CDs that you can play back in a CD player in your home or car.

In this chapter, I'll help you learn the ins and outs of Windows Media Player, with a special emphasis on its musical capabilities.

Windows Media Player at a Glance

Windows Media Player does an amazing number of things, especially when you consider it's included free with every copy of Windows. Most people learn all they need to know by clicking on various buttons and watching what happens. If you feel like exploring, go ahead. To open Windows Media Player, click its icon on the Quick Launch toolbar, just to the right of the Start button; if the Quick Launch toolbar is hidden, you'll find the Windows Media Player shortcut by clicking Start, clicking All Programs, and then choosing Accessories and Entertainment.

> **Note**   In this chapter, I assume you're using Windows Media Player version 8, which is included with Windows XP and is not available for any earlier Windows versions. At the time I wrote this book, Windows Media Player version 9 was in the wings. Although it should look and act much like version 8, you might discover some features that work differently from those described here. You can find out which version you're using by choosing About Windows Media Player from the Help menu.

To switch among the different functions and features available in Windows Media Player, use the buttons on the Features taskbar on the left side of the Windows Media Player window. Each of these seven buttons has a specific role:

■ **Now Playing**   When you click this button on the Features taskbar, the central pane displays content that's appropriate to whatever you're watching or listening to, as in the example shown on the next page. If you're watching a broadcast from the Web or playing back a saved video file or a DVD, the Now Playing pane shows your movie or video clip. If you're listening to a CD, the pane shows information about the album, including its title and the name of the artist, as well as any cover art that Windows Media Player downloaded from the Internet. This is also where you can see *visualizations*, which are splashes of color and geometric shapes that whirl and dance about in time with the music, like a light show from a 1960s rock concert.

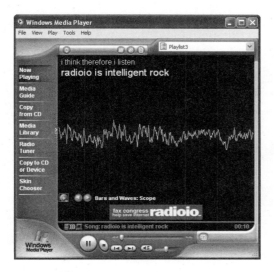

Tip   To view a visualization, click Now Playing on the features taskbar, choose Visualizations from the View menu, and then select any entry from the long list of available visualizations. If you get tired of the built-in visualizations, choose Download Visualizations from the Tools menu.

- **Media Guide**   This link turns the main window into a Web browser that displays content from Microsoft's WindowsMedia.com. You'll find music and video downloads, links to movie previews, and much more here, all updated regularly.

- **Copy From CD**   Use this button to transfer songs from a CD to digital music files on your computer. I explain exactly how to do this in the section "Copying CDs," on page 254.

- **Media Library**   All your downloaded music files and songs you copy from CD are organized neatly here, along with custom playlists you can create by mixing and matching tracks from the collection. I explain how to use this part of Windows Media Player in the section "Organizing Your Music Collection," on page 262.

- **Radio Tuner**   No antenna required! Instead, click the links here to find radio stations that "broadcast" their signals over the Internet. The Featured Stations list includes links to stations hand-picked by

WindowsMedia.com. You can also use the links and Search box in the Find More Stations list to scroll through hundreds of stations, ranging from news and talk to world music and alternative rock. After you select a station, click the Play link to begin listening. If you like it, click the Add To My Stations link, as shown below, to add it to your My Stations list, which appears just below the Featured Stations list after you click the link.

■ **Copy To CD Or Device**   Click this button to begin transferring songs from a CD to your local disk drive, or to copy songs you've already recorded onto a custom CD or a portable music player. I provide details about this in the section "Creating Your Own CDs," on page 264.

■ **Skin Chooser**   Don't like the look of Windows Media Player? Change it! By selecting a skin from the list here (or downloading additional skins from the Internet), you can completely change the look and feel of Windows Media Player. After you select a skin from the list, look at the preview to the right of the list, as shown on the next page. If you like the look, click Apply Skin. To switch between the full Windows Media Player view and the "skinned" view, use the options on the View menu. Or use the keyboard shortcuts Ctrl+1 (Full Mode) and Ctrl+2 (Skin Mode).

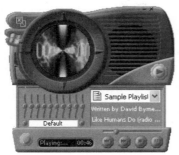

Playing Music CDs on Your Computer

When you slide a music CD into your computer's CD drive, Windows Media Player should open and begin playing the CD immediately. If this doesn't happen, adjust your CD AutoPlay settings so that Windows automatically recognizes the new CD and starts Windows Media Player. If this is the first time you've played a music CD, Windows displays the Audio CD dialog box shown here and asks you for instructions.

Choose Play Audio CD Using Windows Media Player, select Always Do The Selected Action, and click OK.

If this dialog box doesn't appear automatically, you can adjust AutoPlay settings for music CDs by following these steps:

1 Open the My Computer window, right-click the CD drive icon, and choose Properties.

2 On the AutoPlay tab, choose Music CD from the drop-down list at the top of the dialog box.

3 In the Actions box, click Select An Action To Perform and choose Play Audio CD Using Windows Media Player.

4 Click OK to save your changes.

> **Tip** If you install a music playing program other than Windows Media Player, you have the option of setting it as your preferred player for CDs and songs that you save in digital format. In the AutoPlay Properties dialog box, look for an option that refers to using that program to play music CDs and select it.

When Windows Media Player opens and begins playing a CD, you see a window like the one shown in Figure 11-1.

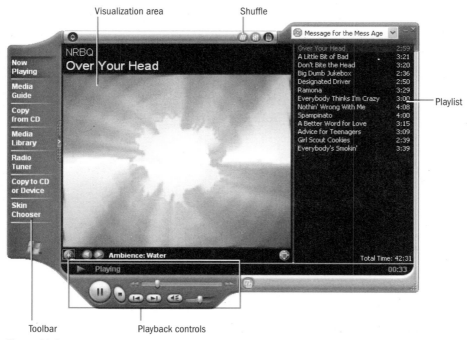

Figure 11-1 Use these Windows Media Player controls to control playback and view album information.

The Now Playing button at the top of the Windows Media Player taskbar should be selected, and your CD drive icon should appear at the top of the playlist. (If it isn't visible, use the drop-down list to select the CD drive.) If you're connected to the Internet, Windows Media Player automatically downloads the album title and the names of all the tracks on the CD and displays them for you. The next time you play the same CD, Windows Media Player finds the saved information and displays it, even if you're not connected to the Internet.

Use the playback controls, shown in Figure 11-2, to start, stop, and pause the CD, adjust the volume, and skip from song to song.

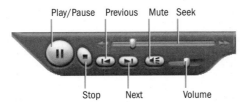

Figure 11-2 These playback controls work just like the ones on the CD player in your home audio system.

What do you do when you're listening to a CD and the phone rings? The Play button becomes a Pause button while Windows Media Player is playing music; click this button to stop the CD playback. When you're ready to resume listening, click Play to pick up right where you left off. To turn the sound down to a low volume, slide the Volume control to the left. You can also click Mute to silence the speakers temporarily while the CD continues to play. Click Mute again to restore the audio.

Don't like a particular song? Skip right past it by clicking Next. You can also drag the Seek slider left or right to jump to a different part of the song that's currently playing.

Windows Media Player plays all the tracks on your CD, in order, unless you turn on Shuffle or Repeat (or both):

- Click the Shuffle button (or press Ctrl+H or choose Shuffle from the Play menu). With Shuffle turned on, Windows Media Player moves through the contents of the CD in a random order. The order is different each time you play the CD.

- If you want the current CD to play continuously, choose Repeat by pressing Ctrl+T or by choosing Repeat from the Play menu.

Managing a Digital Music Collection

Using Windows Media Player to play your CD collection is all well and good, but it requires that you keep your CD collection close at hand, and it doesn't give you the freedom to play disc jockey. If you want to play two tracks from one CD, another three tracks from a different CD, and two more tracks from yet another CD, you can spend more time flipping CDs and clicking track titles than actually listening to the music. Fortunately, you have an alternative: Use Windows Media Player to copy tracks from your CD collection and store them in digital format on your disk drive, where you can listen to them any time in any order.

Copying CDs

Using Windows Media Player, you can copy tracks from a music CD and store them on your hard disk—a process sometimes referred to as "ripping" tracks to disk. Later, you can listen to the saved tracks, download them to a portable music player, or create a custom playlist and burn your own CD. To copy one or more CD tracks to your hard disk, insert the music CD into your computer's CD drive and then choose Copy From CD on the taskbar in Windows Media Player.

Note Did Windows Media Player start playing your CD as soon as you inserted it? No problem; you can play and copy a CD at the same time.

Using your Internet connection, Windows Media Player retrieves details about the CD you inserted, including the album title, the name of each track, the performer, and the genre. (If you weren't connected to the Internet when you inserted the CD, don't worry. After making a connection, click Get Names on the Copy From CD screen.) Figure 11-3 shows the resulting display.

Tip The online music guide has listings for more than half a million CDs, so your CD is probably there. If the listings are incorrect or if Windows Media Player doesn't recognize your CD, you'll see generic titles, such as Track 1. In that case, enter details for each song (title and artist, in particular) manually before recording. Press Ctrl+A to select all the songs in the list, right-click, and choose Edit from the shortcut menu. Use the Tab key to jump to the next field after entering each bit of information.

By default, Windows Media Player selects all the songs on your CD. If you just want to copy one or two tracks from the CD (or if you want to skip that one annoying song on an otherwise wonderful CD), click to clear the check boxes to the left of the songs you don't want to copy. After you've made your selections, click Copy Music to begin copying the selected tracks to your local drive. Look at the Copy Status column in the track listings to see how the task is progressing.

Click here to begin copying.

Select these boxes to copy songs.

Figure 11-3 Don't want to copy one of these tracks from CD? Clear the box to the left of the song's title.

Tip By default, Windows Media Player copies tracks to the My Music folder, which is in your personal profile. If you share your computer with other people and you want everyone to have access to the same music collection, choose Options from the Tools menu, click the Copy Music tab, and click Change under Copy Music To This Location. In the Browse For Folder dialog box, choose My Computer, then Shared Documents, and finally Shared Music. Click OK to save your changes. You can also use this technique if you're running out of room on your primary disk drive and you want your recordings to be stored on a secondary disk drive that has more capacity.

The first time you copy tracks from a CD, Windows Media Player displays the dialog box shown on the next page. If you click OK at this point, all your saved tracks will be copy protected. This makes it difficult to copy them to a portable music player and nearly impossible to share with other people. Furthermore, if you ever have to reinstall Windows, you'll find that your saved tracks will not play back on your new installation, even if it's the same computer! To avoid all these hassles, clear the Do Not Protect Content check box and then click OK.

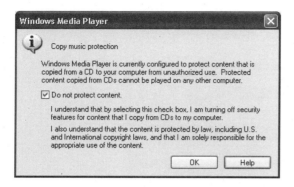

Choosing a Music Format

When you copy CD tracks using Windows Media Player, the saved files are stored using the Windows Media Audio (WMA) format at 64 kilobits per second (Kbps). Although Windows Media Player refers to this setting as CD quality, most audio aficionados would disagree. The 64 Kbps setting is efficient, and it sounds good enough on the small speakers that most people attach to their computers or the headphones used with a portable audio player. However, if your PC audio components are better than average, or if you want to burn your recorded tracks to a CD and play it back on a high-quality home audio system, you'll want to increase the quality level. Just keep the tradeoffs of quality versus storage in mind: Higher *bit rates* equal higher audio quality, but they also require more room on your disk drive.

Lingo   Digital music uses *bits* to store information about each song. The more bits per second (bps) of music, the more information is available to play back that song. When you reduce the number of bits reserved per second of music (the *bit rate*), Windows Media Player has to throw out some information about the track to squeeze it into the smaller space. Let your ears help you decide whether the tradeoff is worth it.

To adjust quality settings for all subsequent recordings, choose Options from the Tools menu in Windows Media Player. On the Copy Music tab of the Options dialog box, shown on the next page, move the slider control under Copy Settings—to the right for higher quality, to the left for more efficient storage at the expense of audio quality.

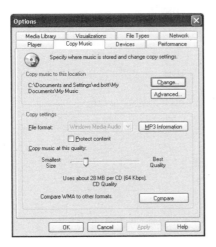

What if you prefer the MP3 audio format? Microsoft's goal in developing the Windows Media Audio format was to devise a way to store music that sounds great without consuming your entire disk drive. As a result, the WMA format is more efficient than the MP3 format. If you want to use Windows Media Player to record tracks using MP3 format (so you can share them with devices or programs that don't recognize WMA format), you'll need to purchase an audio plug-in for this purpose. On the Copy Music tab of the Options dialog box, click MP3 Information to visit a Web site where you can learn more details.

Changing Song Title Formats

When you rip tracks from a music CD using the default settings in Windows Media Player, the saved tracks appear in your My Music folder. Each artist gets a subfolder, and each album gets a subfolder within the artist's folder. Each recorded track file is saved using the track number, followed by a space and the song title (which might also include one or more spaces), as downloaded from the Internet. Normally, this level of detail is fine. In fact, additional details about each track are stored within the saved file itself, and you can view these details any time by opening Windows Explorer and looking at the contents of the folder that contains your songs.

As Figure 11-4 shows, the contents of subfolders in the My Music folder appear in Tiles view by default. This lets you see the artist and album name beneath the name of each track. If that's not enough detail, aim the mouse pointer at a track icon and wait for a Screen Tip to appear, with even more details about the track, including the bit rate at which it was recorded.

Figure 11-4 Aim your mouse pointer at any recorded CD track to see additional details about the song and the recorded file.

If you share music files with other people who don't use Windows XP, or if you want your file listings to include more information, you can set up Windows Media Player so that it automatically names your files differently. Follow these steps:

1 Choose Options from the Tools menu and click the Copy Music tab.

2 Click Advanced.

3 In the File Name Options dialog box, shown on the next page, select the check boxes for the information categories that you want to include in your file names and clear the other check boxes. Use Move Up and Move Down to change the order in which the selected pieces of information appear.

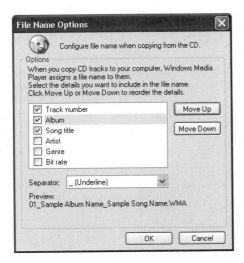

4   If you don't want spaces in your file names, use the Separator list to choose a different character (dashes, dots, or underlines) to separate elements of the name.

5   Use the Preview area to see how the names appear using your new format. When the results are satisfactory, click OK.

Downloading Songs from the Web

The Web is an amazing source of content, and music is one of its strong suits. With even a simple search, you can probably find dozens of sites that allow you to download music that you can integrate into your Media Library. Some of these sources are commercial—for instance, many online CD sellers provide song files that you can download as a try-before-you-buy sample. You can also purchase songs from authorized sources, paying for the rights to download and play the tunes in your collection. Windows Media Player includes a set of technologies to help you manage these *digital rights*. Finally, you can exchange music files directly with other people, either one-on-one or through online file sharing services.

Caution   When downloading music to your collection, make sure you don't inadvertently get more than you bargained for, including viruses and Trojan horse programs. You should be especially suspicious of underground file-sharing services, because no central authority has the responsibility for scanning and checking the files available through these channels to make sure they're safe. It's especially important to use an up-to-date virus scanner when using services such as these.

When you click the Media Guide link in the Windows Media Player taskbar, you can go to Microsoft's Web site and search for downloadable songs. The selection, organized alphabetically by artist, is huge. If you need a digital license to play back the song, Windows Media Player handles the details for you. (You might need to download and install an updated Windows Media Player component first.) After you fill in a few blanks, you see a dialog box like the one shown here.

In some cases, your license to play the downloaded song is restricted. You might be allowed to play it only on the computer you originally used to download it, for instance, or the license might expire after some period of time (30 days, in the example shown here). What if you purchased a license for a song that allows you to play it only on your own computer and you want to move it to another computer? You can usually move the song (giving up your right to play it on your current computer) by backing up your licenses and then restoring the licenses on the new computer.

To see the terms of the license for a given song, open Media Library, right-click the song title, and choose Properties. The information you're looking for is on the License Information tab, shown on the next page.

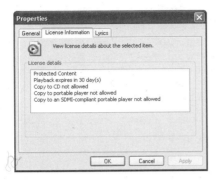

Try This! If you have any licensed songs on your computer, it's a good idea to back up your licenses even if you don't plan to copy the songs to another computer. Backing up the song files themselves does not back up the licenses. Even if you restore the song files, you lose the ability to play back the songs if you can't restore the licenses, too.

To back up all of your media licenses, follow these steps.

1 From the Tools menu in Windows Media Player, choose License Management.

2 In the License Management dialog box (shown in Figure 11-5), click Browse and then choose a location for your backup. (I recommend that you use a floppy disk, a Zip disk, or another type of removable storage for this task.)

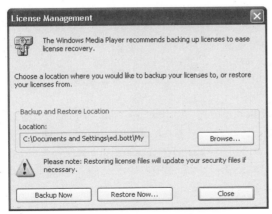

Figure 11-5 Use the License Management dialog box to make backup copies of your digital licenses.

3 Click Backup Now.

To restore the licenses to a different computer, repeat these steps, but locate the backup file instead and click Restore Now as the final step.

Caution   Your digital rights are not unlimited. Each time you restore a digital license to a new computer, Windows Media Player sends a unique identifier to Microsoft's servers. You can restore your backed-up licenses to four unique computers before being locked out. If you reformat your disk drive, Windows Media Player considers the newly formatted drive to be different from the original computer.

When you download music files from other online sources, save them in the My Music folder. (Create a new subfolder if you want to keep them separate from your existing files.) To add the new files to your Media Library, open Windows Media Player and choose Search For Media Files from the Tools menu. To limit the search to the location where you saved your downloaded files, open the Search On drop-down list and select <User-Selected Search Path>. Then click Browse and choose the appropriate folder from the Browse For Folder dialog box.

Organizing Your Music Collection

Whenever you add a music file to your collection, either by recording it from a CD or downloading it from the Web, Windows Media Player adds it to your Media Library. This outlined list makes it easy to locate music and video files for playback (or for other uses, such as copying to a CD). Each album that you record automatically appears in Media Library, categorized by album title, by artist, and by genre. In addition, you can create custom *playlists* of your favorite tracks.

To view the contents of your Media Library, click the Media Library link in the Windows Media Player taskbar. As Figure 11-6 shows, this list consists of two panes: on the left is an outline, showing albums, video clips, custom playlists, and radio tuner presets; on the right is a detail pane, which shows the contents of the item that is currently selected in the left pane.

A playlist is a customized collection of media files that Windows Media Player can play back in the order you select. Each album listed in Media Library's left pane is a playlist. When you choose a name from the Artist category, the playlist consists of all tracks from all albums in your Media Library by that artist. Likewise, you can see all tracks in a particular genre by selecting an item from the Genre category.

Figure 11-6 The Media Library appears as an outline list, organized by album, artist, and genre.

You can create custom playlists to combine your favorite tracks, to reorder tracks on a favorite album, or to mix and match tracks for use in a custom CD. Follow these steps to create a custom playlist.

1 Click New Playlist at the top of the Media Library window.

2 In the New Playlist dialog box, enter a descriptive name for your play-list, and then click OK.

3 Select one or more tracks from the right pane of the library and drag them to the new playlist entry in the left pane.

Playing DVDs

Windows Media Player can play back more than music. It can also turn your PC screen into a personal theater capable of playing movies from DVD disks—but only if you have a DVD drive and a *decoder*. If you purchased your PC with a DVD drive and Windows XP already installed, you might already have both of these pieces. If you upgraded an older computer to Windows XP, however, you might need to download and install a software decoder from the Internet. Does your PC have what it takes? For starters, make sure you have a DVD drive. You can't always tell just by looking at the drive itself, because CDs and DVDs are identical in size and shape. To make sure, look for a DVD label on the drive icon in the My Computer window, or inspect its Properties from the Device Manager window, as I explain in the section "Inspecting Your Hardware with Device Manager," on page 85. To find out whether you have a decoder installed, pop a DVD disk into the drive. If the decoder is missing, Windows Media Player displays an error message with a link to its DVD Troubleshooter. Follow this link to locate a list of compatible decoders.

Lingo   As you might guess from the name, a *decoder* takes the output from your DVD drive and translates it into a format that Windows Media Player can use to display the pictures and sound on the screen. In the early days of DVD technology, decoders were often hardware-based cards that you installed inside your computer. Today, however, you'll typically get better results (with a lot less hassle and expense) from a software decoder that installs just like any other program.

Playing a DVD movie in Windows Media Player is similar to playing a music CD. Your DVD movie should start playing automatically as soon as you insert the disk. If it doesn't, start Windows Media Player, choose DVD Or CD Audio from the Play menu, and choose your DVD drive from the submenu.

Creating Your Own CDs

If you've created a custom playlist from music tracks saved on your computer, you can burn the songs to a CD using Windows Media Player. Naturally, you need a CD-R or CD-RW drive that is compatible with Windows XP to do this, and you'll need a blank CD as well. You don't need any additional software or hardware.

Should you use Windows Media Player to make CDs? Although this method is convenient, it might not be the best choice, especially if you have a third-party CD burning program that has more capabilities. Ask these questions before you begin burning:

- Do you want to make an exact copy of a CD? If so, use your third-party software instead. Using Windows Media Player converts the file twice, first into WMA format and then back into the format used on music CDs, causing a loss in quality. Most third-party programs can copy a CD more quickly, without any loss of quality.

- Do you mind a two-second gap between songs? Windows Media Player automatically adds this gap between tracks, and this setting cannot be changed. Most third-party programs allow you to eliminate this gap.

To begin creating a CD, select the playlist you want to use and then click Copy To CD Or Device in Windows Media Player's taskbar. A window like the one below opens. Your playlist appears in the left pane, with all tracks selected. This list also shows the total playing time for the selected tracks. The right pane shows the current content of the CD, if any.

Compare the total time figure at the bottom of the left pane with the available time figure at the bottom of the right. If the total time exceeds the available time, the Status column displays the message Will Not Fit for some tracks. Clear the check box to the left of one or more tracks to adjust your selection until all the tracks fit.

When you're ready to copy, click Copy Music in the Copy To CD Or Device window. The CD-burning process might take longer than you expect: Windows Media Player checks the license for each track, converts it to a temporary file (in uncompressed CD Audio format), and then burns the contents of the playlist to your CD.

Key Points

- Windows Media Player can automatically begin playing a music CD as soon as you insert it into the CD drive on your computer.

- You can copy (or "rip") tracks from a music CD and save them as digital audio files on your computer.

- Windows Media Player connects to the Internet and downloads information about CDs you play, including album and song titles.

- For the best audio quality, increase the bit rate that Windows Media Player uses when copying music tracks to your computer. Higher bit rates require more storage space.

- When you download music from the Internet, the digital license might restrict your ability to play back the song.

- If you have any licensed music on your computer, be sure to back up your licenses.

- You can create custom playlists to combine your favorite tracks, to reorder tracks on a favorite album, or to mix and match tracks for use in a custom CD.

- To play back a DVD in Windows Media Player, you must have a decoder.

- After creating a custom playlist from saved music tracks, you can burn a custom CD with Windows Media Player.

Chapter 12

Picture-Perfect Digital Photography

Nothing shows off the amazing capabilities of your PC better than a digital camera. Snap all the pictures your memory card can hold. Then plug the camera into your PC and let Microsoft Windows XP do its magic. With the help of a handy wizard, you'll have your photos neatly organized in no time, ready for a place of honor on your screen or in a picture frame. Now, if you can just remember where you left the lens cap...

Out of the Camera, Onto the Computer

Some of the most impressive new features in Windows XP make it easier for you to connect your digital camera to your computer so that you can download images and begin working with them immediately. For most new cameras, getting your digital pictures out of the camera and onto the PC is practically effortless.

Note   In this chapter, I'm assuming your camera is compatible with Windows XP and that you're not using any special software that came with the computer or camera. However, if your camera is more than two years old, it's possible it won't be able to communicate with Windows XP, in which case you may have no choice but to use that third-party software to manage your camera. An even better option for transferring pictures to your computer from an older camera is to buy an inexpensive memory card reader that plugs into your PC's universal serial bus (USB) port. Pop the card out of the camera, plug it into the reader, and take advantage of most of the features I describe in this chapter.

As with any hardware device, you'll need to set up your camera first. If you're lucky, Windows already includes a *driver* for your camera, and it installs automatically when you first connect the camera to your computer's USB port and switch on the power. If Windows can't find a suitable driver in its collection, you'll have to download the correct driver from the camera maker's Web site and supply it when prompted by the Add Hardware Wizard.

See Also   *For more details about drivers and step-by-step help setting up a new hardware device, see Chapter 4, "Microsoft Windows and Hardware."*

After the correct driver is installed, you'll find a new icon in the Scanners And Cameras folder in My Computer, like the one shown here. Each time you connect the camera to the computer, the Scanner And Camera Wizard should start automatically. To start the wizard on your own, double-click the camera icon.

The wizard's job is to help you copy pictures from your camera to your computer. Here's how:

1   Click past the Welcome page.

2   On the Choose Pictures to Copy page, shown in Figure 12-1, you see thumbnail images of every photo stored on your camera's memory card. By default, all images are selected. Adjust the selections, if necessary, and click Next.

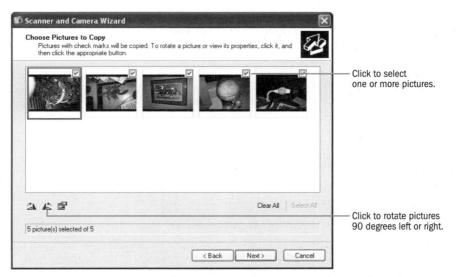

Click to select
one or more pictures.

Click to rotate pictures
90 degrees left or right.

Figure 12-1 Decide which pictures are keepers; clear the check box for any that you don't want to copy to your PC.

3 On the Picture Name And Destination page, enter the name you want to use for all downloaded pictures (the wizard tacks on a three-digit number—001, 002, and so on—at the end of each name). Choose the location where you want the photos to be copied and click Next.

Tip Should you select the Delete Pictures From My Device After Copying Them option? Only if you're certain that the pictures can be successfully transferred to your computer. If you're still experimenting with your new camera, don't delete the pictures until you're sure they've made it safely across the cable.

---

4 As the wizard transfers your photos, it displays the dialog box shown on the next page. At a glance, you can see a large preview of each image, along with a summary of the file name and location where it will be stored. After the wizard finishes copying pictures, click Next.

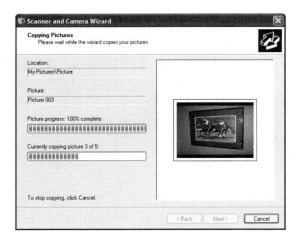

5 On the final page, choose whether you want to publish the pictures to a Web site (such as MSN Groups), order prints from an online photo site, or just close the wizard. Click Next to finish.

Although the wizard is quick and easy, there's a faster, smarter way to get your pictures onto your computer without using the wizard at all. You can configure Windows XP so that when you connect the camera, Windows automatically creates a new subfolder in My Pictures, using the current date as the folder name, copies all your pictures to that folder, and deletes them from the camera after the transfer is complete. To set up this hands-free configuration, right-click the camera's icon in the Scanners And Cameras folder and choose Properties. Click the Events tab and set the options as shown here.

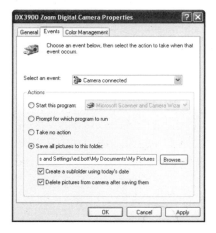

Organizing Your Images

As I noted in Chapter 9, "Making Windows Work Your Way," the My Pictures folder is one of several system folders that Windows XP uses to store specific types of data files. Your digital camera automatically downloads its pictures into this location unless you specify otherwise, and if you have a photo-editing program, it probably defaults to this location as well when opening and saving files.

When you open the My Pictures folder in a Windows Explorer window, you'll probably notice the Picture Tasks pane, shown below, right away. The list of options varies, depending on the current selection.

Tip   Do you have a favorite picture that you never tire of looking at? Then why not use it as the background image on your Windows desktop? In the My Pictures folder, select the image and then, in the Picture Tasks list, click the Set As Desktop Background option.

In the My Pictures folder, different views offer different perspectives on your digital photo collection. For instance, in Filmstrip view, you can select a single image from the list along the bottom and see it in a large preview pane at the top of the window. In Details view, you can still see preview images of each picture. Look at the bottom of the Task pane: the Details pane previews the selected image and provides details about its size, the date on which the photo was taken, and so on.

Putting Your Pictures on Paper

Digital pictures are great for e-mail, but how do you show them off when you run into a friend at the market or the mall? With an inexpensive color printer and some high-quality paper, you can turn out good-looking images that are suitable for framing (or for carrying in your wallet). With the help of a professional photo-finishing service, you can turn high-resolution photos into eye-popping museum-quality prints.

Printing digital photos on a color printer isn't that different from printing any document on any printer. The unique challenge with color printers, however, is to keep costs down by making the most efficient use possible of expensive color ink and glossy photo-finishing paper. Windows XP can help. When you send a digital photo to your printer, Windows offers a handy wizard that lets you choose exactly which size image you want and squeeze as many pictures as possible onto that expensive paper.

Tip   If you're tired of wasting paper on less-than-perfect prints, get in the habit of performing a test first. Choose the black-ink settings for your printer and use ordinary paper instead of expensive glossy paper. You won't want to keep the resulting images, but you can see at a glance whether the cropping you selected is right for your images.

To use the Photo Printing Wizard, perform the following steps:

1   Select one or more images from the My Pictures folder and in the Picture Tasks list, click Print This Picture or Print The Selected Pictures. The Photo Printing Wizard opens.

2   Click Next to skip the Welcome page.

3   On the Picture Selection page, use the check boxes above each image to confirm that you've selected the right pictures to print, and then click Next.

4   Use the selections on the Printing Options page to choose a printer. If your color printer lets you choose from several paper types, click Printing Preferences and choose the correct one. (In the example shown below, I've selected HP Premium Photo Paper for my Hewlett-Packard color inkjet printer; if you have a different printer, your options will probably be different.) Click Next to continue.

5 On the Layout Selection page, choose the way you want to arrange your photos on the printed page. You can take your choice of a wide range of layouts, as shown in Figure 12-2. Click Next to send the job to your printer.

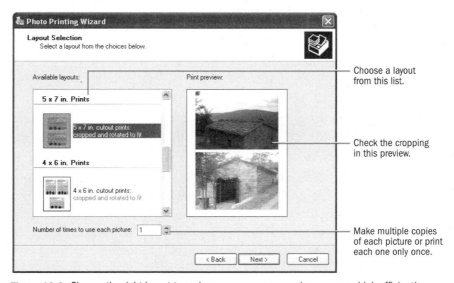

Figure 12-2 Choose the right layout to make sure you use expensive paper and ink efficiently.

> **Caution**   If you're particular about your photos, you'll want to look carefully at the
> results of each layout before selecting it. In all but a few cases, Windows has to *crop*
> the images you selected—that is, trim away a part of the top, bottom, or sides of the
> image—to make them fit in the selected layout. Before you waste paper, check the
> cropping to be sure it's acceptable.

You say your printer turns out less than perfect printed copies? For your very best images, use an online photo-printing service instead. From the My Pictures folder, select one or more images and choose Order Prints Online from the Picture Tasks list to access the Online Print Ordering Wizard, shown below. Follow the instructions to select one of the available photo-finishing firms, choose which sizes you want for your prints, and supply a credit card number. Then all you have to do is wait for your prints to arrive in the mail.

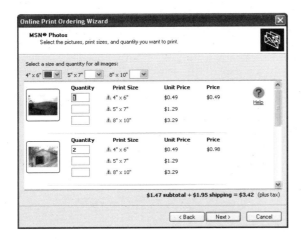

E-Mailing Photos to Friends and Family

Today's digital pictures can capture a staggering amount of data. With 5 *mega-pixels* or more of resolution, they even approach the quality of conventional film. The problem with those super-high-density images, of course, is that the resulting image files are huge! That poses special problems when you want to send a photo to a friend or family member. If you attach the file to an e-mail message, you run the risk that the message will be rejected by one or more mail servers along the line. Not only that, but when the recipients open the attached file, they might discover that it's too large to view comfortably, especially if they're using an older version of Windows and their system is configured to open images in Internet Explorer.

Lingo A *pixel* is a single dot of color in an image. A *megapixel* is a unit of measurement that equals 1 million pixels. The more megapixels your camera can capture on each image, the more detail you'll see. Of course, those high-resolution images also take up tons of disk space, and high-resolution cameras cost significantly more than those that are limited to lower resolutions. Make the tradeoffs based on your budget and how you plan to use your camera.

So how do you shrink the pictures to a manageable size that's safe for sending?

No problem. Just perform the following steps:

1 From the My Pictures window, select the image or images you want to send.

2 Right-click and choose Mail Recipient from the Send To menu.

3 In the Send Pictures Via E-Mail dialog box, click Show More Options. This expands the dialog box so that you see the three choices under Make My Pictures This Size, as shown below. (To restore the smaller, simpler dialog box, click Show Fewer Options.)

4 Select the size you want to use for the converted images. When in doubt, choose the Small option.

5 Click OK. After a brief pause as the files are converted, a blank e-mail message window opens, with the selected (and now shrunken) images attached.

6 Address the message, add any text to the body of the message, and click Send.

When you use this trick, your files are converted, if necessary, to JPEG format, shrunk in size, and compressed. The results can be very impressive. When

I used this option on an original digital image in bitmap format, it went from more than 800 kilobytes (KB) in size to approximately 56 KB, a reduction of more than 90 percent!

Tip   Using this technique causes some loss of image quality in the shrunken copy. If you're intent on sending the best possible copy, use the Compressed Folder feature, found on the Send To menu, to zip the picture or pictures and send that zipped archive through e-mail. You won't save as much space, but the recipient can see the full, original image with no loss of detail.

Posting Your Pictures on the Web

When you want to share a collection of photos with a group of people, e-mail is a woefully inefficient distribution mechanism. Instead, post the pictures to a free or inexpensive Web-based service and send a link to that site through e-mail. This technique offers several advantages over the e-mail route: You can use thumbnails to let your audience quickly preview pictures and then download the larger, high-resolution versions of only those they're really interested in. Your audience can view the pictures from any Web browser, even if they're away from the computer where they receive e-mail. In most cases, you can restrict access to the Web site to only those persons you select, by using logon credentials and a password to protect the site.

Note   If you're a skilled Webmaster, you can also post your images to a personal Web site that you purchase from a Web hosting service. You don't have to go to that extent, however, if all you want to do is share pictures with other people. The two services currently available through the Web Publishing Wizard are simple to manage and convenient to use. In addition, you can find a variety of third-party alternatives, including Shutterfly (*http://www.shutterfly.com*), Ofoto (*http:// www.ofoto.com*), and PictureTrail (*http://www.picturetrail.com*), to name just a few. To find many more, go to a good Internet search engine and search for *free photo services*.

The Web Publishing Wizard built into Windows XP lets you post pictures directly to either of two Web-based services: MSN Groups (a free service) or XDrive Plus (a paid service). (By the time you read this, additional options might be available.) In either case, you must sign on with a Microsoft Passport to access the account. If you select the MSN Groups option, you can choose to upload your files to a private folder, or you can create a new group and make it visible in the public directory, where others can find it and view it.

The wizard's steps are straightforward. Before uploading the photos, it offers to adjust the sizes of your pictures, as shown on the next page. This process is similar to the wizard you use to shrink and compress images for sending through e-mail.

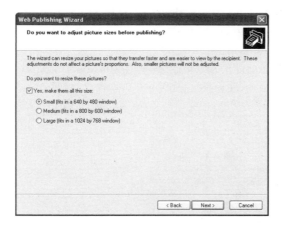

Tip As a general rule, I recommend resizing images to 800 × 600 resolution for posting on the Web. A large number of Windows users have their screens set to this resolution, so if you choose the larger 1024 × 768 size, they'll be forced to scroll to see the entire image.

When you're finished with the Web Publishing Wizard, your photos are available for you at the URL listed on the wizard's final screen. Using options at this address, you can share the site with other people.

Note Don't mistake this Web Publishing Wizard with the tools you use to send files to a Web site created using Microsoft FrontPage or other professional-quality Web site development tools. The purpose of the Web Publishing Wizard is to help you quickly transfer files to and from a standard storage location. For more intricate Web site development tasks, you'll need more powerful tools.

Slide Shows and Screen Savers

After you've built up a big enough collection of digital photos, you might want the option to display those photos on the screen using something other than Windows Explorer. In addition, you might want to create slide shows for special occasions, taking a group of images and converting them to a format that you can display one after the other, using the entire screen, without requiring any input from the viewer.

For these tasks, Windows offers two useful tools. The first gives you the ability to create a slide show on the fly, using a group of pictures you select. To choose this option, open the My Pictures folder and select the images you want to use for your slide show. Then, in the Picture Tasks list, click the View As A Slide Show option. The first image you selected appears on the screen, with each additional image following a few seconds after the previous one. The slide show view is cool because it adds a dramatic black border around each image, clearing away all the normal Windows screen elements. As Figure 12-3 shows, you can use the VCR-style controls to start or pause the slide show and to move through the pictures one at a time.

Figure 12-3 If these play controls aren't visible in your slide show window, just move the mouse pointer.

Tip   Out of the box, Windows XP doesn't include any way for you to package a slide show and save it for other people to view. However, a pair of tools available at Microsoft's Web site lets you do this with ease. Visit *http://www.microsoft.com/windowsxp/pro/downloads/powertoys.asp* and download the HTML Slide Show Wizard or the CD Slide Show Generator from the collection of PowerToys for Windows XP. The latter is an especially effective way to send large collections of photos to people who don't have high-speed Internet access. If you're intrigued by these PowerToys and want to learn more, pick up a copy of the *Microsoft Windows XP Power Toolkit* by Walter Bruce, Paul Thurrott, and David Chernicoff (Microsoft Press, 2002).

Try This! If you have a collection of especially good looking pictures, why not use them as your screen saver? One of the choices in the list of built-in Windows XP screen savers is called My Pictures Slideshow. Follow these steps to customize it for maximum results:

1 Click Start and then click My Pictures on the right side of the Start menu.

2 In your My Pictures folder, click Make A New Folder from the File And Folder Tasks list in the left pane. (If this link isn't available, choose New and then Folder from the File menu.)

3 Give the newly created subfolder a descriptive name, such as My Screen Saver.

4 Select the photos you want to appear in your screen saver and move or copy them into the newly created folder.

> **See Also** If you need a refresher course on moving and copying files, see the section "Organizing Files," on page 236.

5 Click Start and open Control Panel. Click the Appearance And Themes category and then click Choose A Screen Saver from the Pick A Task list. (If you're using the Classic view of Control Panel, double-click Display and click the Screen Saver tab to reach the exact same place.)

6 On the Screen Saver tab of the Display Properties dialog box, choose My Pictures Slideshow from the Screen Saver list and then click Settings.

7 In the My Pictures Screen Saver Options dialog box, shown below, select the options you want for your screen saver. If you're not sure what an option does, click the question mark icon in the top right corner of the dialog box and then click the option to see a pop-up help message.

8 Click Browse, select the subfolder you created at the beginning of this procedure, and click OK.

9 Click OK again to close the My Pictures Screen Saver Options dialog box.

10 In the Display Properties dialog box, adjust the Wait time, if necessary, and then click OK to save your changes.

Now, keep your hands off the keyboard and mouse for a few minutes and wait for your screen saver to kick in. When it does, you'll see the pictures from your new subfolder, with nifty transition effects and a tasteful black border.

Key Points

- Thanks to Plug and Play, most new digital cameras work directly with Windows XP.

- To adjust settings for your digital camera, find its icon in the Scanners And Cameras folder.

- The My Pictures folder is the default storage location for all image files in Windows XP.

- Use the Picture Tasks list in the My Pictures folder to order prints online or upload them to a Web site.

- When you print digital photos from Windows XP, the Photo Printing Wizard lets you make efficient use of expensive paper by laying out the images intelligently.

- When sending photos to friends and family through e-mail, use the Windows XP option to make those images smaller.

- If you have a large collection of images, you can post them on the Web and grant access to friends or family members so they can see the photos from any Web browser.

- You can create a slide show from your favorite digital photos and send the saved file to friends and family members.

- Take your favorite digital photos and use them as a screen saver, with slick transitions and a sharp black border.

Chapter 13

Managing User Accounts

In Microsoft Windows XP, user accounts make it easy for each person who uses a computer to have his or her own customized work environment. Each user can make all manner of settings to customize the appearance and operation of Windows—selecting a desktop background, color schemes, mouse pointers, and so on. More importantly, various program settings and options are unique to each user account. For example, Favorites (bookmarked Web sites) in Microsoft Internet Explorer are stored on a per-user basis and separate e-mail accounts can be set up for each user. And each user has a dedicated area for storing documents and other files.

User accounts also impose security—keeping one user from clobbering another user's files, for example—that wasn't available in the user profiles feature included with Windows 95, Windows 98, and Windows Millennium Edition (Windows Me).

In this chapter, I'll show you how to set up a user account for each person who uses your computer. Then I'll explain how to store your documents so that you can share the ones that you want others to be able to access—and keep your personal documents safe from prying eyes and inexperienced users.

How User Accounts Control Access to Your Computer

In addition to personalization, user accounts form the basis of security in Windows XP. Every object on a Windows XP–based computer—files, folders, and printers, for example—includes a list of which users are allowed to access the object and what each user who has access is allowed to do. (For example, a file might be configured so that certain users can read the file but not modify it.)

Note   Only folders and files on NTFS–formatted disk drives have this sort of security. Disk drives formatted using the FAT or FAT32 file systems are wide open to any user who wants to look at, modify, or delete folders and files—whether maliciously or inadvertently. This is one of the key reasons I strongly recommend that you use NTFS rather than FAT or FAT32.

When you log on by clicking your name on the Welcome screen (and entering your password, if one is required), Windows knows who you are, and each time you try to access an object, Windows checks to see what you're permitted to do with that object. The most significant benefit of user accounts, therefore, is the ability to ensure that only authorized users have access to files you want to protect.

See Also   Of course, providing this level of protection requires that you assign a password to your account; I explain how to do this in the section "Logging On," on page 25.

This benefit extends to program files and system files as well as documents. Users who log on using limited accounts can't inadvertently delete files in the Windows folder, for example. The setup routine for some programs configures the program to ensure that only certain users can run the program and to ensure that the program's files can't be mistakenly deleted.

This user-based security applies to each user's work space. Each user has a private desktop and My Documents folder, along with similar personal folders, such as My Music, My Pictures, and so on. Only that user has full access to these personal files; other users have limited access or none at all. This form of organization provides convenience as well as security. Your media library, with its well-worn classic rock albums, won't be cluttered with your son's hip hop collection. Your kitchen remodeling plans are safely segregated from your daughter's poetry and other musings.

I recommend that you set up an account for each person who uses your computer. Aside from the benefits I just outlined, user accounts control the amount of system access (and, by extension, the amount of damage a user can inflict) granted to each user. You'll probably want to set up an account for yourself and another for your computer-savvy spouse as computer administrators. Your trusted teenager might need computer administrator privileges (for example, a computer administrator account is required to install most programs), whereas you're better off creating a limited account for a young child.

> **See Also** For information about different account types, see the section "Computer Administrator vs. Limited: What's the Difference?" on page 284.

Creating a New Account

When you install Windows XP from its original CD-ROM on a new computer, the setup program gives you an opportunity to create an account for each user. However, if you've already installed Windows—or if Windows was preinstalled by your computer manufacturer—that opportunity is past. What you see on the Welcome screen represents your current collection of user accounts. Creating a new account at any time is a simple process, however.

To create a user account—and to perform many other account-management tasks—use the User Accounts option in Control Panel. It's one of the easier ones to find. A User Accounts icon appears whether you use Category view or Classic view. Figure 13-1 shows the User Accounts window.

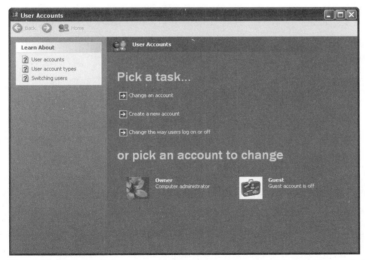

Figure 13-1 In User Accounts, you can pick a task from the list at the top or click an existing account name to perform other common account-management tasks.

> **Note** If you use Windows XP Professional and your computer is joined to a domain, you'll see a different version of User Accounts—one that looks more like an ordinary Properties dialog box. In this situation, management of user accounts is best left to your network administrator, because you'll ordinarily use a domain user account (one that's stored on a network server called a domain controller) instead of a local user account (one that's stored only on your computer).

With User Accounts open, here's how to create a new account:

1 Under Pick A Task, click Create A New Account. (Big surprise, huh?)

2 On the next screen, type the user's name in the New Account text box and click Next. You can type the new user's full name—that is, first name followed by a space and the last name—but I recommend that you don't. Instead, just use the first name. If you need to add something to uniquely identify the user (to differentiate Ed and Ed Jr., for example), don't include a space. Although Windows allows you to include spaces in user names, doing so can cause problems with some applications. I'll show you how to safely insert spaces or make other changes to the name *after* you create the account.

3 Select either Computer Administrator or Limited and then click Create Account. The following section describes the important differences between these two types of accounts.

That's all there is to it. Windows creates the necessary folders to store the new user's *profile* and his or her name now appears on the Welcome screen, ready to log on. Nevertheless, you'll probably want to make some changes to the account before long. (For example, you might want to insert a space or change the name some other way to make it more legible.) I explain how in the section "Changing an Existing Account," on page 286.

Lingo   A *user profile* contains all the settings and files for a user's work environment. Most of the user's settings—everything from the user's desktop background choice to e-mail account settings—are stored in a portion of the Windows registry dedicated to that user. A profile also includes all of a user's personal files—the ones on the desktop as well as those in My Documents and similar folders.

Computer Administrator vs. Limited: What's the Difference?

The User Accounts option in Control Panel lets you set up two types of accounts: computer administrator and limited.

Computer administrators are the most powerful, of course, and have full control of all the computer's resources. Computer administrators' privileges include the ability to

■ Create, change, and delete user accounts.

■ Access all files.

■ Install programs and start or stop services.

■ Share folders so that other users can access them across a network.

- Install or remove hardware devices and make other system configuration changes.

- Log on in Safe Mode.

Limited users, by contrast, have a number of restrictions to prevent them from inflicting harm. Limited users can

- Change (or remove) the logon password and associated Microsoft .NET Passport for their own user account.

- Change the user account picture, desktop theme, and other desktop settings.

- Use programs that have been installed on the computer.

- Create, change, and delete files in their own document folders.

- View files in shared document folders.

For the best security, you should give all users limited accounts. That's because when you're logged on as a computer administrator, you have virtually unlimited power over the computer. This power can be used for evil as well as good, of course. If you open an e-mail attachment that installs a Trojan horse program, it runs without a hitch and allows a hacker to take over your computer from across the Internet. However, if you're logged on using a limited account, Windows prevents the program from inflicting widespread damage. For this reason, you might consider creating a new computer administrator account just for your computer management tasks, and then demoting your own everyday account to limited status. If you find this arrangement too constraining or you find it necessary to frequently switch to your administrative account to perform maintenance tasks, you can always abandon this strategy and change your account back to computer administrator status.

In short, the difference between computer administrator and limited accounts comes down to a tradeoff between convenience and safety.

Using the Guest Account

The Guest account is a special account that's intended for use by occasional users to whom you want to provide secure, limited access. You might find it useful to configure the Guest account for use by a visitor, houseguest, or babysitter, for example.

The Guest account has access to your computer's programs, to files in the Shared Documents folder, and to files in the Guest profile. This gives a guest sufficient tools to check e-mail, browse the Web, and work on his or her own documents as well as those stored in Shared Documents. However, a Guest account user can't view or modify other users' documents, nor can a Guest user modify system settings, install programs, create or modify the Guest password, or otherwise damage your computer.

To enable the Guest account, you must be logged on as a computer administrator. In Control Panel, open User Accounts, click Guest, and then click Turn On The Guest Account. Thereafter, Guest appears with the other accounts on the Welcome screen, and anyone can log on as Guest simply by clicking the Guest icon. No password is required.

You can't delete the Guest account with User Accounts, but you can disable it if you no longer want it to appear on the Welcome screen. Open User Accounts, click Guest, and then click Turn Off The Guest Account.

Changing an Existing Account

With the User Accounts option in Control Panel, you can change any of several user account settings. If you're logged on as a limited user, you can make changes only to your own account. If you're logged on as a computer administrator, you can make changes to all other accounts as well as your own.

To make changes to a user account, open User Accounts in Control Panel. If you're logged on as a computer administrator, at the bottom of the window, click the name of the account you want to change. (If you're logged on as a limited user, opening User Accounts takes you directly to the change window for your own account, as shown here.)

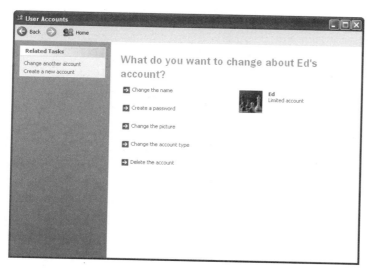

Tip   Don't waste your time clicking Change An Account under Pick A Task. That merely displays a list of accounts like the one below the Pick A Task links. You'll then have to click the account you want to change—just as you can do on the User Accounts home page.

Changing a User's Name

The full name associated with an account appears on the Welcome screen and on the Start menu. Therefore, you'll probably want to make the name read normally—that is, with normal capitalization, spacing, and so on. You can even use periods, hyphens, and certain other symbols that sometimes appear in names. (You can't, however, include a comma.) If your name is Katie McAskill-White, for example, you can have your whole name appear on-screen. (Of course, if only members of your own family use your computer, a surname might be superfluous.)

Tip   If Windows came preinstalled on your computer, the only account name visible initially is called Owner. Why not change *Owner* to your own name? Just remember that when you create a user account or change its name, the length of the name is limited to 20 characters.

When you first create an account, the full name is the same as the user name. Internally, Windows uses the user name to identify your account and determine which files you're allowed to use. The user name is also the one you use if Windows asks you to enter your user name and password or if you use certain *command-line utilities*.

Lingo   *Command-line utilities* are programs that run in a Command Prompt window. A Command Prompt window, which you open by choosing Command Prompt from the Accessories folder under All Programs on the Start menu, displays a bare prompt, similar to the one in the old MS-DOS operating system. Instead of having a menu of commands to choose from, as in most programs for Windows, you must know exactly what to type in. But if you *do* know what to type, command-line utilities often provide a fast, powerful alternative for performing a variety of tasks.

To change the name, click Change The Name (or Change My Name if you are logged in as the user account whose name you're changing), type the new name, and click Change Name. Doing so changes only the full name (the one that appears on the Welcome screen and Start menu), leaving the user name unchanged. This option is available only if you're logged on as a computer administrator.

Assigning or Changing an Account Password

If your computer is located where someone else can access it, you should seriously consider assigning a password to each of your accounts. At the very least, password-protect your computer administrator accounts. Doing so makes it significantly more difficult for an untrusted visitor to sneak into your office and read your e-mail or poke around in your private files. It also protects your computer from inadvertent damage by less-experienced users (your kids, perhaps, or even your cat walking across the keyboard) who log on to your account with a single click or keystroke. Keep in mind that computer administrator accounts are all-powerful. They can access, modify, or delete any folder or file, and they can run any program. Even if you don't store classified secrets on your computer, you (or another user on the computer) undoubtedly have some files or information that would be difficult to replace—and are therefore safer if a password is required to log on to your account.

To assign a password to an account, follow these steps:

1 Click the account name in User Accounts and then click Create A Password.

2 Type your password two times (because the characters you type are obscured, typing it twice ensures that you type it the same each time) and type a password hint, as shown below. (If you're stumped at the Welcome screen because you can't remember your password, you can display the hint by clicking the blue question mark.) Then click Create Password.

3 If you're creating a password for your own account (an Administrator account), on the next screen, click Yes, Make Private if you want to prevent users with limited accounts from viewing your files (the ones in your My Documents folder and its subfolders). Otherwise, click No. For more information about this option, see the section "Making Your Files Private," on page 293.

Tip Creating a logon password for Windows provides a good level of security, but if you forget your password, you cannot log on to access your own files. Windows XP provides a solution: a password reset disk. To create one, click the Prevent A Forgotten Password link in the Related Tasks pane at the left side of the What Do You Want To Change About Your Account? page. (This link appears only for your own account; each user must create his or her own password reset disk.) For details, see the section "Logging On," on page 25.

If you've already assigned a password to the account, the process for changing the account is similar. In the window that lists things you can change, click Change The Password or Remove The Password. (If you are changing your own password, the option is Change My Password.) If you do this for an account other than your own (you must, of course, be logged on as a computer administrator to do this), you'll remove access to that user's personal *certificates* and to any stored user name/password combinations that person uses to access Web sites or network resources. (This is a security measure that prevents an unscrupulous computer administrator from changing another user's password and then gaining access to the user's deepest, darkest secrets.)

Lingo A *certificate* is a record that's used by secure computer systems to prove one's identity or to encrypt information so that others can't read it. Certificates are used by a variety of applications (Microsoft Outlook Express, for example) as well as Windows itself.

If you use Windows XP Home Edition, chances are good that you (or others who use your computer) don't have critical certificates or a large number of stored passwords—so the risk of locking someone out of their own information isn't great. Nonetheless, if you're changing or removing the other person's password because it's been forgotten, you're better off using a password reset disk.

Try This!   Next to your name on the Welcome screen and the Start menu, you'll see a small picture—perhaps a snowflake, a chess piece, or a soccer ball. Windows picks the picture from a limited
set, and I'm willing to bet that you don't closely resemble any of those. Here's how you can change
the picture to one that you choose, whether it's a picture of yourself of simply a picture that makes
you smile each time you see it:

1   Open the Start menu and click the picture to the left of your name at the top of the
menu. This nifty shortcut takes you to the same window that appears when you click
Change The Picture in User Accounts, as you can see here.

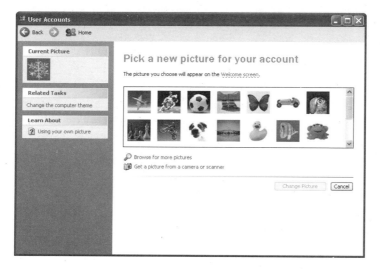

2   If a picture shown in the window strikes your fancy and is an appropriate match for your
personality, select it. If you want to use a picture that's not shown, click either of the two
links below the predefined pictures:

- Browse For More Pictures lets you select any picture stored on your computer. You
can use pictures in bitmap, GIF, JPEG, or PNG format.

- Get A Picture From A Camera Or Scanner lets you select a picture from an attached
camera or scan one using an attached scanner.

3   Click Change Picture.

When you select a picture from a file, a camera, or a scanner, Windows creates a copy of the
picture that's reduced to fit the picture box. If you want to fill the allotted space, use an image-editing
program to crop the picture to a square shape before you select it.

Working with Passwords and Passports

User Accounts is the place to manage your passwords (for logging on to Web sites and network resources that require you to enter a user name and password) and your .NET Passport. Unlike the other user account items you can change, which I described in the preceding sections, you can make the following changes only for your own account—the one with which you're currently logged on:

■ To work with your stored passwords, click the Manage My Network Passwords link in the Related Tasks pane at the left side of the What Do You Want To Change About Your Account? page. The Stored User Names And Passwords dialog box shows the names of sites and domains for which you have saved a user name and password (typically by selecting Remember My Password in the logon dialog box for a site or resource that's compatible with this feature). If you're using Windows XP Home Edition, you can review or delete user name/password combinations that Windows has stored for you automatically. With Windows XP Professional, you can also add credentials for other sites by clicking Add.

■ A .NET Passport is a service that lets you use an e-mail address and a password to log on to any .NET Passport–participating Web site. With a .NET Passport, you don't need to remember a different password for every site, nor do you need to re-enter your name, e-mail address, and other information at each site. The service is provided by Microsoft (and, indeed, you must have a .NET Passport to use certain Microsoft services and Web sites), but it's also used by hundreds of other sites. To associate a .NET Passport with your Windows account (and create one if you haven't already), click Set Up My Account To Use A .NET Passport on the What Do You Want To Change About Your Account? page. The .NET Passport Wizard leads you through the procedure. Thereafter, you can change your .NET Passport information or even switch to a different .NET Passport by clicking Change My .NET Passport.

Note The Stored User Names And Passwords feature remembers only passwords that you enter in logon dialog boxes. It is not related in any way to the AutoComplete feature, which stores user names and passwords you enter directly in text boxes on Web pages. For details about this feature, see the section "Filling In Forms and Remembering Passwords," on page 143.

Deleting an Account

Each user account consumes a chunk of disk drive space (the amount depends on how much the user stores in the My Documents folder, among other factors) as well as a bit of real estate on the Welcome screen. In addition, every user account is a potential entry point for someone trying to break into your computer. Therefore, you should delete any user accounts that you no longer need. If your spouse no longer needs to use your computer or if the kids have gone off to college, delete the unused accounts.

You can delete any account except one that is currently logged on, and it's a simple process: In Control Panel, open User Accounts, click the name of the account you want to delete, and then click Delete The Account. You need to be aware of a few wrinkles, however.

First, to delete an account, you must be logged on as a computer administrator.

When you click Delete The Account, you must decide what to do with the files in the account's user profile, as shown below.

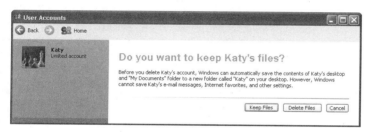

If you click Keep Files, Windows copies all files and folders on the user's desktop and in the user's My Documents folder to a folder on your desktop. The files and folders then become part of your profile and remain under your control. Everything else in the user's profile, including e-mail messages, Internet favorites, and settings stored in the registry, will be deleted after you confirm your intention in the next window that appears. Clicking Delete Files does just what you'd expect: Windows deletes all files in the user's profile, including the My Documents folder, desktop items, and everything else.

So, under what circumstances should you delete an account and all its files? Only when you're absolutely, positively certain you won't need those files again. When in doubt, err on the side of caution. Let's say you set up an account on your computer for a friend who's visiting for the holidays. You've swept up the New Year's confetti and driven her to the airport. When you sit down to your computer again, you might be tempted to delete your friend's account and all the files. Why not wait a few weeks instead? That way, you'll be covered if your friend calls, frantically searching for an important file or e-mail message she created while visiting you. Even better, let the account remain dormant. Change the password to something that's impossible to guess (after creating a password reset disk, of course), and set the account status to Limited. When your friend makes a return visit, you won't need to re-create the account; it's already set up.

> **Tip**   If you use Windows XP Professional, you can disable an unused account, making it impossible for anyone to use it until you enable it again. To disable an account, right-click the My Computer icon and choose Manage from the shortcut menu. In the Computer Management console, choose Local Users And Groups from the console tree on the left. Double-click the Users icon on the right, and then double-click the icon for the user account you want to disable. Choose Account Is Disabled and click OK. To re-enable the account, repeat the process and clear this option.

Making Your Files Private

A default installation of Windows XP includes security settings that make all the files in your profile visible to anyone who logs on using a computer administrator account. As Figure 13-2 shows, the My Computer window that a computer administrator sees displays an icon for each user's My Documents folder (conveniently identified with the user's name). With the default settings, a computer administrator can open any of these folders and view, modify, or delete another user's personal documents.

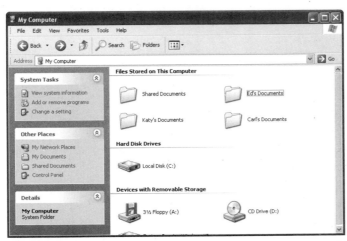

Figure 13-2 A user with an administrator account sees the My Documents folder of all users on your network.

By contrast, limited users have access only to files in their own profile. Other users' document folders do not appear in a limited user's view of My Computer. If a user with a limited account uses Windows Explorer to display another user's profile folder, an error message like the one shown on the next page blocks the attempt.

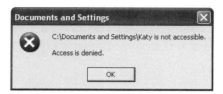

While this low-security setup provides a convenient way for people who share a computer to collaborate on projects, you might not want to allow unfettered access to all your files. For example, you might want to keep financial data and other private files locked out of the reach of your kids—not just to ensure privacy, but also to prevent accidental changes or deletion.

No matter which type of account you use (computer administrator or limited), you can designate folders in your profile to be private. When you do that, any other user (including a computer administrator) who tries to open your private file is rebuffed with an "access denied" message. To make a folder private, right-click the folder, click Sharing And Security, and select the Make This Folder Private check box, as shown here.

If you haven't already protected your account with a password, Windows warns you of the insecurity of a "private" folder that anyone can access by displaying the dialog box shown on the next page. Clicking Yes takes you directly to the page in User Accounts on which you can create a password.

Private folders are effective and easy to implement, but you should be aware of this feature's limitations:

■ The Make This Folder Private option is available only for folders within your own profile. Although some programs store documents you create in other folders, you can't make private a data folder stored outside your profile. Similarly, you can't make another user's folders private; individual users must make their own folders private.

■ Privacy protection applies to all files and subfolders (including the files and subfolders within the subfolders) within the folder you make private. You can't protect individual files.

If you want to make private your entire profile—which includes your My Documents folder, Start menu, desktop folders and files, Internet Explorer favorites, cookies, and other personal data—follow these steps:

1 Open the Start menu and choose Run.

2 In the Run box, type **%userprofile%** and click OK.

3 In the Windows Explorer window, click Up or press Backspace.

4 Right-click the folder with your user name and choose Sharing And Security from the shortcut menu to display the folder's Properties dialog box.

5 Select the Make This Folder Private check box.

6 Click OK to apply your changes and close the dialog box.

With your entire profile made private, your folders won't appear in the My Computer window of other users—even computer administrators.

Lingo Why do you need to add percent signs when entering *%userprofile%*? Those characters tell Windows to look for an *environment variable* instead of simply looking for a folder named *userprofile*. Environment variables are special shortcuts that can be different for each user. Typing *%userprofile%* guarantees that Windows will open the correct folder for the account under which you logged on.

Key Points

- User accounts provide a customized work environment, storage area, and security for each individual user.

- The security benefits of user accounts are available only if your disk drive has been formatted with NTFS.

- Computer administrator accounts have full control of the computer and all its files, whereas limited accounts provide greater security by restricting access to files and settings outside the limited user's profile.

- You create and manage user accounts with the User Accounts option in Control Panel. (If you have Windows XP Professional, you can also use the Local Users And Groups option in the Computer Management console for some tasks.)

- To create a new user account, open User Accounts and click Create A New Account.

- The Guest account allows convenient ad hoc use by occasional users without jeopardizing the security of your files.

- To change an account's name, password, picture, or other settings (or to delete an account), open User Accounts and then click the name of the account you want to change.

- You can change an account's picture by clicking the picture at the top of the Start menu.

- If you don't fully trust everyone who has physical access to your computer, assign a password to each account—at least to each computer administrator account.

- If you have a .NET Passport (for access to certain Web sites), you can associate it with your user account so that you log on automatically to those sites.

- Unless you make folders in your profile private, other users with computer administrator accounts can view, modify, or delete your files.

- To make a subfolder within your personal profile private, right-click it, choose Sharing And Security, and select Make This Folder Private.

Chapter 14

Setting Up and Running a Small Network

Once upon a time, you needed an engineering degree, a shelf full of technical manuals, and a couple of voodoo dolls to connect two or more computers in a local area network (LAN). Thanks to Microsoft Windows XP, those days are history. Setting up hardware can still be a challenge, but once you get the cables and network cards sorted out properly, a wizard handles the work of configuring your network. The result is that even a moderately experienced Windows user can hook up two or more computers running Windows XP in a matter of minutes.

And once you have your network set up, you can start reaping the benefits immediately, including the convenience of sharing files and printers with other users. You can even share an Internet connection, which can save you money in the long run. You don't have to surrender your privacy if you have a network, either—with Windows XP, you can have your own customized work space, and you can share documents that you want to make available to other users while keeping your private documents from prying eyes.

Do You Need a Network?

If you have more than one PC in your home or small office, you can share resources between them by setting up a LAN. Even the most basic two-PC network can offer some significant advantages:

- **Shared storage space**   By sharing certain folders on your computer, you allow anyone on the network to open a shared report or play a music file in Windows Media Player.

- **Shared printers**   Do you have a laser printer connected to one computer and a color inkjet printer connected to another PC? By sharing those printers, you allow everyone else on the network to use whichever printer they want.

- **Shared Internet connection**   This benefit is especially important if you have a fast Internet connection, such as a cable modem. With a little extra hardware, you can share the Internet connection with every other computer on the network.

- **Games**   Do you like the head-to-head action of multiplayer games? Over a fast LAN, these games take on a whole new dimension.

What Hardware Does Your Network Need?

So, you've decided you want to set up a network. Now what? Before your computers can communicate with one another, you need to add the right hardware. Each computer needs a device called a *network adapter*, which transmits and receives *packets* of information among other computers on the network. In addition, you probably need a hub, switch, or other central connecting point.

Lingo   When Windows sends data across a network, it chops the transmission into manageable chunks called *packets*, each of a fixed size. Each packet has an envelope, which contains the address of the destination computer and information about how to reassemble the packets into the file or message that was originally sent.

Here's a quick shopping list:

- **Network adapters**   You'll need one of these devices for each PC on your network. Some newer computers (especially portable PCs) include built-in network adapters. For a newer desktop computer, you can install an internal card into an open slot. If you'd rather not hassle with taking the cover off the computer, get a network adapter that plugs into the universal serial bus (USB) port instead. With portable computers, you also have the option of using a network adapter in the PCMCIA format, commonly referred to as a PC Card.

Tip   When buying a network adapter, be certain it is compatible with Windows XP. Also, make certain all adapters can communicate at the same speed. Typically, network adapters used in small networks can transmit and receive data at either 10 megabits per second (Mbps) or 100 Mbps. For maximum flexibility, you should get adapters that can work at either speed—look for 10/100 in the name or product description. Make sure your hub or switch is rated at the same speed as the network adapters on your network!

■   **A hub or switch**   As you might guess from the name, this is the part of your network where everything comes together. Each computer plugs into the hub or switch—a small box that contains some electronic components, a few flashing lights, and LAN ports with RJ-45 jacks. For a simple home network, a four-port hub is fine. Some hardware manufacturers now offer devices that combine the functions of a router and a hub in a single box. If you plan to share a high-speed Internet connection, this is an excellent way to do so.

■   **Cables**   For a standard network, you need unshielded twisted-pair (UTP) Category 5 cabling, with an RJ-45 connector on either end. This wire (sometimes called a patch cable) looks a lot like ordinary insulated telephone wire, except that it includes eight individual color-coded strands instead of four. Each computer needs to connect to the hub through its own run of cable. Make sure each cable is long enough to accommodate your physical arrangement.

Tip   If your home network consists of only two computers, you can skip the expense of a hub or switch and connect them directly, using a *crossover cable* plugged into each computer's network adapter. Although a crossover cable looks exactly like a standard network cable, the internal wiring is different, with the connections on one pair of wires reversed. As soon as you add a third computer to the network, though, you'll need to add a hub or switch and replace the crossover cable with a standard patch cable.

Think of any logistical hassles you're likely to face. If your two computers are side-by-side in the home office, you can put the hub on the desk between them and plug both computers directly into it, using two short cables. On the other hand, hooking the kids' computer in the basement to Dad's upstairs PC forces you to think about more creative wiring techniques, such as a wireless network (a more expensive option than a wired network, although costs of wireless networks have dropped dramatically in recent years) or one that lets your networked computers connect over your existing telephone or power wiring. If you choose the latter option, be absolutely certain that the hardware you select is compatible with Windows XP.

Making Network Connections

Setting up your network is a two-step process. First, you must install the required hardware and drivers. Then, you use the Network Setup Wizard to configure the Windows networking components so that computers on the network can communicate with one another. In this section, I assume that you're using a standard network adapter in each computer and hooking up the network through a hub or switch.

Tip   To set up any network components, you must be logged on as a member of the Administrators group. If you're the owner of the computer, this should be no problem. If someone else set up your user account as limited, you'll need to ask that person's permission to proceed.

Setting Up Your Hardware

To set up your network adapter, follow the instructions in Chapter 4, "Microsoft Windows and Hardware." If you've plugged in a USB network adapter, you'll see a Plug and Play message almost immediately, alerting you that Windows has found a new device. If you've installed an internal network adapter, Windows should detect the new card after you restart your computer and display Plug and Play messages as it installs a driver.

For network adapters whose drivers are included with Windows XP, no further configuration is necessary. If Windows can't find a suitable driver for your new hardware, click Have Disk when Windows asks you to select a driver. If you downloaded an updated driver, point Windows to that location; otherwise, use the floppy disk or CD that came with your network adapter.

After setting up the network adapter on each computer, plug in one end of a Category 5 cable to the network adapter's RJ-45 port and connect the other end to the hub. When you've finished this process for each computer on the network, you're ready to run the Network Setup Wizard.

Checking Your Network Configuration

After you've successfully installed your networking hardware, Windows automatically creates a local connection that includes all the networking components you need to start. To see the settings for your computer, open Control Panel and choose Network Connections. (You'll find this link in the Network And Internet Connections category.) Right-click Local Area Connection and choose Properties.

Note   If you have more than one network adapter installed in your computer, you'll see multiple connections in the LAN Or High-Speed Internet category. Look at the text under the connection name to see the brand name of the network adapter, which offers one clue. If that doesn't work, unplug one cable. The text under the connection name tells you which one you just disconnected. The text under the connection name is visible only if you've selected Tiles from the View menu.

Figure 14-1 shows the networking components installed as part of a standard installation of Windows XP Professional, as follows:

- **Client For Microsoft Networks**   This piece of software allows your computer to connect to another computer running just about any version of Microsoft Windows, including Windows 95, Windows 98, and Windows Millennium Edition (Windows Me).

- **File And Printer Sharing For Microsoft Networks**   This service allows other computers on your network to connect to shared resources on your computer.

- **QoS Packet Scheduler**   This component is installed only on systems running Windows XP Professional and is not available on Windows XP Home Edition. It enables Quality of Service (QoS) features on corporate networks and is not used on small networks.

- **Internet Protocol (TCP/IP)**   Transmission Control Protocol/Internet Protocol (TCP/IP) is the default *network protocol* used by Windows XP. It allows you to connect your computer to other computers on your network as well as to the Internet. For most network configurations, you can use the default TCP/IP settings.

Figure 14-1 When you install a network adapter, Windows XP automatically installs the components you need to connect to the rest of the computers on your network.

Lingo   A *network protocol* is the language that computers use to transfer data over a network. To successfully communicate on a LAN, all computers must use the same protocol.

Running the Network Setup Wizard

After you verify that you have set up your LAN properly, it's crucial that you complete the job by running the Network Setup Wizard. Do not skip this step, even if your network appears to be operating correctly! The initial configuration that Windows XP does automatically allows basic communication between computers on the network, but that's all. Running the Network Setup Wizard finishes the job by doing the following tasks:

■ Setting permissions on shared folders so that other people can access them

■ Adding essential information to the registry

■ Turning the Internet Connection Firewall on or off

■ Adjusting system policies so that file sharing works properly over the network

After you initially set up your network hardware, Windows should detect the new network connection and offer to run the Network Setup Wizard for you.

You can also start the wizard by opening the Network Connections folder and choosing Set Up A Home Or Small Office Network from the Network Tasks pane (if the Network Tasks pane is not visible, choose Network Setup Wizard from the File menu).

Tip When you set up your network for the first time, always run the Network Setup Wizard first on the computer that is sharing its Internet connection. If your network doesn't include a shared Internet connection or if you use a router or residential gateway to share the Internet connection, run the wizard first on your computer before setting up other network computers.

The Network Setup Wizard is extremely simple to use. Just point and click your way through its options, which vary depending on how you've configured your network to work with your Internet connection, as follows:

- If you're using the Internet Connection Sharing (ICS) feature built into Windows XP, set up the ICS host first. (You'll find the instructions in the section "Sharing Your Internet Connection," on page 131.) Then run the wizard on other computers on your network; for computers that are not running Windows XP, use the Windows XP CD to start the wizard.

- If you're using a hardware router or residential gateway to share your Internet connection, run the wizard on each computer in your network, choosing the second option in the dialog box shown here: This Computer Connects To The Internet Through Another Computer On My Network Or Through A Residential Gateway.

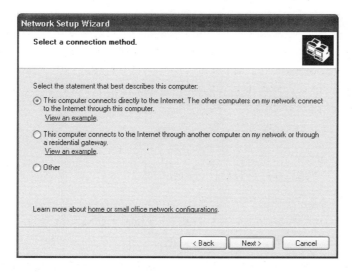

If you use ICS, the Network Setup Wizard enables the Internet Connection Firewall (ICF) on your connection to the Internet and disables it on the connection to the rest of your network. This provides essential protection against hackers and other potentially dangerous forces on the Internet. If you use a hardware router or residential gateway, the hardware device provides this protection, and the firewall is disabled on your LAN.

See Also   *For more details on how the Internet Connection Firewall works, see the section "Keep Hackers Out with a Firewall," on page 190.*

When you use the Network Setup Wizard on additional computers after you've set up ICS, the wizard automatically detects the presence of the ICS host and makes setup extremely easy. When prompted, choose Yes, Use The Existing Shared Connection For This Computer's Internet Access. The wizard automatically sets up the correct network and firewall settings.

One particular network configuration presents insurmountable security problems, however. If you plug your cable modem or DSL line directly into the hub or switch along with all the computers on your local network, you'll need to choose the Other option from the Select A Connection Method page of the Network Setup Wizard and then click Next. Then, on the Other Internet Connection Methods page, shown below, you select the top option, This Computer Connects Directly To The Internet Or Through A Network Hub. Other Computers On My Network Also Connect To The Internet Directly Or Through A Hub.

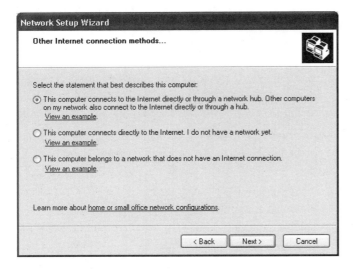

When you click Next, the wizard displays the stern warning shown here. If you continue with the wizard, you'll discover that your network doesn't work.

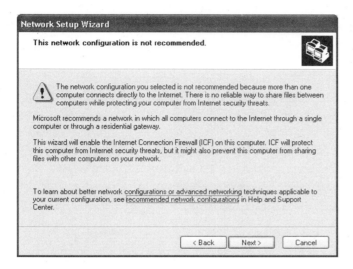

What's wrong with this configuration? Simply this: it allows packets of data from the Internet to travel on the same connections as those used for your local network. Unfortunately, Windows has no way of knowing which of those packets comes from one of your trustworthy network neighbors and which comes from a potentially dangerous attacker on the Internet. To safeguard your computer, the wizard therefore turns on the Internet Connection Firewall, which protects you from hackers but also blocks any traffic between computers on your network.

Caution   Although you can work around this restriction if you're persistent, I strongly discourage doing so. The risks are just too great. Instead, add another network card to one computer on the network and set it up as an ICS host, or invest in a hardware router to protect your network.

Naming Your Computer and Workgroup

No matter which option you select when using the Network Setup Wizard, you'll be asked to name your computer and your workgroup as part of the process. On the Give This Computer A Description And Name page, you'll notice that the computer name is already filled in; this name was assigned during the initial setup of Windows XP. You can add a description here, to make it easier for other network users to identify your computer when browsing for shared resources in the My Network Places folder, as shown on the next page.

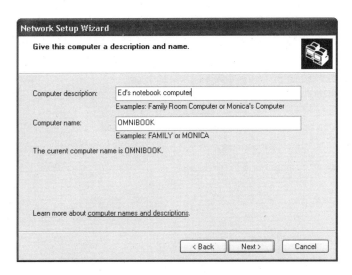

What if you don't like the name assigned to your computer? Although you can change its name at any time, doing so can have adverse consequences. It can cause problems with some Internet service providers (ISPs), for instance, especially cable companies, which often use the computer's name to establish your Internet connection. Unless the computer name is a serious problem for you, leave it alone and use the description to help other people identify it on the network.

Note   Your computer name cannot be the same as your logon name. Try using a variation of your logon name—if my user name is EDB, my computer name might be EDB_PC.

As for the workgroup name, you can choose any name you want. Just make sure it's the same on all computers on your network. The default name, MSHOME, is the easiest choice; however, you can select a different name if you want. Don't use spaces; do keep the workgroup name to 14 characters or fewer.

Setting Up a Wireless Network

If you have a portable computer, how do you keep it connected to the network? You could try snaking a 100-foot-long cable from your office into your living room, although you'd get tired of tripping over it after a day or two. A much better option is to install a wireless network adapter in your computer and a wireless access point on your network. Using this combination, you can maintain a network connection without any wires.

The good news is that wireless networking hardware has plummeted in price in recent years; the hardware still costs more than the wired alternatives, but with careful shopping and some technical help you can find deals that make wireless networks relatively affordable. Even better news is that Windows XP can automatically detect and configure your wireless adapter. You need to follow the hardware manufacturer's instructions to set up the wireless access point. After you've accomplished this task, connect the wireless adapter by sliding it into the PCMCIA slot on your portable PC or plugging it into a USB connector on a notebook or desktop PC. When you do, Windows displays the Connect To Wireless Network dialog box, as shown in Figure 14-2.

Figure 14-2 Windows XP automatically detects your wireless access point and configures your wireless network adapter.

Choose the name of your wireless network from the Available Networks list and click Connect. If you've set up the Wired Equivalent Privacy (WEP) option on your wireless access point, you'll need to enter your encryption key in the Network Key text box before you can make the connection.

If you have trouble connecting to your wireless network, try the following troubleshooting steps:

- Check with the manufacturer and make sure you have the latest drivers for Windows XP.

- If the wireless network includes its own configuration software, you must disable the "wireless zero configuration" feature in Windows XP. From the Network Connections folder, right-click the wireless connection icon and choose Properties. Then, on the Wireless Networks tab, clear the Use Windows To Configure My Wireless Network Settings option, as shown on the next page.

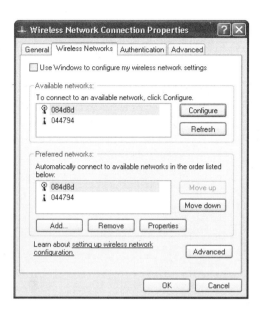

■ If the ID for your access point doesn't appear in the Available Networks frame, consult the documentation for the access point and change its settings so that the ID is automatically broadcast.

Troubleshooting Network Problems

What can go wrong with a LAN? In general, when your network stops working, the problem is likely to be relatively straightforward to diagnose and fix. Start by looking for other computers on the network. Open the My Network Places folder on each computer and browse through the computers you see there. Double-click on a computer icon to see the available shares for that computer. If you don't see anything in this folder, you still might be able to connect to other computers. Click Start, choose Run, and enter the name of another computer on the network, preceded by two slashes in the Run text box. If you're at a computer called BLUE and you want to reach the computer called RED, type the command **RED** and press Enter.

If you can't communicate, the first thing you should try is an automatic repair. In the Network Connections folder, right-click the icon for your balky network connection and choose the Repair option. Repair runs through common networking diagnostics and attempts to fix settings and configurations that report problems. If the repair procedure succeeds, you'll see a message almost immediately. If the operation is unsuccessful, you'll see an error message that might help you identify the problem further.

Fixing Physical Problems

When your network is knocked out, the first thing you should check is the physical connection. Look at the network adapter itself and at the hub or switch. Most have one or two lights that indicate the status of the network connection; a green light means you have a proper physical connection, and you should see flashing lights on the adapter when data is flowing between points. Next, look in the Network Connections folder. If you see the message "Network cable unplugged," as shown below, try removing and reinserting the cables at each connecting point. If you have a loose connection, this action could fix the problem immediately.

TCP/IP Problems

On a network that uses TCP/IP, configuring each machine's *IP address* is a crucial step.

Lingo   The *Internet Protocol (IP) address* is a unique identifier that consists of four numbers, each between 0 and 255, separated by dots. If you use ICS, for instance, the computer serving as the ICS host will assign an IP address of 192.168.0.1 to the network adapter that connects to the LAN. Other computers on the same network have addresses in the same subnet, such as 192.168.0.2.

IP addresses serve the same function on a network as ZIP codes do to the postal service. Each packet of information sent across the network is encoded with the IP address of the sender and the receiver, to ensure that it reaches its destination safely.

On the Internet, IP addresses have to be registered with the Domain Name System (DNS). The fact that a Web server is always at the same unique IP address allows any computer to reach it reliably from the Internet.

On your home network, however, only your router or the computer serving as the ICS host needs a registered (public) IP address. On the local side of the network, you don't need to use registered IP addresses, because you're not going to allow the entire world to access your network. Instead, you can use IP addresses from a range of numbers set aside for use on private networks. You must make sure that each address from within these ranges is unique on your network, but you don't need to worry if other people on the Internet are using those same addresses, because your network will never communicate directly with those networks. These address ranges are as follows:

- 10.0.0.0–10.255.255.255
- 172.16.0.0–172.31.255.255
- 192.168.0.0–192.168.255.255

In addition, all versions of Windows, including Windows XP, reserve a block of addresses in the range 169.254.*x.x* for private use.

Why should you care about these numbers? If you use Windows XP, you don't need to. When you first set up TCP/IP, each machine automatically assigns itself a unique address that is compatible with other computers on the network. This feature is called Automatic Private IP Addressing (APIPA), and as the name suggests, it automatically sets up these crucial networking components. Likewise, if you turn on the ICS feature, it handles all the details of assigning IP addresses to all other computers on the network, regardless of which Windows version they use.

To see the IP address in use for any computer on your network, open the Network Connections folder and double-click your connection to the Internet. Click the Support tab to see the current IP address and *subnet mask* for the local computer, as shown here.

Lingo The *subnet mask* is a set of numbers that distinguishes the network ID (which must be the same on each computer on the network) from the ID for each host computer (which must be unique for each computer on the network). A subnet mask of 255.255.0.0, for instance, means that the network ID is the first two numbers, and the host ID is the last two numbers.

By itself, the IP address doesn't tell you much. But if you compare the IP addresses for two computers on your network, you might learn why the computers aren't talking. The two addresses must be in the same range, as defined by the subnet mask. So with a subnet mask of 255.255.0.0, your two computers must have the same two numbers as the first part of the IP address, with different numbers for the last two numbers. If these numbers aren't in the same range, try running the Network Setup Wizard again.

Tip   You can use the Ping command to test the connection between two computers. Click Start, choose Run, type **cmd** in the Open text box, then click OK. In the Command Prompt window, type the command **ping *ip_address***, where *ip_address* is the IP address of the other computer on your network. You should see a series of four responses from the other computer. If you see the message "Destination host unreachable," you must repair either the physical connection or the networking components.

How File Sharing Works

Now that you've got your network up and running, it's time to learn about all the great things you can do with it. One of the key features of Windows XP is the ability to securely allow or prevent access to files, printers, and other resources. Windows controls the use of files by maintaining for each file a list of which user accounts are permitted access and exactly what type of access is allowed for each account.

Windows XP Professional offers two sharing models, Simple File Sharing and classic sharing. (Windows XP Home Edition uses Simple File Sharing exclusively.) Simple File Sharing uses a simplified interface that makes it easy to set up common sharing arrangements. Classic sharing offers granular control over access to each object on a computer, but it requires understanding concepts and navigating an interface that are beyond the needs of most home and small office users.

Simple File Sharing

Behind the scenes, Windows manages the access control lists (ACLs) for each folder and file on your NTFS-formatted drives. With Simple File Sharing enabled, Windows hides the complexity by reducing the options to a limited few:

- You can set permissions only at the folder level. You can't apply permissions to individual files.

- You can share a folder and the files it contains with all others who log on to your computer, with all other users on your network, or with nobody. You can't pick and choose which users get access.

■ Only two types of access are available for shared folders: full control, in which users can create, read, modify, rename, and delete files; and read only, in which users can view files but not change them in any way.

Note   If you previously shared folders on a computer running Windows 95, Windows 98, or Windows Me, you might be accustomed to adding one or two passwords to each shared folder, allowing you to restrict access to only those people who can supply the Read Only password or the Full Control password. In Windows XP, this option is gone. When you share a folder on a computer using Simple File Sharing, anyone who can access your computer over the network can view the contents of that folder. As I explain in the next section, you can also specify whether network users can change those files, but this setting, too, is an all-or-nothing proposition.

Classic Sharing

Classic sharing is the method of securing folders and files that's used in Windows NT and Windows 2000. Designed for use in complex enterprise computing environments, it offers explicit control over who is allowed to access each file and precisely what they're allowed to do with it.

Although classic sharing greatly increases your flexibility, it comes at the cost of a significant increase in complexity. Aside from the business of understanding and applying permissions—a daunting topic that has baffled many a professional network administrator—using classic sharing requires a fundamental change in the way you work with user accounts in a network environment. Unless your LAN includes a Windows domain controller (a high-end server typically found only on large corporate networks), you must create identical user accounts for each user on each computer. In addition, when you use classic sharing and share a folder over the network, you must apply network share permissions (to control who can access the folder over the network) *and* NTFS permissions for the folder and its files—and understand how these different sets of permissions interact. If you make a mistake, you could end up locking yourself and other authorized users out.

This stuff isn't rocket science, but it's not for the faint of heart, either. My advice? Unless you have security needs that are unusual for home and small office environments, stick with Simple File Sharing. If your computers are networked and you need the additional security options provided by classic sharing, consider setting up a server as a domain controller. If you want to know more about the benefits, pitfalls, and details of using classic sharing, whether on a standalone computer or in a network environment, check out *Microsoft Windows XP Inside Out*, by yours truly and Carl Siechert (Microsoft Press, 2001).

Try This! In this book, I describe only the procedures for sharing resources using the Simple File Sharing option. But if you use Windows XP Professional and you want to get a glimpse of the differences in classic sharing, here's how:

1 In My Computer (or any Windows Explorer window), open the Tools menu and choose Folder Options.

2 In the Folder Options dialog box, click the View tab and scroll down to the last item in the Advanced Settings list box.

3 Clear the Use Simple File Sharing (Recommended) check box, and then click OK.

Now when you look at the Properties dialog box for any folder (by right-clicking the folder and choosing Sharing And Security), you'll see separate Sharing and Security tabs. You set network share permissions on the Sharing tab, and NTFS permissions on the Security tab. Each of these tabs, shown in Figure 14-3, provides more options than the Sharing tab that appears when Simple File Sharing is enabled, as shown in Figure 14-5 later in this chapter.

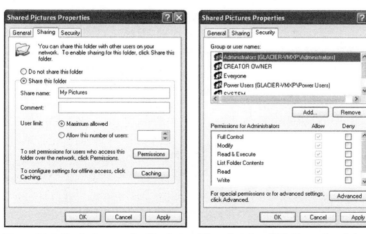

Figure 14-3 The buttons on the Sharing and Security tabs of this Properties dialog box lead to still more arcane settings.

In addition, the Properties dialog box for each file (right-click the file and choose Properties) includes a Security tab similar to the one shown in Figure 14-3, allowing you to set explicit permissions on each individual file.

When you've finished your exploration of classic sharing, reenable Simple File Sharing by returning to the Folder Options dialog box and selecting the Use Simple File Sharing (Recommended) check box.

Using the Shared Documents Folder

The easiest way to share files with others who use your computer is through the Shared Documents folder. Anyone who logs on to your computer—whether using an administrator account or a limited account—can display the contents of the Shared Documents folder. Along with each user's documents folder, Shared Documents appears as a top-level folder in My Computer, as shown in Figure 14-4.

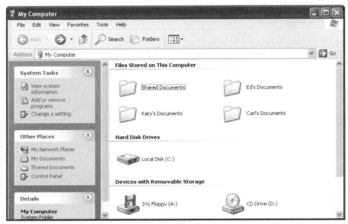

Figure 14-4 You'll find a link to Shared Documents in the task pane (under Other Places) as well as in My Computer.

Any user can store documents in Shared Documents and its subfolders, either by saving a new document in the folder or by copying or moving an existing document to the folder. What each local user is allowed to do with a document in Shared Documents, however, depends on the account type.

■ Computer administrators have full control over all files in Shared Documents. A computer administrator can read, modify, rename, or delete any file.

■ Users with a limited account have full control over files that they create in Shared Documents. Limited users can only read files created by another user; they cannot modify, rename, or delete any one else's files. They can, however, make changes to a document and save it using a new name or copy a document to their own My Documents folder, where they have full control.

If you enable network access to your computer, as I describe in the following section, Windows automatically sets up the Shared Documents folder so that network users have full access to it. If you want Shared Documents to be available only to users on your computer but not to users who connect over the network, right-click Shared Documents, choose Sharing And Security, and clear the Share This Folder On The Network check box.

Caution   You should be aware of one other important change that occurs when you enable network access to your computer. The restrictions on limited users' access to files in Shared Documents no longer apply. All users—computer administrators and limited—have full control over all files in Shared Documents.

Sharing a Folder with Other Network Users

The Shared Documents folder provides a convenient way to share documents with other people who use your computer. In this section, I'll show you how to share documents (in the Shared Documents folder or elsewhere) with other users on your network.

Enabling Network Access to Your Computer

On a clean installation of Windows XP, network sharing is disabled. The easiest way to enable network sharing is to run the Network Setup Wizard, as discussed earlier in this chapter. If you haven't yet run the wizard, when you attempt to share a folder the Network Sharing And Security frame on the Sharing tab in the folder's properties dialog box displays the explanatory message shown below.

You can click either link in this box. The first link, of course, launches the Network Setup Wizard, which enables sharing and also ensures that computers in your network use the same workgroup name. This link also configures a shared, firewall-protected Internet connection. If you've already configured your network without using the wizard, you can click the second link. Doing so displays a dialog box that offers another chance to run the Network Setup Wizard, as shown here.

If you're confident that your Internet connection is secure (because you've set up a firewall or an equivalent measure), you can safely bypass the wizard and select the second option shown here, Just Enable File Sharing.

Note   You must be logged on as a computer administrator to share a folder over the network. After a folder has been shared, however, the share is available to network users no matter who is logged on to your computer—and even when nobody is logged on.

Sharing a Folder

Once network sharing has been enabled, as I described in the preceding section, the necessary controls for sharing a folder across the network become evident in the Network Sharing And Security frame on the Sharing tab of a folder's properties dialog box. Figure 14-5 shows an example.

You can share any of your computer's folders except Program Files and Windows. (You can share subfolders of Program Files, but not subfolders of Windows.) Here's how to share a folder so that other network users can access its files:

1   Open the folder you want to share and then click Share This Folder (under File And Folder Tasks in the task pane at the left side of the window). Alternatively, right-click the folder you want to share and choose Sharing And Security.

2   In the Network Sharing And Security frame, shown in Figure 14-5, select the Share This Folder On The Network check box.

3 Accept the proposed share name or type a new name for the shared folder in the Share Name text box. The name you specify here is what other network users will see when they browse to your computer. It doesn't change the name of the folder on your computer.

4 Select or clear the Allow Network Users To Change My Files check box, depending on your needs as follows:

- Select the check box if you want network users to be able to create and modify files in your shared folder.

- Clear the check box if you want to allow network users to view files in your shared folder and its subfolders, but not allow them to create or modify files.

5 Click OK.

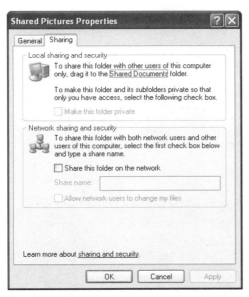

Figure 14-5 The Sharing tab changes in a minor, yet important, way after you enable network sharing.

Sharing a Printer

When you share a printer, all users on your network can use the printer. This means a single printer can serve all the computers in your home or office. When you use the Add Printer Wizard to install a new printer, one of the wizard's pages asks if you want to share the printer with other network users. If you're still in the process of setting up a printer, select the Share Name option and, optionally, modify the name that Windows suggests, as shown on the next page.

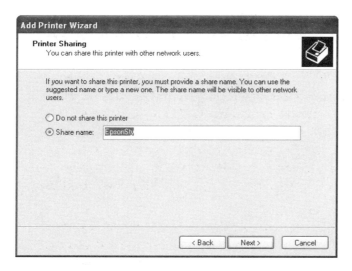

If you didn't set up your printer for network sharing when you installed it, you can do so at any time later. To do that, you must be logged on as a computer administrator. Here's how to share a printer with other network users:

1   Open Control Panel, click Printers And Other Hardware (if you use Category view), and then click Printers And Faxes.

2   Click the printer you want to share and then click Share This Printer, as shown below.

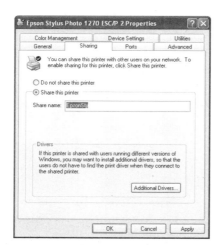

3   Change the text in the Share Name text box to something that'll be meaningful to other people on your network. The name that Windows suggests has no more than eight characters, with no spaces. This is done so that computers running MS-DOS or Windows 3.1 can connect to your printer—but if all the computers on your network have more current versions of Windows, you aren't bound by these restrictions.

4 If other computers on your network are using versions of Windows other than Windows XP, click Additional Drivers. Select the Windows versions in the Additional Drivers dialog box; Windows might prompt you to provide a disk with the driver file. By installing drivers for other Windows versions on your computer, when users of those systems connect to your printer over the network, Windows automatically installs the appropriate driver on their computers; they don't need to have a driver disk.

5 Click the General tab and make entries in the Location and Comment text boxes, as shown below. This step is optional, but the text you provide here is visible in each network user's Print dialog box, and it might help them understand more about your printer.

6 Click OK.

Accessing Shared Folders and Printers on Your Network

Once a user has shared a folder or printer on the network, all network users can use these resources. You can access folders and printers through the My Network Places folder. To open My Network Places, click Start and then click My Network Places. If it doesn't appear on the Start menu, open My Computer.

You'll find a link to My Network Places under Other Places in the task pane at the left side.

By default, My Network Places shows all the shared folders and printers on your network, as in the example shown below. (If shared folders do not appear, open the Tools menu and choose Folder Options. Click the View tab and then select the first check box in Advanced Settings, Automatically Search For Network Folders And Printers.)

You work with documents in a shared network folder exactly like you work with documents on your own computer: open the folder where the desired document is stored and double-click it.

To use a shared network printer, you must first connect to it, which you can do in either of two ways:

- Right-click the icon for the shared printer and choose Connect. Follow the wizard's instructions to complete the connection. (If the printer doesn't appear in My Network Places, click View Workgroup Computers. Double-click the name of the computer that the printer is connected to, and the printer should appear.)

- From Control Panel, open Printers And Faxes. Click Add A Printer to invoke the Add Printer Wizard, which leads you through the process of connecting to a printer connected to another computer on your network.

> **Tip** You can also start the Add Printer Wizard from within the Print dialog box of most programs. Choose Print from the File menu and then, in the Select Printer box, double-click Add Printer. If you try to print a document on a computer where no printer is currently installed, Windows informs you that you need to install a printer before you can continue. Click Yes to proceed to the Add Printer Wizard.

Once you've connected to a network printer, you use it just like any other printer.

> **See Also** *This chapter has only scratched the surface of the topic of home networking. For detailed information on all the ins and outs of setting up and using a small network at home, see This Wired Home: The Microsoft Guide to Home Networking, Third Edition, by Alan Neibauer (Microsoft Press, 2002)*

Key Points

- To set up a network with Windows XP, you need a network adapter for each computer.

- If you use standard network adapters, you must plug them into a hub or switch, using standard patch cables. On a two-computer network, you can use a crossover cable instead.

- Windows XP automatically configures basic settings for your network, allowing computers on the network to communicate with one another. To finish configuring your network, be sure to run the Network Setup Wizard.

- Sharing an Internet connection requires that you install a router or set up Internet Connection Sharing on a computer running Windows XP.

- To set up a workgroup, all computers on the network must use the same workgroup name.

- Windows XP automatically configures wireless network adapters.

- To troubleshoot Windows networking problems, first check for physical problems, then make sure that the TCP/IP settings are correct.

- By default, Windows XP uses Simple File Sharing; Windows XP Professional users can opt for the more complex classic sharing instead.

- You enable and disable Simple File Sharing in the Advanced Settings list box on the View tab of the Folder Options dialog box.

- With Simple File Sharing, you can share folders with all users of your computer, all users on your network, or with nobody (that is, you can make certain folders private).

- You can restrict folders that you share over the network so that other network users can only read files but not modify them in any way.

- When you share a folder, you're sharing all its files, all its subfolders, and all the files and subfolders they contain.

- The Shared Documents folder provides a convenient place to share documents with everyone who logs on to your computer.

- To share a folder or printer with other network users, you must enable network access to your computer; the easiest (and safest) way is to run the Network Setup Wizard.

- To share a folder, open it and then click Share This Folder (under File And Folder Tasks in the task pane). If the task pane isn't visible, right-click the folder icon and choose Sharing And Security from the shortcut menu.

- To share a printer, select it in the Printers And Faxes folder and then click Share This Printer (under Printer Tasks in the task pane).

- To find a shared folder or shared printer on another computer on your network, open My Network Places.

- To use a shared printer, install it (choosing Network Printer in the Add Printer Wizard) or connect to it from the shortcut menu (right-click it in My Network Places and choose Connect).

Index

Ed Bott

Ed Bott is a best-selling author and award-winning computer journalist with more than 15 years of experience in the personal computer industry. He's written extensively about Microsoft Windows, Microsoft Office, and the Internet in leading magazines and on the Web. For nearly a decade, Ed wrote *PC Computing*'s annual "Windows SuperGuide," a compendium of tips, tricks, and in-depth explanations that won rave reviews and multiple awards. Ed has written more than 15 books, all on Windows and Office, for novices and experts alike, and his work has been translated into dozens of foreign languages.

Ed is a two-time winner of the Computer Press Award and has won the prestigious Jesse H. Neal Award, sometimes referred to as "the Pulitzer Prize of the business press," three times. After spending three years living just around the corner from Microsoft's headquarters in Redmond, Washington, Ed and his wife Judy exchanged the gray and damp of the Northwest for the sunny Southwest and have never been happier.

The manuscript for this book was prepared and submitted to Microsoft Press in electronic form. Pages were composed by nSight Inc. using Adobe FrameMaker+SGML for Windows, with text in Garamond and display type in ITC Franklin Gothic Condensed. Composed pages were delivered to the printer as electronic pre-press files.

Cover designer:	Tim Girvin Design
Interior Graphic Designer:	James D. Kramer
Principal Compositor:	Patty Fagan
Project Manager:	Susan H. McClung
Copy Editor:	Marcia Allen
Technical Editor:	Bob Hogan
Proofreaders:	Jan Cocker, Jackie Fearer, Robert Saley
Indexer:	Edwin Durbin

Work smarter—
conquer your software *from the inside out!*

Hey, you know your way around a desktop. Now dig into Office XP applications and the Windows XP operating system and *really* put your PC to work! These supremely organized software reference titles pack hundreds of timesaving solutions, troubleshooting tips and tricks, and handy workarounds in a concise, fast-answer format. They're all muscle and no fluff. All this comprehensive information goes deep into the nooks and crannies of each Office application and Windows XP feature. INSIDE OUT titles also include a CD-ROM full of handy tools and utilities, sample files, an eBook links to related sites, and other help. Discover the best and fastest ways to perform everyday tasks, and challenge yourself to new levels of software mastery!

MICROSOFT® WINDOWS® XP INSIDE OUT
ISBN 0-7356-1382-6

MICROSOFT WINDOWS SECURITY INSIDE OUT FOR WINDOWS XP AND WINDOWS 2000
ISBN 0-7356-1632-9

MICROSOFT OFFICE XP INSIDE OUT
ISBN 0-7356-1277-3

MICROSOFT OFFICE V. X FOR MAC INSIDE OUT
ISBN 0-7356-1628-0

MICROSOFT WORD VERSION 2002 INSIDE OUT
ISBN 0-7356-1278-1

MICROSOFT EXCEL VERSION 2002 INSIDE OUT
ISBN 0-7356-1281-1

MICROSOFT OUTLOOK® VERSION 2002 INSIDE OUT
ISBN 0-7356-1282-X

MICROSOFT ACCESS VERSION 2002 INSIDE OUT
ISBN 0-7356-1283-8

MICROSOFT FRONTPAGE® VERSION 2002 INSIDE OUT
ISBN 0-7356-1284-6

MICROSOFT VISIO® VERSION 2002 INSIDE OUT
ISBN 0-7356-1285-4

MICROSOFT PROJECT VERSION 2002 INSIDE OUT
ISBN 0-7356-1124-6

Microsoft Press® products are available worldwide wherever quality computer books are sold. For more information, contact your book or computer retailer, software reseller, or local Microsoft® Sales Office, or visit our Web site at microsoft.com/mspress. To locate your nearest source for Microsoft Press products, or to order directly, call 1-800-MSPRESS in the United States (in Canada, call 1-800-268-2222).

Prices and availability dates are subject to change.

Microsoft
microsoft.com/mspress

Learn how to get the job done every day—
faster, smarter, and easier!

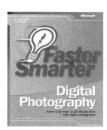   

**Faster Smarter
Digital Photography**
ISBN: 0-7356-1872-0
U.S.A. $19.99
Canada $28.99

**Faster Smarter
Microsoft® Office XP**
ISBN: 0-7356-1862-3
U.S.A. $19.99
Canada $28.99

**Faster Smarter
Microsoft Windows® XP**
ISBN: 0-7356-1857-7
U.S.A. $19.99
Canada $28.99

**Faster Smarter
Home Networking**
ISBN: 0-7356-1869-0
U.S.A. $19.99
Canada $28.99

iscover how to do exactly what you do with computers and technology—faster, smarter, and easier—with FASTER SMARTER
ooks from Microsoft Press! They're your everyday guides for learning the practicalities of how to make technology work
he way you want—fast. Their language is friendly and down-to-earth, with no jargon or silly chatter, and with accurate how-
 information that's easy to absorb and apply. Use the concise explanations, easy numbered steps, and visual examples
 understand exactly what you need to do to get the job done—whether you're using a PC at home or in business,
apturing and sharing digital still images, getting a home network running, or finishing other tasks.

Microsoft Press has other FASTER SMARTER titles to help you get the job done every day:

Faster Smarter PCs
ISBN: 0-7356-1780-5

Faster Smarter Web Page Creation
ISBN: 0-7356-1860-7

Faster Smarter Microsoft Windows 98
ISBN: 0-7356-1858-5

Faster Smarter HTML & XML
ISBN: 0-7356-1861-5

Faster Smarter Beginning Programming
ISBN: 0-7356-1780-5

Faster Smarter Internet
ISBN: 0-7356-1859-3

Faster Smarter Digital Video
ISBN: 0-7356-1873-9

Faster Smarter Money 2003
ISBN: 0-7356-1864-X

To learn more about the full line of Microsoft Press® products, please visit us at:

microsoft.com/mspress

Get a **Free**
e-mail newsletter, updates, special offers, links to related books, and more when you
register on line!

Register your Microsoft Press® title on our Web site and you'll get a FREE subscription to our e-mail newsletter, *Microsoft Press Book Connections.* You'll find out about newly released and upcoming books and learning tools, online events, software downloads, special offers and coupons for Microsoft Press customers, and information about major Microsoft® product releases. You can also read useful additional information about all the titles we publish, such as detailed book descriptions, tables of contents and indexes, sample chapters, links to related books and book series, author biographies, and reviews by other customers.

Registration is easy. Just visit this Web page and fill in your information:

http://www.microsoft.com/mspress/register

Microsoft®

Proof of Purchase

Use this page as proof of purchase if participating in a promotion or rebate offer on this title. Proof of purchase must be used in conjunction with other proof(s) of payment such as your dated sales receipt—see offer details.

Faster Smarter Microsoft® Windows® XP
0-7356-1857-7

CUSTOMER NAME

Microsoft Press, PO Box 97017, Redmond, WA 98073-9830